THE POLICE

every little thing

Also by Caroline and David Stafford

Fings Ain't Wot They Used T'Be: The Life of Lionel Bart
Cupid Stunts: The Life and Radio Times of Kenny Everett
Big Time: The Life of Adam Faith
Maybe I'm Doing It Wrong: The Life and Music of Randy Newman
Halfway to Paradise: The Life of Billy Fury

THE POLICE

every little thing

THE ADVENTURES OF STING, STEWART AND ANDY

Caroline & David Stafford

OMNIBUS PRESS

London / New York / Paris / Sydney / Copenhagen / Berlin / Madrid / Tokyo

Dedicated to Trisha Wilson and her boys Harry and Mike

CONTENTS

CHAPTER ONE

THE REUNION TOUR

'I don't want to be doing this when I'm 40. I mean, look at someone like Mick Jagger. He's wasted his life. His whole life has been taken up by The Rolling Stones. It's deadly. I don't know how he's managed to keep going. He's just going through the motions of being Mick Jagger, which is a bit of a caricature.'

Sting, *Melody Maker*, 1980

In October 2003, Sting celebrated his 52nd birthday.

Earlier that year, the Police had been inducted into the Rock and Roll Hall of Fame. There was, as they say, a lot of love in the room that night, a lot of forgiveness and forgetting.

Gwen Stefani, who introduced them, said, 'The Police was the first big concert I ever went to – and I was at the Hollywood Park on their *Synchronicity* tour.'

She told a tale of chasing after Sting to get his autograph. 'I was this little chubby 13-year-old girl from the suburbs of Orange County. I was in love with him. He wasn't even looking at me. He was totally grumpy. He didn't want to sign my poster. But he didn't burn me off too bad.'

After Gwen's induction, Sting, Stewart and Andy played together for the first time in 18 years. That's what Sting said in his announcement, anyway. Actually, they'd played at Sting's wedding 11 years earlier, but that didn't count. The three-song set – 'Roxanne', 'Message In A Bottle' and 'Every Breath You Take' – was a little ragged, but they rose to the occasion.

Three years later, Stewart edited the miles of Super 8 film he'd shot back when the band were together into a documentary, *Everyone Stares: The Police Inside Out*, and showed it at the Sundance Film Festival. Andy Summers came along. To everyone's surprise, Sting turned up too, and the three of them huddled at the after-show party.

'There was a vibe,' Stewart told *Rolling Stone*. 'Three blond heads sticking out of an inky blackness as one thing.'

Andy's hair was brown by this time, and Stewart's white, but that night they all felt blond.

'Things, I suppose, were brewing,' said Sting.

Another year went by. At the 49th Grammy Awards in February 2007, they opened the show.

'Ladies and gentlemen, we are the Police, and we're back,' Sting said, before blasting into 'Roxanne'.

The following morning, 12 February 2007, they held a press conference/concert at the Whisky a Go Go club in West Hollywood. As they came on stage, the PA system played a recording of the interview in which Sting, in reply to the question of whether the Police would ever do a reunion tour, said: 'I think that would be good cause for having me certified insane.'

'Yes,' he said, as he approached the mic. 'I am certifiably insane.'

He, with his bandmates Andy Summers and Stewart Copeland, tore into 'Message In A Bottle'. Then he said, 'So, okay, we're gonna come clean. We're gonna go on tour.'

A huge cheer greeted the news, but it's doubtful whether the announcement was a surprise to anybody in the audience.

Sting gave thanks to various people who'd brought them to this position, including Miles Copeland III, Stewart's big brother, their former manager and chief architect of the band's greatness. Miles, sitting among the press, looking like the unholy love child of Andy Warhol and Draco Malfoy, grimly acknowledged the shout.

Miles would not be involved in the reunion. Later he told the *Guardian*, 'They had a bunch of lawyers who said, "Let's keep Miles out. You're going to save money." I still get my royalties, but I thought it was undermining the essence of what the Police was.'

Miles, at the time, was managing the Bellydance Superstars, who did a sort of *Riverdance* show, but (obviously) without the rigid spines.

★ ★ ★

'I woke up one morning in November last year,' Sting told John Pidgeon of the *Independent*, 'and the John Dowland record had just gone in the charts.' The 'John Dowland record' was his 2006 *Songs from the Labyrinth*, an album of music written by the 16th-century English composer he'd made in collaboration with the lutenist Edin Karamazov. It had gone to number 24 in the UK album chart.

'So, I was very happy about that, and I thought, "What do I do now? Should I do that again? No, that'll paint me into a corner. Do I do another Sting album? No, I'm not really ready for it. What do I do to surprise people? Or surprise myself, even?" And this little voice said, "You reform the Police." And another little voice said, "Don't be ridiculous, you don't want to do that."

'We phoned Andy and Stewart, and they didn't believe it either, because I'd been so adamant. If you'd asked me the day before, I would've said, "You're out of your fucking mind. I don't want to do that." But suddenly everybody clicked with it, it just triggered something, and the timing was perfect.'

There was also, perhaps, an air of 'now or never' about it. At the end of 2006, Andy Summers had celebrated his 64th birthday. He was in very good shape, but bus passes and free prescriptions were only a year away and the immortality that seemed to have been bestowed on Keith, Mick, Paul and Cliff could not be taken for granted.

There was also clearly a lot of money to be made.

Billboard magazine reckoned that the Rolling Stones, the well-established Kings of the World Touring circuit, had, in 2006 alone, made $234,064,920. 'With their radio and album-selling heyday behind them (their 2005 release *A Bigger Bang* spent only three weeks in the Billboard 200), the Stones rake in more dough than ever by taking their reputation as the world's greatest rock'n'roll band on the road.'

Others raking it in included Madonna, U2, Bon Jovi, Elton John and Aerosmith.

There was no certainty, of course, that the Police could effortlessly jump on the same gravy train.

Sting's albums still charted: his 2003 release *Sacred Love* had gone gold in the UK and platinum in the US. But Q magazine's 2007 round-up of the '100 Best Singers' featured the Icelandic singer Jon Thor Birgisson, Sigur Rós's frontman, and one of the Cocteau Twins. Elvis Presley was number one even though he'd been dead for 30 years, but Sting did not feature at all.

Q magazine also took a straw poll of readers' reactions to the impending reunion.

'Anything that'll get Sting off the lute music and wake him up!' said Mike.

'Sting finally woke up and realised that it's the Police stuff that people love and not that elevator music he's been churning out for the last decade. Hopefully we'll get some new music and not just a tour,' said Shawn.

'Remember them for what they were. The Police knew when to say when. It's still when,' said Chili.

★ ★ ★

There would, they decided, be no backing singers, horn sections or offstage keyboard players. It would be just them. The three of them.

Months of rehearsal in Vancouver and at Il Palagio in Tuscany – the place Stewart called 'The Magic Stingdom' – brought some good things to the surface.

'I was pleasantly surprised at the first rehearsal,' Sting said. 'Although it certainly wasn't polished, there were still moments of, "Oh, that's why we were good, that's why we were successful." So, rehearsal was just about joining those moments together and expanding them.'

As if it was all going to be nicey-nicey, easy-peasy.

The film of the tour includes footage shot at those rehearsals. Stewart does a drum fill. Sting pulls a face.

'What?!' Stewart says. 'That drum solo will be on the fucking cover of *Drum!* magazine. It's going to be fucking devoted to that drum fill, you cunt.'

Sting smirks. 'It's amazing that you can play that drum solo in nine beats… It's fantastic.'

'Just cos you got lost! Just cos it's a little confusing for the bass-playing element.'

Stewart and Sting, the two little ones, needle, jostle and squabble. Big brother Andy gave up trying to keep the peace years ago.

Sometimes they claimed the squabbling and name calling was a vital part of the creative process, that it was all about the music, that it helped make it better, but it should be remembered that the London Symphony Orchestra turn out some fairly decent stuff without calling each other cunts.

'It's all in the detail,' Sting said. 'Andy and Stewart may disagree with me. They think we should jam more. I want the details to be precise.'

'We are not falling apart,' Andy told *Rolling Stone*, his teeth clenched. 'The motor is purring nicely. But at the same time, we are a rock band and by definition you have to be somewhat at the edge.'

'It's not a democracy,' Andy said. 'It's an egocracy. We all have one.'

'There's going to be shit. There's going to be turbulence. You have to get a mantra going that you're going to get through this.'

★ ★ ★

Reputedly, tickets for the entire British leg of the tour sold out in half an hour, although in other parts of the world the sales dragged on for as much as an hour and a half.

After a trial run for fan-club members, the tour opened on 28 May 2007 at the General Motors Place, Vancouver (now the Rogers Arena), with a crowd of nearly 40,000. They were supported by Fiction Plane, with Joe Sumner, Sting's son, on bass and vocals, just like Dad.

The gig was, in Stewart's words, 'unbelievably lame'.

Stewart tripped as he came on stage. They got half a bar out of sync with each other in the opening number, 'Message In A Bottle'. On 'Never Mind', Stewart kicked into the chorus while Sting was still on the verse. They had to stop and start again. In song after song there were fluffs, mistimings. They'd changed the keys of some of the songs to accommodate Sting's more mature vocal range. This caused confusion too.

Few of the fans in the crowd would have noticed the fluffs, but Andy, Stew and Sting did. It threw them. 'It usually takes four or five shows on a tour to get to the disaster gig,' Stewart said, 'but we're the Police, so we're a little ahead of schedule.'

A couple of months and 33 gigs later, they hit Fenway Park in Boston.

'Nearly everything was reworked or stretched out to let Sting, drummer Stewart Copeland and guitarist Andy Summers find their way around each other instrumentally,' said music critic Brett Milano in the *Boston Phoenix*. 'That sense of real-time exploration made the two-hour show's peaks grand and its lags excusable.'

'But...,' he went on, 'the shows... could also use some new material, at least a song or two that could represent where the band stands today. Sure, plenty of bands have done quick-grab reunion tours without writing anything new; but even with its dead spots, the first Fenway show proved that the Police are still too good to take the easy way out.'

There had been talk at one point of Sting writing a couple of new songs, but it never happened.

Clearly, there would have been a market for a new album or even a new single. Sell a copy to everybody at, say, 10 of the gigs they'd played and there's a million.

But what kind of record? What kind of new material?

As Stewart told *Sound Vapors*, much of the power of the songs they were playing lay in their age. They'd been around for 30 years. They were packaged with the smells, the emotions and the snows of yesterday that evoke lost youth. 'At the front, we used to have a lot of teenage females fainting,' Stewart said. 'Now we have grown men weeping... I look out there and they're weeping inconsolably.'

And the last thing those grown men wanted to hear was 'stuff from the new album'.

And, besides, 'Sting writes a great song. The wrong place for it is the Police. Why should he be arguing with Stewart about this, or Andy about that? Why should he be struggling with that when he knows exactly how to make a record. That song that he's got, he knows exactly what to do with it.' On the other hand, 'It is very liberating. If we were thinking, "Gosh, I hope Sting writes an album and sticks around for another tour," then we'd have to kiss his ass every day.'

★ ★ ★

Forty gigs in the US and Canada, three weeks off, then Sweden, Denmark, England, Germany, the Netherlands, Switzerland, Austria, Germany again, Portugal, Spain, France, Italy, Ireland, Belgium, Wales, and England again. In 2008, they did Argentina, Chile, Brazil, Australia, New Zealand, China and Japan – 151 stadium gigs in 15 months. Every night, a few hundred thousand people – 3.7 million in all – came through the turnstiles and a few more million dollars went into the tills. The total gross, worldwide, was estimated at something in excess of $360 million, a chunk of which went to various charities, including to WaterAid, an organisation that provides sanitation and clean water in poor countries.

Outside the tour bubble, one of the worst financial crises of the past 200 years was brewing. Banks were going bust. Stock markets were panicking. The middle-aged, middle-class, late baby boomers – the Police demographic – were in crisis, too, worried about their pensions, their kids' college funds, the value of their homes. But the band played on, simultaneously soothing frazzled nerves and boosting their own millions – just in case.

Stewart celebrated his 55th birthday in Cleveland, Ohio, and was still on the road for his 56th in Concord, California. Sting celebrated his 56th birthday in Turin, Italy. Andy had his 65th during the six-week break they took over Christmas and New Year, between gigs in San Juan, Puerto Rico and Wellington, New Zealand.

At Twickenham, they played for 104,000. In Paris, at the Stade de France, they did 158,000 and, for the encore, Henri Padovani, the original guitar player who was 'the Police' with Stewart before even Sting was in the band, joined them for an encore on 'Next To You'.

At 30 of the gigs, their support act was Elvis Costello and the Imposters. Sometimes Sting joined Elvis on stage and they'd sing a couple of numbers together, two ageing veterans of the new wave.

They played their last UK gig at Hyde Park on 29 June 2008.

'While Sting may wish to go down in popular memory as a man who raised awareness of the rainforests,' David Cheal wrote in the *Daily Telegraph*, 'I suspect that he will be remembered by most people for the gloriously meaningless mantra that rang out from his mouth and from thousands more in the crowd last night: "Eee-yoh-ohhh!"'

At the very last concert in Madison Square Garden, New York, the audience – Michael Bloomberg, the mayor, among them – rose to their feet as soon as the band appeared and never sat down again.

'It's been a huge honour to get back together,' Sting said. He thanked Stewart and Andy for 'your musicianship, your companionship, your friendship, your understanding, your patience with me. The real triumph of this tour is that we haven't strangled each other. Not to say it hasn't crossed my mind.'

Stops were pulled out on that last night. Sting, who'd grown a beard over the last months of the tour, left the stage for a moment and appeared on the screens being shaved and manicured, after which he returned shirtless and hairless to ecstatic applause. The NYPD Police Band joined them on stage, as did various children.

After they left the stage, a 'fat lady' in full operatic kit came on to sing an aria from *Aida*, which segued into the Looney Tunes theme and Porky Pig stuttering, 'Th—That's all Folks!'

'I thought we went out and totally proved that we were as great as we always were – possibly, we played better than we'd ever played,' Andy told *Rolling Stone*. 'Clearly that tour was amazingly successful beyond our wildest dreams. That was a more satisfying place to leave it, in a way, that we went out for a couple years and just creamed everything in sight.'

CHAPTER TWO

SONS OF THE CIA

In March 1949, Husni al-Za'im, Chief of Staff of the Syrian Army, led a military coup d'état, overthrew the country's existing government and installed himself as president. The extent of US involvement in the planning and execution of this coup is disputed. The CIA's 'man in Damascus' at the time was Miles Copeland II, so the version of the story told by his son, Stewart, born three years after the coup, is probably as inaccurate as any other.

'They thought the guy running Syria was an asshole,' Stewart said, 'and they could do better. Someone said, in effect, "How about it, then?" And my father thought, "Let's give it a go."'

A plan was hatched to engineer a bit of a riot. This would establish that the government had lost control and, if only for reasons of public safety, the army would have no option but to assume power. Miles II suggested that the conspirators should hire some hoodlums to come and shoot up his house, which was American Embassy property. This would not only add credence to the 'government out of control' narrative, it would also create a diplomatic incident, and establish that the CIA (i.e. Miles II) had absolutely nothing to do with the coup.

The family – which at this time consisted of Miles' wife Lorraine and their son, Miles III – were sent out of town while Miles II waited for the mayhem to start.

The hoodlums were late. And, when they did arrive, they were using real bullets.

Miles II phoned the conspirators, 'Hey! You forgot to tell them to use blanks. They're making a terrible mess of the furniture. I'll have to hang up now. They're shooting at me.'

Miles was close to those conspirators. A month or so after the coup, Lorraine went into labour with their second son. Things did not go well, so Adib al-Shishakli, one of the army officers who had engineered the coup, loaded her into his car and drove her to the hospital. In gratitude, Miles and Lorraine named their second child Ian Adib Copeland.

Adib (al-Shishakli, not Ian) eventually became president of Syria. Then he, too, was overthrown and escaped to Brazil where, 10 years later, he was assassinated.

A few years after that first Syria coup, Copeland helped orchestrate Operation Ajax, the coup that unseated Mohammad Mossadegh in Iran and reinstated the Shah. He was also involved in the coup that unseated King Farouk of Egypt.

'Nobody,' he later said, 'knows more about changing governments by force than me.'

★ ★ ★

Miles Copeland II was born in Birmingham, Alabama, the son of a doctor. He didn't distinguish himself academically at school, but claimed he 'could outsmart the other kids so as to get whatever I wanted from them'. He sold them forged stamps for their collections, fake raffle tickets, aphrodisiacs they could try on their sweethearts and 'subscriptions to a zoo of Alabama's fauna to be made up of animals to be trapped by a local Boy Scout troop'.

He got caught, but instead of punishing him the school principal said, 'The victims should thank me because I had taught them a lesson that would be invaluable to them later in life when they entered the real world.'

Eventually, after various adventures, he joined the National Guard, then got sent to the organisation in Washington that later became the Office of Strategic Services (OSS). In one of his appraisal tests, they asked whether he hated anybody. He said, 'If you want me to ice somebody, I'd be happy to do it. Just don't ask me to hate them.' That showed he had the right stuff.

They sent him to London. He helped with the planning of Operation Overlord and the liberation of France, and met and married Lorraine Adie, a Scot and fellow spook, working with British military intelligence.

After the war, he was instrumental in turning the OSS into the CIA, and was posted to Damascus along with Lorraine and toddler son, Miles III, where they lived in luxury – a seven-bedroom house with cook, chauffeur, nanny, maid and beautiful furniture – until the hoodlums came to shoot it up.

In a 1986 interview with *Rolling Stone*, he grumbled that the trouble with the modern CIA was that it 'isn't overthrowing enough anti-American governments or assassinating enough anti-American leaders, but I guess I'm getting old'.

One would be tempted to add, 'They don't make them like that any more' – but they do.

★ ★ ★

Stewart, the youngest child, was born in Alexandria, Virginia, on 16 July 1952 during one of dad's 'retirements' from the service. Dad kept on the move. When Stewart could barely walk, the family relocated to Cairo, where Miles II was helping Nasser – the general who overthrew King Farouk – to set up his own secret service.

In 1957, they upped sticks again, went to Beirut and had a ringside seat for the 1958 civil war in which Muslim insurgents tried to overthrow the pro-Western government.

'I was just a toddler,' Stewart says, 'but I remember explosions in the night, sandbags and tanks in the street, gangs fighting and gunfire at any time. We were living in an apartment with the rooms full of food and bathtubs full of water.'

★ ★ ★

There were three sons and a daughter. The daughter, Lorraine, usually known as Lennie, was smart. She went to Vassar, the 'most selective' college in the US, and later became a movie producer and writer. The sons, among many other achievements, all did their bit to turn the Police into a global industry.

In his memoir *The Game Player*, Miles II quotes Nat Samuels, an international lawyer, who, speaking of politics and slightly mixing his metaphors, said, 'There'll always be players, but they can't make any meaningful moves on the board until someone gives them the music, puts the orchestra together and hires the hall. There you have the two categories of people who make things happen in this world.'

Stewart became a player, Miles and Ian each became 'someone who gives them the music, puts the orchestra together and hires the hall'. Together, they made things happen.

It's tempting to suggest – as many have – that the boys learned everything they knew at the feet of their father; that their techniques for achieving world domination with a three-piece band weren't dissimilar to those he'd used to overthrow governments. The parallels are inescapable.

The CIA and the music industry are both fighting the same battle for hearts and minds. Convincing the world that the American brand of capitalism is the best system of government available isn't that different from convincing the world that 'Walking On The Moon' is the best record ever made and, if only we'd all dye our hair blond and shout, 'Eee-yoh-ohhh!', peace would come and the planet would be saved.

In 1980, when the Police played India, Miles III, their manager, said, 'It's obviously a good thing for the Police to play the Third World because it gets to the youth of those countries, people who will one day be running them. And, if they are Western-orientated because they like Western music, then it's good from our government's point of view. I happen to believe in the old values of the West. I believe in free enterprise capitalism. I'm not saying we are perfect, but we are definitely better.'

The Copeland brothers never, as far as we know, overthrew a government in order to stop it falling into the hands of Elvis Costello, but that's not to say they wouldn't have, or couldn't have, if *Almost Blue* had outsold *Ghost in the Machine*.

Dad gave them a global perspective, too, and perhaps a reluctance to be impressed by power. When they were in Beirut, dinner guests might include Kim Philby, the British spy who later became a general in the KGB, Gamal Abdel Nasser, the aforementioned president of Egypt, or Adnan Khashoggi, the billionaire wheeler dealer who, essentially, ran the world from one of his private yachts. If, when you were a kid, your dad was on first-name terms with the great, the good, the evil and the notorious, it's less likely that you'll be browbeaten by the ents secretary at Aston University or impressed when the boss of Cheapskate Records refills your glass with Tesco whisky and promises great things.

Years later, when the Police played Egypt and their gear was held up by customs, Miles III put a call through to Hassan Tuhami. When Miles was a kid living in Cairo, Hassan was his next-door neighbour and working as Nasser's bodyguard. He used to come round to show the lad his favourite machine guns. He had since risen to become Egypt's deputy prime minister. The gear got through customs. Brian Epstein could never have done that.

The Copelands could have invented the 'can-do' attitude. They liked to excel and often did. Self-doubt was something you kept secret.

★ ★ ★

Miles III, the eldest son, was groomed for greatness, equipped with a library of inspirational books and reams of advice.

Dad advised him, for instance, to stay away from the spy business, principally because there was no money in it. Similarly, he turned him against politics. Candidates for the US presidency have to be born in the USA, he told him. Miles was born in London. What's the point in entering any profession knowing you'll never get the top job?

There was a suggestion that maybe he could go into the oil business. So, Miles took a degree in History and Political Science in Birmingham, Alabama, then another in Economics at the American University of Beirut. He spoke fluent Arabic and was smart as a whip.

But it was 1968 by then. The Beatles had proved that there was a new way of making money, potentially more lucrative than espionage or politics, maybe not so good as oil, but certainly more fun than any of them. The music business was still largely run either by gentleman amateurs, like Brian Epstein, or by old-time pros who still saw pop as a subsection of good old variety and who hadn't noticed that the Rolling Stones didn't do panto. In other words, it was a wide-open field for a boy with CIA know-how, the Copeland can-do attitude, a lick of sense and a degree in Economics.

Miles started promoting concerts at the university in Beirut, with light shows and so forth to provide as near to the full *14-Hour Technicolor Dream* psychedelic experience as he could manage with the limited resources at his disposal. His work brought him to the attention of a local promoter, who was importing a band, Rupert's People, from the UK for a string of gigs. Could Miles work some of his trippy magic on them? Of course he could. Miles acquired the requisite strobe and UV lights, put non-compatible coloured fluids between two sheets of glass and projected their mind-blowing interactions all over the place, and generally recreated the popular image of an LSD trip for the Lebanese punters. He also looked after the business interests of Rupert's People, making sure they got paid. When, a little later, Miles moved back to London, Rupert's People persuaded him to be their manager. He was good at it. Finding bands, finding venues, putting the former in the latter. Piece of cake.

Ian, the second brother, ran with the bad guys. In Beirut, they called him 'Jodang', the 'Little Rat'. He joined a biker gang, 'riding', as big brother Miles put it, 'with the King of Death'. Miles decided that the best way of saving Ian from his bad company and outlandish ways was to sell his motorcycle. When Ian found out, he ran away from home.

In 1967, Ian rode with the King of Death for real by joining the US army and shipping out to Vietnam with the 1st Infantry Division. He made sergeant. He won a medal. They called him 'Leroy Coolbreeze'.

He survived.

'Somehow,' he said. 'I believed there is no way in hell they were going to get me, because this was my movie. How could the star get killed?' It was a strategy that failed for a quarter of a million other soldiers in Vietnam, but, miraculously, it worked for Ian. After the army, he joined his big brother in London and started finding bands and venues of his own.

Stewart was the baby of the family. He was a late developer, small for his age, slightly geeky, and he wore glasses. He found it hard to make friends even at the American School. He was also hopelessly overshadowed by his two magnificent brothers, the smart one and the wild one. He was destined, it seemed, never to have an identity of his own, and possibly never even a name. He would be known forever only as either 'Miles' geeky brother' or 'Ian's geeky brother'.

Dad, in his youth, had played trumpet with the big bands so fashionable at the time, and hoped that one of his kids would show some interest in playing an instrument. Miles III didn't, Lennie didn't, Ian did occasionally, but not if it interfered with his social life. Stewart had a few trombone lessons, but quickly revealed his true passion was for hitting things. He nagged his mother to get him a snare drum, then his dad rented a full kit with a faded champagne sparkle finish. It became an obsession.

'The power of noise was endlessly thrilling and empowering. When I wasn't drumming or air drumming, I was that kid who drives everyone insane with persistent foot-tapping or thigh-slapping. It was the nervous twitch from hell.'

By the age of 12, he was in a band. They were called the Nomads, or the Black Knights and played gigs at the American Embassy Beach club organised by brother Ian, doing James Brown covers and the Kinks and the Animals.

On the whole, the kids were left to their own devices.

'When I remember what I was getting up to at that early age it... er... really shocks me. We were sort of neglected, I guess, with our parents being such important people. There was a totally decadent, hedonistic society among the kids of the American community.'

The lad took a precocious interest in sex and believed in the aphrodisiac qualities of the beat.

'Well, here I am, the skinny runt of the litter, but as long as I drive the beat, I'm a hairy-assed silverback motherfucker banging tree trunks. I'm swinging through the trees. My voice is a manly roar.'

The story that the first night he played in a band was the night he lost his virginity has often been told. After the gig, apparently, three big girls led him to the beach and showed him how to play rude buckets and spades.

There is a notion – not widely respected among psychiatrists, but convincing enough in pubs – that whatever a man is doing the first time he gets laid forms his personality for the rest of his life. If he pleads, he will be forever needy. If he jokes, he will be a joker. If he plays the drums, he will be a drummer. Those three big girls on the beach sealed Stewart's fate.

As well as sex, drums gave him a proper identity, something that set him apart, something that made him different from his brothers, maybe even better.

In the mid-1960s, the family moved back to London and Stewart was taken out of the American School in Beirut and sent to Millfield School, a couple of miles from Glastonbury in Somerset.

Millfield is a co-educational school that believes in nurturing the 'whole' person rather than single-mindedly pursuing academic excellence. Its alumni include several noted sportsmen and women, the DJ Tony Blackburn, the singer Lily Allen, journalist and *Strictly Come*

Dancing contestant John Sergeant and, just 12 days younger than Stewart, the young Maha Vajiralongkorn, who, in 2016, became the King of Thailand.

Stewart took piano lessons and played drums in the school orchestra. His dad had arranged for him to have drum lessons with Max Abrams, then in his fifties, who'd served with Jack Hylton, Caroll Gibbons' Savoy Orpheans and, in the 1950s, Humphrey Lyttelton. Abrams taught him to read drum parts from big-band charts and gave him complicated coordination exercises.

'Learning to uncouple the hands so as to free them for independent activity is the goal,' Stewart said, 'but uncoupling my brain is the result.'

He was left-handed. Some left-handed drummers, like Phil Collins and Micky Dolenz of the Monkees, set up their kit in mirror image, with the snare and hi-hat on the right and the floor tom on the left. Others, like Ringo Starr and Stewart, set it up the regular, 'right-handed' way, and either force the coordination to flip-flop, or adapt to play some things with the 'wrong' hand (some of Ringo's more quirky fills result from his leading with the left), or, most likely, a combination of the two. Any way you do it demands a fair amount of brain-uncoupling, but no effort is too great if there's a chance it might lead to three big girls on a hot beach.

The first proper gig Stewart saw in the UK was Jimi Hendrix (another lefty) at the Saville Theatre.

Everybody was in awe of Hendrix. Eric Clapton and Pete Townshend used to follow him around, like groupies, from gig to gig, trying to get a spot near the front so they could see his hands. Just his presence was magnificent – he was only 5'10" but always looked at least a foot taller. The Cuban heels had something to do with it, and the hair, but mostly it was just the presence.

Jimi played at the Saville several times. Brian Epstein, who'd taken a lease on the theatre, put straight plays in there, as well as rock concerts.

As we shall see, all of the Police saw Jimi play live in 1966 or 1967, and they included his 'Purple Haze' as their first encore on that last ever gig of the reunion tour at Madison Square Garden.

Stewart went on 27 August. Jimi had been booked for two nights. If Stewart had booked for the second night, he'd have been disappointed: Brian Epstein died, and the show was cancelled. Stewart wasn't quite so blown away as he'd have liked to have been, mostly because the sound was so terrible. He remembers thinking, 'I wish they would turn everything off so I could hear what's going on.' Nevertheless, he said, 'My mind was blank for three days.'

After school, Stewart went to college in San Diego and took classes in piano and composition at the School for the Performing Arts, later moving up to Berkeley and taking Communications and Music. He was American-born, but still felt as much a misfit in Southern California as he had in Beirut.

In composition classes, his technique was sketchy, but the raw talent shone through. His teacher, having played through one of his exercises, said, 'Stewart, you have parallel fifths in the measures three, seven and eleven but, more important, this is actual music. You have a voice.'

Some years later, that exercise became 'Does Everyone Stare', track 5, side 2, on *Reggatta de Blanc*. Nobody bellyaches about parallel fifths in rock'n'roll; they just call them 'power chords'.

At Berkeley, he experienced an odd change of personality.

'One moment I was lacking in imagination,' he says in his 2009 autobiography *Strange Things Happen*, 'the next I was a bright spark, I started thinking and accomplishing. I hate to say it and I would never recommend it because I know of too many casualties, but the only thing it could have been was LSD. I don't take it any more. It did really open my eyes though. Probably an inspiring book might have done it, but it wouldn't have occurred to me to read an inspiring book.'

Whenever he was in the UK, during breaks from college, his brother Miles put him to work. He gave him a job roadie-ing – or tour managing – for Rupert's People, who, by this time, had been rechristened Stonefeather. They went to France and Paris and the French Riviera. As holiday jobs go, it beat the hell out of working as a factory cleaner.

It happened every holiday after that. Miles always had a band in need of a driver who knew how to avoid the A14 around Huntingdon or the Périphérique around Paris, could carry a 4x12 cabinet up three flights of stairs, set up a drum kit and tell the bass player to stop doing that before somebody gets hurt.

For a while, Stewart worked with a band called Cat Iron, the drummer of which was Kim Turner – who, as time went on, would make his own vital contribution to the Police's world domination.

Stewart doubled as roadie/performer. Cat Iron specialised in outrage. At one point, Stewart, dressed as a policeman, would invade the stage and pretend to bust the venue. In response, Kim Turner would leap over the drum kit and grab Stewart. The rest of the band would pull a fake penis from Stewart's trousers and Kim would cut it off with garden shears.

The year after that, Miles hired him to roadie for a (then) up-and-coming Joan Armatrading. This, according to brother Ian, was fine, except that after the shows Stew and Joan often found themselves chasing the same girls.

★ ★ ★

Brother Miles' career as a manager/promoter was on the up and up. He eventually set up a company, BTM (British Talent Managers), and a record label, BTM Records.

At the Country Club, in Hampstead, London NW3, just down the side of Belsize Park tube station (soft drinks only, so make sure you get tanked up in advance), he discovered a bass player and a drummer whose guitar player had gone home to Torquay, and paired them, by means of the customary *Melody Maker* ad ('no breadheads, no timewasters'), with a couple of guitar heroes. Between them they came up with a name, Wishbone Ash.

The B-side of their first album had just two tracks, the way albums did in 1971, but nobody felt short-changed because it was perfect for taking the edge off a too-epic high. It made the Top 30 in the album chart.

Their fourth album went to number three. That one had three tracks on the A-side and four on the B. *Sounds* readers voted it the 'Best Rock Album of the Year' and *Melody Maker* 'Top British Album'. They were never a singles band, because a 7-inch could not contain them.

Miles found further success with Renaissance, a band that had gradually evolved, with many personnel changes, from the Yardbirds.

Blessed by the piano playing of John Tout and the voice of Annie Haslam from Bolton, they provided quality prog for the discerning listener, and averaged six tracks per album. Miles encouraged them towards a more orchestral sound that skimmed the outer edges of MOR with which they scored some Top 40 hits in the US album charts and a three-night gig at Carnegie Hall with the New York Philharmonic.

This was the big time. And it brought the very big time irresistibly close.

The talent stable grew to include, among others, Climax Blues Band from Stafford, the magnificent Squeeze from Deptford, and Curved Air, a crushed-velvet art-rock band – which is where the story really starts.

Darryl Way, a classically trained fiddle player, and Francis Monkman, an organist and harpsichordist who also played guitar, joined forces with the extravagantly named old Etonian Florian Pilkington-Miksa, a drummer, Nick Simon, a pianist, and Rob Martin, who played bass, and formed a band called Sisyphus. They added a singer to the line-up, Sonja Kristina, who'd previously starred in the musical *Hair* (she's on the original UK cast recording singing the show's best lyric, 'Frank Mills'), and changed the band's name to Curved Air.

They made waves, picking up a £100,000 advance from Warner Bros and releasing the first proper picture disc ever, *Air Conditioning*.

John Peel gave them his stamp of approval. A single, 'Back Street Luv', went Top 5. The second album, called *Second Album*, went to number 11 in the album charts. They toured the US and developed a cult following, which, in the time of prog, was the only kind of following worth having. The third album brought the usual musical differences. Francis wanted to wig out more. Darryl didn't. They split.

A new Curved Air line-up was tried, but failed to do the business. Sonja went off to become a croupier at the London Playboy Club. Darryl formed a new band, initially called Darryl Way's Wolf, managed again by Miles. They recorded three magnificent, mostly instrumental albums, seven tracks each, of classical-drenched prog,

Darryl's new band rehearsed in the basement of the Copelands' parents' house on Marlborough Place in St John's Wood, the same place where Stewart liked to hit things. When Wolf's drummer left the band, Darryl, reckoning (at least according to Ian) that there might be advantages in having the manager's brother in the line-up, hired Stewart. He renamed the band Stark Naked and the Car Thieves, stealing the name from a band that Ian had played with in Vietnam.

Stewart Copeland was at last a professional musician, playing with other professional musicians in a professional band. His joy was unconfined, but short-lived.

In 1974, Curved Air were sued by Chrysalis (who'd been promoting their concerts) for breach of contract. And the taxman was after them. The quickest way, and possibly the only way, to raise the sums required was to reform with the essence of the old line-up, including Darryl. So, Stark Naked and the Car Thieves broke up and Stewart was no longer a professional musician. As a consolation prize, he was appointed Curved Air's tour manager.

The tour was a smash, and the live album that came out of it made a few quid as well – enough, all told, to pay off the debts. Job done, Francis and Florian left again, but Sonja and Darryl hung on to the Curved Air name and reformed yet again, this time with Stewart on drums.

As soon as Stewart joined the band, they went off for some gigs in Europe, '...and it was very quickly apparent I was jumping in a bit ahead of myself. I really wasn't quite up to it. I was quite convinced I was going to be sacked.'

So, to make himself more attractive to the band, he tried to work up a bit of self-publicity in a bid to become their celebrity drummer. Under assumed names, he wrote letters to the music papers, commenting on the brilliant drumming of the guy in Curved Air.

'Dear Melody Maker [19 April 1975 issue], I saw Curved Air in Glasgow and would like to know the name of the new drummer and what bands he has been with. Where did he get his see-through drums which not only look spectacular but have an amazingly heavy sound? Is this because of the material or some other factor – Shown Donnell, Glasgow.'

On behalf of 'Shown', *Melody Maker* phoned Stewart and he kept them talking long enough to get six column inches or so cataloguing his entire life story ('I was born in the Middle East') and detailing the exact sizes of his tom-toms and the weight of his sticks ('They're all 10-lug drums fitted with Evans Weathermaster Heads, the sticks are Percussion Services C').

Similarly, when journalist Phil Sutcliffe – later to become important in the story of the Police – wrote a review of a Curved Air concert for *Sounds*, Stewart followed it up with a letter, again written under a pseudonym, praising Sutcliffe's 'astute insight' for spotting the brilliance of Curved Air's new drummer.

★ ★ ★

Like a lot of young men at the time, with and without ex-army greatcoats and roll-ups, Stewart was in thrall to Sonja. 'She moves like smoke across the stage,' he wrote, 'hardly seeming to move at all, but undulating in slow motion. Who cares what the band is doing? As a muso I've never bothered with singers, considering them to be musical passengers. How wrong I've been! She's not even singing yet, and she owns everything.'

'I first met Stewart in Ian's flat, but then he became our tour manager,' Sonja said. 'He didn't make that much of an impression on me to start off with. I was actually in a mini relationship with Ian before I met Stewart. The magic happened when Stewart came along for a rehearsal. That was when I thought he was really, really interesting. We got together during that tour... There was just all this linking of Copelands, and it sort of randomly all came together in a pattern.'

Stewart and Sonja stayed together for 16 years.

Eventually, Miles went for the very big time and overreached himself. He invented a peripatetic rock festival called 'Startruckin' 75', which was supposed to send most of his own acts, together with Tina Turner, Lou Reed and John McLaughlin's Mahavishnu Orchestra, all around the world. Somehow, he underestimated travel and accommodation costs, and the dubious reliability of rock stars.

The venture was a financial black hole.

The biscuit was taken when, in New Zealand, Lou Reed locked himself in the toilet and wouldn't come out.

Miles went bust. His company, BTM, was finished. It was time for something new.

CHAPTER THREE

I THINK MOST OF THESE GROUPS WOULD BE VASTLY IMPROVED BY SUDDEN DEATH

The old and the frail shrivelled up and died in the hot, dry summer of 1976. Crops failed. Hurn Forest in Dorset burned to the ground. When you turned on your tap, nothing came out: you had to queue with a bucket by the standpipe at the end of the street if you wanted to make a cup of tea. But, all the same, it was a lovely summer.

At your local reservoir, you could ride a Chopper bike from one bank to the other without getting wet. At lunchtime, besuited accountants paddled in metropolitan fountains. On TV, grinning local news reporters fried eggs on pavements. When sunset came, couples high on love and Hirondelle jostled for lying-down space in parks. And when you kept your windows open at night – as you had to – always, three streets away, Kiki and Elton would be cranking out 'Don't Go Breaking My Heart'.

But all through those months of glorious summer, just beneath the surface glow of Hirondelle and Elton, something dark and dirty was festering.

★ ★ ★

Malcolm McLaren, after an unconventional upbringing and sporadic schooling, had developed an intelligent and wayward curiosity in the ways – particularly the more perverse ways – of the world. This led him, while he was a student at Chiswick Art College, to discover the doings of Guy Debord and the Situationist International.

To offer the *Reader's Digest* condensed version, the Situationist International was a group of (mostly French) artists, intellectuals and political theorists who subscribed to the notion that capitalism had absorbed every aspect of human experience – every idea, emotion and social interaction – and turned them into commodities, like saucepans or socks.

This reduced the average Jill or Joe's role to that of spectator, passive consumer of music, art, philosophy, beauty, love – which the Situationists describe as 'the Spectacle'. Our only access to these things is via monetary exchange, and the only way we can make money is through work.

In order to disrupt 'the Spectacle', Situationists became interested in anti-art, anti-music, anti-films and 'pranks' of one kind or another. Films were made of nothing, just a blank screen. Some Situationist artists embraced surrealism or Dadaism, the anti-art movements of the 1910s and 1920s, others decided that the only valid art was revolution and, instead of painting pictures, threw stones at policemen.

Malcolm McLaren's main areas of interest were anti-clothes and anti-music.

He opened a shop on the King's Road and, with his then girlfriend Vivienne Westwood, started selling clothes – initially, under the name Let It Rock, retro and repro Teddy boy wear; and eventually, under the name SEX, fetish and bondage wear. Malcolm and Vivienne went to America for a while and worked as stylists/managers with the New York Dolls, a proto-punk band who made a noise that Norwegian death metal addicts still find a little hard on the ears.

Back in the UK, McLaren put a band together called Masters of the Backside – which essentially involved the personnel who went on to become the Damned plus Chrissie Hynde, who went on to front the Pretenders, but they fell apart after one gig (or maybe one and a half).

Then, one day, a young man called John Lydon wandered into the shop on the King's Road, and the rest is a version of history.

There are other versions. Punk was one of those things in the zeitgeist. To the untrained eye, sometimes the distinction between a punk band and a pub-rock band can seem very blurry. It's hard to believe that, if there had been no Malcolm McLaren, punk wouldn't have happened anyway, although possibly with fewer buckles and razor blades.

Word soon got round that punk was the howl of disenfranchised working-class youth, outraged by their barren employment prospects and the gloom of the recession-crushed 1970s teenage wasteland. Others suggest that there was something much smarter going on. Rather than a straightforward reaction to unemployment and gloom, it was a 'dramatisation' of it, tinged with irony and maybe a smidgen of postmodernism. In the greater scheme of things, though, any suggestion that punk had one inspiration, one cause, or that it was in any sense a movement is, of course, bollocks.

There were as many variations of punk as there were punks, and mostly – in keeping with the overall ethos, if there was such a thing – they hated each other. The tribes did, anyway, tending to be fiercely judgemental. You could be condemned for living in the wrong kind of squat, for taking the wrong kind of drugs, buying records when you should be stealing them: any number of errors of dress, hair, deportment, piercings or level of disengagement could brand you a plastic punk, a weekend punk, a part-time punk.

King's Road punks were snubbed by Camden Town punks, Leeds punks by Manchester punks, Swansea punks by Cardiff punks, Cumbernauld punks by Glasgow punks. Even Taunton punks, who barely had the nous to tear their own T-shirts, could sneer at Tiverton punks, who pogoed only *after* they'd done their homework.

The only thing that united them all – in the late 1970s, anyway – was trousers. Though punks found it impossible to unite under an anti-capitalist, anti-sexist, anti-racist, anti-royalist or pro-anarchist banner, their unity against flares was unshakable. They hated them more than anything. Except prog rock. And art-rock, fusion, Abba and Tubular bloody Bells. And Biba. And Felicity Kendal in *The Good Life*.

'I hate shit,' said Johnny Rotten, 20. 'I hate hippies and what they stand for. I hate long hair. I hate pub bands. I want to change it so there are rock bands like us... I'm against people who just complain about *Top of the Pops* and don't do anything. I want people to go out and start something, or else I'm wasting my time.'

Pissing people off was always a vital part of the mix.

'My personal view on punk rock is that is nauseating, disgusting, degrading, ghastly, sleazy, prurient, voyeuristic... I think most of these groups would be vastly improved by sudden death,' said Bernard Brook-Partridge, Conservative Chairman of the Greater London Council Arts Committee.

The *Sunday People* ran a three-week probe into the 'sick', 'sinister', 'dangerous' new phenomenon. The *Sunday Mirror* demanded that somebody should 'Punish the Punks'.

Perhaps the best expression of British punk's odd mixture of hype, howl, danger, domesticity, fury, fun, madness and music hall was seen in Kipper Williams' Christmas 1976 cartoon on the front page of *Melody Maker*. It showed a Johnny Rotten lookalike dressed mostly in safety pins, sitting among Xmas decorations, watching, on TV, a show called *The Blank Generation Game*.

This was the modern world.

★ ★ ★

By 1976, Miles III's company, BTM, had pretty much had it. Miles was still managing Squeeze and Curved Air, but Curved Air had pretty much had it too.

'It had reached the point where we had no new material,' Stewart said. 'We didn't have much in common and there was little hope of improvement. So, we just decided to round off our schedule and leave it at that.'

In December 1976, the band played its last gig before lying dormant for 14 years.

'Stewart and I were both going through the same transformation,' Miles said, 'sort of embittered with our previous situation: worked a long time, what have we got? Empty pockets, debts mounting up, squandering money.'

Stewart was living with Sonja and brother Ian in a ritzy flat in Mayfair. The flat was owned by Marcy, a friend of their dad's. There was a tenant, a titled lady, young but grand, living in the flat downstairs whom the owner wanted to be rid of. So, Dad suggested that Marcy should move a couple of his sons in and encourage them to fill the place with 'Arab cronies, loud musicians and hoodlum friends'. Which they willingly did.

In either the autumn of 1976 or at New Year – memories are understandably hazy – Ian, Stewart and Sonja hosted a party. Al Stewart, the singer-songwriter, was there, along with a bunch of music industry people – many of them in flares.

Caroline Stafford, a friend of a friend (and co-author of this book) says, 'I remember the buzz of excitement and maybe fear when the Sex Pistols showed up. I can't remember whether this was before or after "Anarchy In The UK" was released. I knew who they were, anyway. I'd seen them at the 100 Club and the Nashville. At some point I drifted upstairs. The talking party was upstairs. The noise party was downstairs.'

A fight developed in the noise party. Ian, the Vietnam vet, moved in to sort it out. The trouble had started because one guest wanted to put the Average White Band on the turntable, while another, a punk and possibly a Sex Pistol, wanted 'Blank Generation' by Richard Hell and the Voidoids.

'This punk finally convinced me to let him play it,' Ian said, 'I said, "Okay, after the next James Brown Record."'

So, he put it on, and all the punks went crazy while the rest of the room looked on in amazement.

The following morning, when Stewart and Ian were clearing up the debris, they noticed that 'Blank Generation' was still on the turntable. They put it on. When they listened properly, they grew excited. This is not surprising. It is a wonderful track. The lyric is about a nurse fiddling with her garters while some triangles fall from the sky. And the guitar solo could be the work of a talented horse. After that, Ian, Stewart and Sonja became unlikely champions of the new music.

'Every time punk music was heard,' Sonja said, 'everybody from the music industry would say, "Oh, no! This is not music! This is terrible!" We'd say, "No, this is just fantastic. This is where the energy is."'

Among those in the music industry who remained unconvinced was Mick Jagger. 'Don't you think the Stranglers are the worst thing you've ever heard?' he told *NME*. 'Christ, I do. They're hideous, rubbishy... so bloody stupid. Fucking nauseating, they are.'

And Pete Townshend, again quoted in *NME*: 'When the scramble is over, something will come from it, but they can't just say, "fuck, fuck, fuck, fuck", that's too easy.'

To which, in the following week's edition, Johnny Rotten replied, 'That's easy? You try saying "fuck, fuck, fuck, fuck" with a mouthful of raw goldfish.'

★ ★ ★

Meanwhile, Miles, still on his uppers, had moved into a grubby little office in a grubby little alley off Wardour Street in Soho called Dryden Chambers – long gone now.

'Miles had a declining empire,' says journalist Phil Sutcliffe. 'Business was what tickled him. The first time he sniffed change was when he shared an office with Mark Perry.'

Mark Perry was a former bank clerk who had founded the fanzine *Sniffin' Glue and Other Rock'n'Roll Habits (for Punks!)*, which happened also to be based at Dryden Chambers. Danny Baker came on board, wrote, typed and stapled. Over the course of a few months – and perhaps thanks to some astute help and advice from Miles – the magazine upped its circulation from 5,000 to 20,000.

And, upstairs at Dryden Chambers, Malcolm McLaren's organisation had an office. The Sex Pistols were frequent visitors.

'Unknowingly,' said Miles, 'I moved to the centre of the punk rock revolution.' He quickly spotted that, from an economic standpoint, punk had one massive advantage over what had gone before.

The back of Pink Floyd's 1969 album *Ummagumma* shows their roadies, Alan Styles and Peter Watts, standing with the band's equipment all neatly arranged on an airstrip. The gear included two bass drums, two timpani, a vibraphone, a gong, a trombone and rows and rows of amps and speaker cabs.

It set the trend.

When the Who toured the US in 1973, 20 tons of equipment came with them, carried in three 45-foot trailers and manhandled by 12 roadies.

In 1977, Emerson, Lake and Palmer had seven 45-foot trailers for the indoor gigs and another three for the outdoor gigs. The trailers were accompanied by three buses – two for the orchestral musicians and one for the choir.

All this cost a great deal of money. And, on top of that, you have to add the mounting costs of the artists' princely demands.

By 1973, Led Zeppelin's rider specified the quality of hi-fi systems that were to be installed in their hotel rooms. Their private jet had a waterbed.

It was not uncommon for entourages to include personal caterers, physiotherapists, art directors, wardrobe supervisors and spiritual advisers for those tricky moments when the soul gets sick.

And, even when they came off the road and went into the studio, the bloated bands racked up the expenses. The Beatles' first album took a day to record and cost about the same as a used Hillman Imp. Queen's *A Night at the Opera* took four months in three different studios and cost a couple of four-bedroom semis in a fashionable part of London.

Punk bands, on the other hand, came cheap. They did not require a fleet of Edwin Shirley trucks and an army of roadies. No art directors. No fancy wardrobe. No light shows. They made records fast for fear of sounding polished. Backstage they needed lager, pills, something to wipe the gob off and a flushing toilet.

For a cash-strapped manager, in Miles' words, 'God had descended and answered my prayers.'

★ ★ ★

Stewart, too, had spotted the economic advantages of size and constraint. He decided his next band would be a three-piece and, like Yul Brynner in *The Magnificent Seven*, began to assemble his team.

★ ★ ★

Henri Padovani (sometimes Henry, but most people call him Henri, so that's what he shall be) was an amiable Corsican hippy.

'Lovely bloke, everybody liked Henri,' says Caroline Stafford. 'Possibly stoned all the time, but in that utterly charming French way.'

Henri's mum and dad were teachers who worked in Algeria, leaving the kids back in Corsica to be raised by grandparents and uncles. It was an idyllic childhood. The island was, at the time, in the process of becoming groovy. During the 1960s, Tom Jones took to spending his holidays in Calvi in the north. Françoise Hardy and Jacques Dutronc bought a house in Monticello. Catherine Deneuve and Petula Clark both fell in love with Cavallo – a little island just off the south coast where they could 'live like gypsies and wash in the sea'.

By that time Henri's parents had moved from Algeria (where independence had happened) to the French mainland, and the kids, including Henri, joined them. But still, school holidays were nearly always spent at Gran's house back in Corsica.

With the coming of the jet set, clubs had mushroomed. Not long after puberty hit, Henri took to climbing out of his bedroom window and hitching with his cousins to wherever the action was. Eventually he scored a job as DJ at a place called Le Club. Then an uncle gave him a cheap acoustic guitar. (The role of uncles bearing cheap acoustic guitars in the history of popular music is a PhD thesis waiting to be written. Their importance crops up many times in this book. See how many you can spot.)

He learned some chords from a 'How to Play Guitar in Ten Minutes' article in a women's magazine, progressed to Beatles songs and was eventually able to take his eyes off the sleeve of Hendrix's *Electric Ladyland* long enough to learn some of the licks and solos.

As soon as he'd figured out how to fit a pick-up to the guitar and turn his dad's radio into an amp, he formed a band at school called Lapsus. They played the school dance, singing hits of the day in what he calls 'yoghurt English', spicing things up now and then by shouting, 'Kick out the jams, Motherfuckers', while the non-English-speaking members of staff tapped their feet and smiled indulgently.

Two events led to his first trip to London.

The first was seeing the Flamin' Groovies, in Aix-en-Provence. He described the Beatles-esque power-pop they were playing at the time as 'perfect rock'n'roll' and afterwards hung with the band, fixing them up with dope. He jammed with them. They gave him their tour book and suggested he look them up elsewhere.

The second was when he and his band played a gig at the Tao Club in Calvi. After the gig, Jean Temir, the manager of the club, introduced Henri to Paul Mulligan, a well-connected airline exec with a passion for music. Paul took a liking to Henri – everybody took a liking to Henri, they couldn't help it – and suggested that, any time he found himself in England, he could crash at his flat in Barnsbury.

So, in December 1976, Henri packed his guitar and amp into his car (obsessives might need to know it was a Jacobacci Studio 3, a Fender Twin Reverb and a Renault L6) and, stopping only to take in a Santana concert in Paris, drove to London.

He arrived on the Wednesday. Pretty much as soon as he'd unpacked the car, he and Paul went to see Meal Ticket at Dingwalls in Camden. A couple of days later, he met up with his pals the Flamin' Groovies in a Paddington pub. The Saturday after that, Paul Mulligan took him to see Curved Air in St Albans.

Paul had spent some of his early years in Beirut and knew the Copelands well. After the gig, he introduced Stewart to Henri and mentioned that he played the guitar. Stewart – as always – was immediately enthusiastic. 'Come round. Let's jam.'

So, the following Sunday, Henri and Paul went to the Mayfair flat – a riot of expensive furniture, guitars, amps, records, unwashed plates and mugs, hookahs, skins and quid deals. Upstairs they found Stewart drumming, Ian playing a Plexiglas bass through a tiny Pignose amp turned up to destruction, and Sonja strumming a Gibson SG and singing.

Stewart was delighted to see Henri. 'Grab a guitar, plug in. Let's play.'

Henri did as he was told. Sometimes Paul grabbed the mic from Sonja and played a mouth organ solo.

They played for two or three hours. Stewart showed them some of his own compositions. 'Henri – I've just written this. It's called "Fall Out". Let's go!!' Stewart told Henri about a band he was planning to put together. He already had a name. They would be called the Police. At the moment he, the drummer, was the only member, but other prospects were under consideration.

Stewart liked Henri. 'He couldn't speak much English,' he said, 'but he'd picked up some musicians' slang and he used to say, "Where can I put my homp [amplifier]?" or "Where do I put my rope [lead]?"'

'He could play guitar better than I could, and I could play guitar better than Joe Strummer... well, in those days.'

To further their collective understanding of punk, they – Stewart, Henri and Paul – took themselves off to the newly opened Roxy club in Neal Street to see the Damned.

Henri saw which way the wind was blowing and decided that, if he was going to make it as a musician in London, he would have to adapt to the spirit of the times. He had his hippy locks cut, shaved his beard and started looking for work. He spotted a 'no breadheads, no timewasters' ad in *Melody Maker*.

A band was being put together by Miles Tredinnick (aka Riff Regan) and Jon Moss (later of Boy George's Culture Club). They needed a guitar player. Henri auditioned. They offered him the job.

He phoned Stewart to tell him.

'Does this mean you're planning to stay in London?' Stewart asked him.

Henri told him he was.

'If you're going to stay in London, why don't you join my band?'

'Because you never asked me.'

'I thought it was understood.'

So now there were two.

Stewart told him that he'd got a potential third member in mind, a bass player from Newcastle.

CHAPTER FOUR

HIS NAME WAS ERNIE

There is a scene in the Hitchcock film *Marnie* in which Marnie, played by Tippi Hedren, visits her mother's house in a terraced street leading down to the Baltimore shipyards. At the bottom of the street is a huge ocean liner. It's actually a badly lit backdrop, but all the same it looms in the way that big ships up close do, and the looming is made all the more intense by the domestic setting – terraced houses, street, dog, pavement, lamp posts, huge ship bigger than all the rest of it put together. It's like having a planet at the bottom of your road, or God.

The *Esso Northumbria*, built in the 1960s on the River Tyne at the Swan Hunter yard at Wallsend, was 300 metres long and the height of a 17-storey building. It blotted out the sun. People had to keep their lights on all day, so Swan Hunter agreed to pay their electricity bills.

Sting, Gordon Matthew Thomas Sumner, born in Wallsend Maternity Hospital, 2 October 1951, lived as a lad in a house rented from Swan Hunter that sat in the shadow of those big ships.

★ ★ ★

The Sumner family – Mum, Dad, Gordon, and later Philip, Angela and Anita – were fine examples of post-war working-class aspiration.

It was a widespread phenomenon. The post-war Labour government had brought free education and free healthcare. Prosperity and invention had brought inside lavatories, washing machines, spin dryers, refrigerators, TV, long-playing gramophone records, wall-to-wall carpets, fitted kitchens and eye-level grills. The aspirational wanted one of each and two of some of them. And maybe a Ford Anglia and a holiday in Devon. And they wanted to possess that intangible thing called 'culture', too – or, if they couldn't possess it, then at least their children could. They could grow up knowing that a French Impressionist wasn't somebody who did impersonations of Maurice Chevalier and that Beethoven was pronounced 'Bay' not 'Bee'. They would grow up to have their dinner in the evening rather than at dinner time and smoke Du Maurier cigarettes without feeling poncey.

In Victorian times they would have talked about wanting their children to become 'gen'lemen' like Pip in *Great Expectations*. By the 1950s, the aspiration was experienced as a more general circumvention of anything perceived as 'common'. Girls who smoked in the street were 'common'. Watching ITV instead of BBC was 'common' (some families taped over the channel-changing knob, the better to avoid temptation). Dropping your aitches was 'common' (although if you went the whole hog and talked like Katie Boyle or Michael Aspel you ran the risk of people asking 'Who d'you think you are?' because there have to be limits).

The Sumners were off to a good start.

Grandad, Mum's father, had done well for himself in the insurance business and drove a Rover.

Mum, Audrey, was a hairdresser (a good few rungs above any sort of factory work) and played the piano – not the classics; she favoured tangos, Broadway musicals and sometimes even the latest pops if they were to her taste. She was a looker, too, by all accounts – in a classy way, but men still whistled in the street.

Dad, Ernest Matthew Sumner, five or six years older than Mum, was ex-Royal Engineers: 'Build bridges, blow 'em sky high and put them up again.' He worked as a fitter with an engineering firm. He was a skilled worker, C2 socio-economic bracket, a proud step up from the Ds, but not white-collar enough to make C1.

Little Gordon's relationship with Mum and Dad tended towards the standard Freudian Oedipal set-up. Mum adored him; Dad resented him. That's the way the boy felt, anyway, so whether they really did or not is of no importance.

★ ★ ★

Mum and Dad both had seagoing ancestors.

A 2015 US TV series, *Finding Your Roots*, turned up Sting's family tree. Back in the 18th century, one ancestor had been a river pilot. Another, Jane Cowell, at 76, had been the oldest stewardess working on the steam packets between the Isle of Man and Liverpool,

In the programme, Sting sifts disconsolately through paperwork and newspaper clippings about forebears who lost their lives at sea or suffered accidents in the shipyards. His great-grandfather, Richard, was only 13 when he was seriously injured, falling 45 feet from a wagon in Sunderland Docks. 'I don't know these people; I've never heard of these people and yet there they are and they're part of me.'

Ernest was a Roman Catholic. Audrey had been brought up Church of England, but, when it came to the matter of little Gordon's immortal soul, both agreed that Catholicism was the way to go.

He learned his Hail Mary, his Our Father and his Creed. Eventually he became an altar boy, one of the last generation to serve the Latin Mass, up the front with the priests in a clean white surplice, freebasing incense and, if you were lucky, dinging the dinger. Once the might and majesty of the liturgy is embedded in your skull, it can never leave. No matter how committed an atheist you subsequently become, the words 'Who made you?' will provoke the immediate, knee-jerk response from the catechism: 'God made me.' And, when you spend your formative years confessing, saying every Sunday and sometimes weekdays too, that you have 'greatly sinned', it's hard to believe that sometimes there might be a day when you haven't.

Bruce Springsteen was a Roman Catholic. He had an adoring mother, too, and a resentful father, and, like Sting, came to discover that consolation and liberation could be found in music. But he remained – to some degree gratefully – haunted by the smell of incense.

'This was the world where I found the beginnings of my song,' he wrote in his 2016 autobiography, *Born to Run*. 'In Catholicism, there existed the poetry, danger and darkness that reflected my imagination and my inner self. I found a land of great and harsh beauty, of fantastic stories, of unimaginable punishment and infinite reward. It has walked alongside me as a waking dream my whole life.'

★ ★ ★

The Sumner family's aspiration really kicked off when Ernest became self-employed. Tommy Close, a friend of Audrey's father, had a dairy and milk delivery business with its own premises. When Tommy retired, Ernest took it over. The premises came with a two-bedroom flat. There were five of them by this time. Sting's brother Philip and sister Angela had come along.

But the change in circumstance exacerbated problems in the marriage. Audrey was 'spontaneously emotional and as prone to tantrums and tears as she was to laughter and the joys of life'. Sting's father, on the other hand, seemed with age to become more emotionally distant. 'My family was always on the point of breaking up. They were always battling. Open bitter fighting.'

Grandma, Dad's mother, Agnes, provided refuge and solace. Agnes was the daughter of an Irish stevedore and had convinced her husband Tom to convert to Roman Catholicism. She had proper books in the house, subscribed to the *Reader's Digest* and prided herself on her ability to do the *Times* crossword.

She worked as housekeeper to Father James Thompson (always 'Father Jim' to Sting) at a convent in South Gosforth. Run by the Sisters of Our Lady of Charity of the Good Shepherd, the convent provided a 'home for penitents and young girls with dangerous surroundings, or who need training'.

Agnes and Tom had a terraced house in the grounds of the convent. Tom, in his old blue dungarees and army beret, was the caretaker. He looked after the laundry vans that picked up the soiled linen for the penitent girls to wash and press under the beady eyes of the Sisters of Our Lady of Charity of the Good Shepherd, and he kept the coke furnace in the cellar going.

Father Jim was a constant presence in Grandma's house. He was a character, Sting later observed, straight from a P. G. Wodehouse novel, posh and opinionated.

By the time he was 7, little Gordon had read his grandmother's copy of *Treasure Island* and was ploughing his way through the other books that lined her shelves.

Then comes what, if this was a major motion picture, would be called the 'inciting incident'.

Agnes' other sons, Ernie's brothers, Stings uncles, were, like Ernie himself, aspirational. Uncle Gordon, after whom little Gordon was named, had sailed off to prospect for gold in Australia. Then another uncle, John, sailed off to seek his fortune in Ontario, Canada. When he went, he left behind his cheap acoustic guitar. It had five rusty strings. Sting saved up for the sixth, started teaching his hands to make chords and watched with pride as the callouses grew on the ends of his fingers.

'Made my life. So, I'm grateful to Ontario for attracting my uncle.'

He had found books. He had found music and he was, by his own account, 'detached, lonely and driven'.

'That's basically where I am now,' he said in 2007, 'detached, really detached.'

★ ★ ★

He was sloughing off anything that might be construed as 'common' and, under the influence of Mum and Grandma, becoming, like them, a cut above.

'Everyone was envious of Gordon,' said another uncle, on his mum's side. 'Unlike us he was a posh kid. His mum dolled him up and he always seemed to have his nose in a book.'

Dad noticed, too.

'I was the bright red apple in my mother's green eye,' Sting said, 'just as I was a thorn in [my dad's] side.'

During school holidays and at weekends, his dad – Ernie, who, one devoutly hopes, drove the fastest milk cart in the west (at least in Wallsend) – would drag Gordon out of bed at 5.00 in the morning to help with the milk round, loading up the van and delivering the bottles in the silent streets of Hill Farm Estate. He'd inherited his dad's big hands, big enough to carry 10 milk bottles all in one go, and later to play the big stretches on the bass guitar.

In 1987, when his father was dying, Sting went to see him. Relations hadn't always been good between them. 'Sting reached out to take his father's hand in his,' says Phil Sutcliffe. 'His father looked down and said, "We do have something in common after all."'

★ ★ ★

St Cuthbert's Roman Catholic Grammar School was the smart place to go, especially if you were a bright Catholic 11-year-old and a cut above. The standard eleven-plus didn't cut the mustard. You had to take a special test as well. And prove you were a proper Catholic. Competition for places was very high. Sting walked it, the only kid in his primary school class to pass the exam.

One of the many things to dislike about St Cuthbert's – for Sting, anyway – was the trek there and back: a train into Newcastle, then a 34 bus to school, an hour each way, in his cap, his grey shorts and his 'claret' blazer.

He was tall for his age. At school, they called him Lurch, after the Frankenstein's monster/butler in *The Addams Family*.

He adapted, the better to fit in. 'The first thing that went was my accent. I realised as soon as I got into grammar school that it had to go. I was intelligent enough to see that to get on I'd have to have a non-accent.'

His accent retained a chameleon quality. In later interviews, if you listen carefully, you can hear the vowel sounds subtly change the better to fit those of the interviewer. A bit posher for this one, a tad Cockney for that. Maybe he's taking the piss. With American interviewers, he tends to become a little more English, not quite clipped, but going that way, because that's what they want to hear. And, of course, when he sang reggae, he channelled Bob Marley.

Anyway, the accent, along with the cap and the rest of the uniform, meant he wasn't a Wallsend kid any more. His primary school mates barely knew him.

Then his mum started an affair with one of the milkmen at his dad's dairy and the atmosphere at home deteriorated further – from difficult to poisonous.

Sting didn't fit in anywhere. The 'detachment' deepened.

St Cuthbert's was a tough school. There were canings, bullying, torture and sadism – routine for the time, but even so St Cuthbert's had a reputation for being stricter than most. Climbing the 13 steps up to the headmaster's office was, for many, like climbing the scaffold to the gallows.

'I was obnoxious, I think,' Sting said. 'I used my intelligence as a weapon.'

When he reached the third form – 13- and 14-year-olds drowning in hormones – the headmaster, Canon Cassidy, said, 'There is a canker amongst us.' The 'canker', according to various accounts, including the canker's own, was subjected to a record number of canings.

Different people can have different interpretations and sometimes entirely different memories of the same event.

A later headmaster at St Cuthbert's Edward Lovell, asked about Sting at school, replied, 'Our records and personal recollections show that he worked hard and, contrary to popular mythology, was well behaved.'

Six of the best, half a dozen of the other.

Gordon was a useful sprinter. 'Sprinting is something you're born with,' he said. 'There's no strategy involved, and not much training.'

At one time he was the county 100 yards champion and was entered for the nationals. In the qualifying heats, he came third and never ran competitively again.

'I realised that there were two people in my age group who were better than I was,' he said, in a distant echo of Miles Sr's advice to his son about there being no point going into politics if you can't be president of the USA. 'And there was no possibility of me beating them. So, I just stopped running.'

Elsewhere he's said that he was only running anyway to try to impress his father. It didn't work. 'I remember going home with the county 100-yard trophy – "Look what I've won" – and he said "Yeah?" and looked out of the window.'

Dad's dairy was doing well. Just after Sting started in the fourth form, the family acquired a car and a nice modern house out on the Marden Farm Estate, in North Shields, out towards Cullercoats. Sting hated that house. For a start, it was nearly twice as far away from school as the house in Wallsend had been. And it was miles out of town and civilisation.

He shared a bedroom with his little brother Philip. Phil had football posters on his side of the room. Sting had the Beatles, Motown stars and Bob Dylan. He could sing all eight verses of 'When The Ship Comes In', Dylan's song about how the oppressed will rise and their oppressors will be left drowned on the shore. Take that, Canon Cassidy.

He was at the age when priorities become clear. Home, family, school, sport faded into the background. Only two things mattered any more, and they were music and girls.

He'd progressed, by this time, from his uncle John's acoustic to an electric guitar that his friend, Pete Bingham, had made. He and Pete would sit around playing blues in their bedrooms.

Watching *Top of the Pops*, 7.30 every Thursday, became a religious observance more sacred than anything he'd known as an altar boy. He studied and learned those songs. They became part of him, the Petula

Clarks and the Jim Reeves as well as the Beatles, Beach Boys, Small Faces and Who. He needed more.

Technically, he was still too young to go to proper clubs. Most of them had an 18 and over policy. But he was tall for his age, and nobody was asking for ID...

The Handyside Arcade on Percy Street was Newcastle's answer to Carnaby Street. Actually, it was better than Carnaby Street. It was a world unto itself, a place where you could hang all day, meet your friends, browse the record racks, buy a shirt, a vial of patchouli oil, a psychedelic poster, a hippy hat, some coffee, some pills. And then, when you were done, go upstairs to the Club A'Gogo.

The Animals, at one time the club's house band, had a song on their first album celebrating the magic and mystery of the Club A'Gogo which name checked some of the artists who played there, including John Lee Hooker, the Rolling Stones, Memphis Slim and Sonny Boy Williamson.

It was true: the American blues heroes and the Rolling Stones – along with the Who, the Yardbirds, Pink Floyd, Fleetwood Mac – everybody played the Club A'Gogo.

It could be rough. John Lee Hooker, who had played some of the meanest dives on Beale Street in Memphis and Hastings Street in Detroit, was scared of the place: 'Fighting outside. And inside. "Oh," I said, "that's it. I ain't gonna play here no more."'

Sting was 15 when he saw the Graham Bond Organisation. A few weeks later, it was John Mayall and the Bluesbreakers. Then, 10 March 1967, came the epiphany.

He'd put a Ben Sherman button-down shirt in his schoolbag and a pair of jeans, and got changed in the lavs at Central Station. He joined the queue and eventually bagged himself a place at the back of the room. The band came on late, the way they always did.

Like Stewart at the Saville Club, he witnessed the greatness and glory of Jimi Hendrix. 'The Jimi Hendrix Experience was an overwhelming, deafening wave of sound that simply obliterated analysis,' Sting later wrote. 'I think I remember snatches of "Hey Joe" and "Foxy Lady", but that event remains a blur of noise and breathtaking virtuosity... I remember Hendrix creating a hole in the plaster ceiling above the stage with the head of his guitar, and then it was over. I lay in my bed that night with my ears ringing and my world view significantly altered.'

Going out to clubs also gave him access to his other priority. There were no girls at his all-boys school, but uptown, in the Arcade and in the clubs, there were hundreds of them.

He'd already had hints that, like sprinting, this was something he was good at when his sister, Angela, noticed she was becoming unaccountably popular with her schoolmates. 'One day it dawned on me,' she said, 'that a lot of my friends were coming round to drool over Gordon. I think Gordon noticed it – he couldn't fail to, really.'

He became, in his own words, 'the Don Juan of North Shields'.

'I'd always be looking for the right one. I suppose we all are, but... I needed a middle-class girl.'

It was the aspirational thing again.

But the search involved a lot of false starts and try-outs. Hearts were broken. One girl – he didn't find out until years later – killed herself. Not directly because of... It was complicated.

Eventually, he found his middle-class girl in the shape of a daughter of a headmaster. Their affair went on for a few years until she dumped him.

'I'd never had that happen to me before. Almost a repeat of what I'd done to other people. So, I learned.' And he wrote songs about it.

At school, after exemplary O-level results, he scored a B in his English A-level and a couple of disappointing Ds in Geography and Economics.

It was enough, though, to get him into Warwick University, then a new and allegedly exciting place.

It didn't take. He dropped out after the first term.

He worked for a year or so on building sites, then applied (in his 'best handwriting') for an office job with the Inland Revenue. That lasted about six months.

Years later, in 1995, his accountant was jailed for six years for filching £6 million of Sting's money.

'And tell me, Mr Sumner,' said the accountant's defence counsel in the trial, 'is it true that you were once employed in a tax office prior to your musical career, and nevertheless did not notice a discrepancy of this magnitude?'

'I think that's why they sacked me,' Sting replied.

After the Inland Revenue had finished with him, he did what people usually do when they're reasonably well-educated and have no idea what they want to do with their life – or the ideas they do have seem like ridiculous pipe dreams. He thought he'd better become a teacher and enrolled at Northern Counties Teacher Training College.

This turned out to be an unexpectedly fortuitous move when he ran into a fellow student called Gerry Richardson, who not only played the piano but was making money playing the piano.

Piano players, particularly piano players who can pick up a tune after one listen and sight-read whatever's put in front of them, are always in demand – weddings, posh birthdays, fancy restaurants, stand-in organist at the working-men's clubs. As long as you can play 'Happy Birthday', 'The Anniversary Waltz', 'Hava Nagila', 'I Can't Help Falling In Love', 'Delilah' and the entire Nat 'King' Cole oeuvre at the drop of a hat, you'll get paid.

Sting had switched from guitar to bass by this time. It seemed the way to go. Perhaps, in the same way as there was no point sprinting unless he could win, there was no point being a guitarist unless he was the best, and Jimi Hendrix already had that sewn up.

With bass players, 'best' is harder to define. Jaco Pastorius was an extraordinarily agile and inventive bass player, but very few bands or styles of music require 'agile and inventive'. They want solid and dependable. So, you can be the most solid and the most dependable, and that makes you the 'best'. Besides which, Sting wanted to sing. Paul McCartney played bass and sang. Jack Bruce played bass and sang. What's good enough for Paul and Jack had got to be good enough for anybody.

Sting saw a kind of nobility there, too. 'It just seemed a kind of quiet heroism. You know, you'd be stoic just there laying it down at the bottom end.'

He and Gerry explored each other's record collections, discovered their tastes overlapped and decided to form a band.

'Frankly I didn't give a toss about Sting's bass playing until we got talking and discovered he knew a drummer who owned a PA and a van,' Gerry said. 'That's what I really wanted, so I sacked my bassist and drummer and we formed this new line-up called Earthrise.'

The line-up was piano, bass, drums, singer and a horn section. No guitars. In the age of Clapton, Page and Beck, a guitarless band was a revolutionary concept. It also informed their repertoire, shifting it away from the usual covers people were thrashing out in their parents' garages towards stuff from the Motown catalogue, Memphis soul and jazz-rock.

The band never gigged much, but at college they rehearsed practically every day.

41

Sting discovered that bass players, if they had a good ear and were versatile, could pick up a few bob here and there, just like piano players, and started putting himself about a bit. He was anybody's.

'I played Dixieland, mainstream, bebop, free-form, I played in a big band, I also played as a backing musician for various cabaret artists. It was a very rich education.'

Two of the gigs were regular.

★ ★ ★

Traditional New Orleans jazz had experienced a huge revival after World War II, and a boom in the late 1950s and early 1960s, when Acker Bilk, Kenny Ball and Chris Barber were up there with Elvis and Cliff. In Newcastle, the Phoenix Jazzmen were still playing it 10 years after the boom had collapsed. Possibly, as the name implies, they thought it was due for another magical rebirth.

It wasn't, although at the time the music was still much admired by heavy drinkers of a certain age and the Phoenix Jazzmen were good at it.

In matching pink shirts and grey slacks, they gigged all over – pubs, working-men's clubs and bingo halls. Sometimes, to cater for all tastes, they included a pop number or two. It is history's tragedy that no recordings have ever surfaced of Sting adding the vocal refrain to the band's cover of the New Seekers' 1971 hit 'Never Ending Song Of Love', a duty he performed, just as he wore the pink shirt and grey slacks, with admirable resilience.

The Phoenix Jazzmen also gifted him his name. One night he showed up in a black-and-yellow striped sweater and Gordon Solomon, the trombone player, said, 'He looked like a wasp.' And that was it. You couldn't have two Gordons in the same band anyway. On old-time dance nights, people would make the obvious joke.

Years later, in the 1990s, Sting's wife, Trudie Styler, found herself sitting next to Princess Margaret at some charity do. HRH quizzed her about the nickname.

'He never liked the name Gordon,' Trudie said, 'and this was a fun nickname given to him when he was a teenager. All his family call him Sting and even his children and grandmother call him Sting, and so I have always called him Sting.'

There was a pause. HRH blew an eloquent smoke ring. 'Pity,' she said. And turned away.

★ ★ ★

The second regular gig – a great deal more challenging for a self-taught bass player – was with the Newcastle Big Band.

Sting remembers the Big Band as '25 pissheads trying to get through to the end of the arrangement'.

They were formidable arrangements, straight from the band books of Duke Ellington, Woody Herman and the like. No busking there, no off-the-cuff-count-of-three-and-all-pile-in. Reading the dots, and sometimes sight-reading the dots, was a given. Even the bass parts were full of odd rhythms and unexpected intervals. He'd take the sheet music home to learn his part, educating himself at the same time in the way they were put together, figuring out the strange mathematics of harmony and counterpoint – the same sort of lessons that Stewart had taken at university. Then he'd show up at the next rehearsal polished and raring to go.

'Another thing about him was the reliability factor,' Andy Hudson, the conductor, said. 'In five years of working with him, he was never late. That's important.'

The band's Sunday afternoon gigs, playing to packed crowds in the bar at Newcastle University, are among Sting's warmest memories. 'MacArthur Park' was always the favourite – a 'massive, rowdy blast'.

Sting kept up his association with the band until 1976, and it was with them that he made his first appearance on record (Wudwink, 1972 – tracks include the Count Basie/Neal Hefti tune 'Li'l Darlin'', Jimmy Webb's 'MacArthur Park', Cole Porter's 'Love For Sale' and the Beatles' 'Hey Jude', on sale at the time of writing for £296.15). Sting's there with his photo on the sleeve, standing between the guitarist and a trumpeter, looking nervously at the conductor. They don't sound like pissheads.

As an apprenticeship, working with the Phoenix Jazzmen and the Big Band could not have been bettered. First, musically, it gave him an intimate acquaintance with some of the core repertoire – the first 40 or 50 years of jazz and American popular music that informed everything that came after, from swing to death metal to industrial house. And, second, he learned crowd control. In later life, he and others often attributed his ability to deal with a difficult audience to his experience as a teacher, but one must never forget that here was a man who had played miners' clubs on drunken Saturday nights.

The musical adventure took a great leap forward when the rhythm section of the Big Band – Gerry on keyboards, John Hedley on guitar (later replaced by Terry Ellis), Ronnie Pearson on drums and Sting on bass and vocals – set up a band of their own and called it Last Exit. They played jazz/fusion/funk – with lots of Fender Rhodes piano, wah-wah guitar and Sting's soaring voice.

They copped a residency at the Gosforth Hotel, a pub on Gosforth High Street in the north of Newcastle – and packed the place every Wednesday night for two years. You cannot, of course, play the same set every Wednesday night for two years without crushing boredom setting in and punters feeling short-changed. On the other hand, hunting down, adapting and rehearsing new material is a fag. So Last Exit started writing their own stuff.

Sting had always messed around with songwriting. Now he had the chance every week to write something, rehearse it and try it with the Wednesday audience.

Again, as an apprenticeship, it couldn't have been bettered. Gerry was writing, too. 'I never had a rival in the way Gerry was a rival,' Sting said. 'He'd write something, I'd write something and vice versa. He says he didn't, but he did write a song a week. He always came up with something and there was always a great little ping-pong match going on.'

Some of the stuff that Sting came up with was later recycled, in sometimes radically adapted form, as material for the Police. 'The Bed's Too Big Without You', for instance (inspired by Sting being dumped by 'the one'), started life as a Last Exit song, 'Truth Kills' morphed into 'Truth Hits Everybody', and 'Fool In Love' (with four-to-the-bar cowbell) had part of the lyric recycled as 'So Lonely'.

★ ★ ★

He moved into a flat with Gerry, a freezing shit-heap in Heaton where they once burned the furniture to keep warm.

College finished. Sting, sans student grant, sans structure to his day, had no option but to start teaching.

His first job was in Cramlington, a pit village, teaching nine-year-olds. 'I never gave a fuck about them learning maths or logarithms,' said Sting. 'I just wanted them to enjoy themselves when they had time.'

It was a Catholic school. A convent school. He was the only male teacher in the place. A lot of the other teachers were nuns, and sometimes it must have seemed that he'd been put there by God to test their vows of celibacy.

The headteacher, Sister Agnes Miller, thought he was 'likable in a distant and hazy sort of way. Gordon was always the last to arrive in the morning and left the second the bell went in the evening. On the other hand, he had terrific charm and a shyness that the other staff – all female – found charming. We probably spoiled him.'

Spoiled by nuns all day, playing in a band a night. Could life get any better?

★ ★ ★

Phil Sutcliffe was a journalist who'd started his professional life on the Newcastle *Chronicle*, but had since gone freelance as a rock journalist – effectively a north-east stringer for *Sounds* and anybody else who'd pay him. It was his business, as well as his delight, to know the Newcastle music scene, the bands and the musicians. He was a regular at the Gosforth Hotel Last Exit gigs, and became instrumental, as we'll see, in the Police existing at all. In 1981, it was he who wrote, with Hugh Fielder, the first proper book about the Police, *L'Historia Bandido*.

'Newcastle had a good pub rock scene, extending to stuff like Last Exit,' he says. 'There were loads of bands. With a bunch of friends who were mostly fans but some working in the media, we organised this thing called Bedrock, which was a loose cooperative of people interested in music and musicians, and we helped to get things happening, encouraging things. There was a great burgeoning of enthusiasm.'

Newcastle was jumping, then, and Last Exit was, by most people's reckoning, the best band in Newcastle.

In June 1974, Sting and Gerry were hired to play in the pit band for a pro-am production of *Joseph and the Amazing Technicolor Dreamcoat* at the University Theatre. 'I closed my eyes, drew back the curtain', six nights a week, for 13 weeks, at £60 a week.

Then, towards Christmas, they were booked at the same theatre for the world premiere of Tony Hatch's new *Rock Nativity*, commissioned by Cameron Mackintosh and Veronica Flint-Shipman. This was a big deal.

Tony Hatch and his wife Jackie Trent had had major hits in America as well as the UK. They'd written Petula Clark's 'Downtown', 'Don't Sleep

In The Subway' and 'I Couldn't Live Without Your Love'. Tony wrote 'Sugar And Spice' for the Searchers. He wrote the theme from *Crossroads*.

The *Rock Nativity*, according to the Newcastle papers, was a massive hit. 'Inspired moments of rejoicing,' the *Newcastle Journal* said. 'Great fun, and the sheer happiness of the evening is hard to resist.'

Sadly, the rest of the world failed to see the joy, and the show never quite made it into the West End. The market for religious musicals has its limits, and Lloyd Webber and Rice seem to have had it sewn up.

All the same, for Sting *Rock Nativity* was a life-changing experience.

In the lead, playing the Virgin Mary, was an Irish actor, Frances Tomelty. Frances was from Belfast cultural royalty – her father, Joseph Tomelty, had co-founded the Belfast Group Theatre and had written two novels and 12 plays. She left Belfast in 1970, and was fast becoming a name. She'd done *Coronation Street*, *Play for Today* and *Callan* on TV and had a major role alongside Albert Finney on the stage in *Cromwell* at the Royal Court.

Sting was no small-town rube. He read books. He knew Proust was pronounced 'Proost' and not 'Prowst' and Goethe was pronounced 'Gerter' and not 'Go-eth'. His gran could do the *Times* crossword.

But Frances was from out there – the place where people chat about the new book they've just published, just like you'd chat about a record you just bought. The place where music, theatre, cinema were not activities to be pursued at the weekend, as an adjunct to real life, but real life itself. She was the antidote to the 'who the hell d'you think you are' voice that plagues all working-class provincial kids with uppity notions. She was living proof that it was possible to make a living without having an actual job. She was smart, beautiful and funny. And there was no doubt in his mind that she was 'the one'.

He was in love.

'He found so much in Frances,' says Phil Sutcliffe. 'Culture, Irishness, ambition. It gave him the impetus and, because she was an actress, she knew that you could have bad patches and push through.'

When *Rock Nativity* came to an end, Sting spent a lot of his time on the road to London and, when Frances wasn't on tour or working in London, she'd come to stay in the freezing shit-heap in Heaton. They even did the place up a bit so that it wasn't quite so shitty.

★ ★ ★

The huge hit of 1974 – in the album charts, anyway – was Mike Oldfield's *Tubular Bells*. It had been released in the previous year, since when it had been nigh on impossible to eat in a restaurant, shop for clothes or go to the pictures (it was the soundtrack of *The Exorcist*) without its jangles and stabs confronting you at every turn.

In February 1975, an orchestral version, played by the Royal Philharmonic, was released. It became a hit all over again and the Northern Concert Orchestra decided to use it as the opening of their 1975–6 season at the Newcastle City Hall. Since Mike Oldfield suffered from severe stage fright, they hired another guitar player to do his parts – a chap called Andy Summers.

Last Exit were booked as support.

It was, by all accounts, a thankless gig. Most nights, the place was half empty.

And what might have been the Livingstone/Stanley moment – 'Mr Summers, I presume' – never happened. Andy caught about five minutes of Last Exit's set, then wandered off to have a cheese roll and a cup of tea. And that was it. Hardly worth mentioning, really.

★ ★ ★

Last Exit became regular visitors at Impulse Sound Studios in Wallsend, at the back of the old Borough Theatre, where the dressing rooms used to be. It was run by Dave Wood, who knew Sting from when Sting used to deliver his milk.

The Big Band had made their album there and Dave had released it on his own Wudwink label.

Last Exit recorded a bunch of stuff at Impulse and sent some of it off to Tony Hatch ('We have a dozen bands in London who can do the same thing much better'). Eventually they released a single on Wudwink, with 'Whispering Voices' on the A-side, and 'Evensong' on the B-side. Both were Gerry's compositions.

The reputation began slowly to build.

They entered the *Melody Maker* 'Battle of the Bands' contest and came third (out of 30). Thanks to Alan Hudson, the Newcastle Big Band conductor, they got to play at the San Sebastian Jazz Festival in northern Spain (Ella Fitzgerald was topping the bill) and won the *Concurso de Aficionados* – the amateurs' contest. Off the back of this, they picked up some gigs in Bilbao.

None of this was making them much money and money became something of a priority when, on 1 May 1976, Sting married Frances at St Oswin's Catholic Church in Front Street, Tynemouth. Gerry played the organ. Joe, their son, came along seven months later.

'I was 28. I needed a baby,' Frances said. 'My whole self was telling me it was the right time. Our careers didn't come into that side of it at all.'

Sting had come back from the San Sebastian/Bilbao adventure proudly bearing the *Concurso de Aficionados* award, but with just a fiver in his pocket. He was teaching but wanted desperately to give it up.

Frances was still getting regular work. The previous year she'd done a feature film, *The Romantic Englishwoman*, starring Glenda Jackson and Michael Caine and directed by Joseph Losey. Admittedly her role – 'Airport receptionist' – was less than beefy, but it all adds up. In 1976, she put food on the table with a five-part kids' series for ATV television called *A Place to Hide*. She played Ann Smith, a bank robber.

But how easily would she be able to keep working when she was pregnant and when she was nursing a baby?

★ ★ ★

The cruise ships beckoned. Cruise ships hire musicians. They're expected to play getting-on-the-boat music, getting-off-the-boat music, being-on-the-boat music, having-your-lunch music, having-your-dinner music, sometimes music for dancing and sometimes music to accompany a singer, comedian, conjuror or talent show. Often the bandleader provides the musicians with a book twice the size and twice as sacred as the Bible, which contains every song anybody on board is likely to request. ('Can you play "The Jewel Song" from Gounod's *Faust*?' 'Page 1,726, lads, and no fuzzbox on the guitar.')

Ronnie, Last Exit's drummer, had done cruises before and knew the form. He fixed it up. 'You've got to understand,' he warned them. 'It'll be foxtrots, waltzes and quick steps. There'll be no room for rock'n'roll.'

'It was hellish,' said Gerry, 'but we were getting £60 a week, and free board and lodging.' And nobody drowned.

★ ★ ★

Frances encouraged, coaxed, provoked and pushed. In Sting's words, she 'transformed my life and was a catalyst in my becoming something completely different'.

'Sting changed when Frances came on the scene,' says Phil Sutcliffe. 'He would say he got more focused. She advised him how to establish stage presence. It was an actorly trick. She'd sit in the audience of the Gosforth Hotel and watch him and give him her advice. "You're trying to make contact with everyone in the room by looking at each one of them in the course of the set. Don't do that. Fix a point in the back of the room to look at. They will look at you." It's a commanding way to deal with being on stage.'

Frances knew the business well enough to know that, rightly or wrongly, London was where you had to be.

'There was no way I could have settled in Newcastle. I'd lived in London before and it held no terrors for me – although perhaps it did for Sting.'

That summer, heavily pregnant, Frances made the rounds of the A&R men in London armed with tapes of Last Exit. She got murmurs of interest from Virgin, Island and A&M. This was encouraging.

In the autumn, Richard Branson and Carol Wilson of Virgin Music came up to see Last Exit support Alan Price at the Newcastle City Hall. The band didn't seem to impress them much, but Carol Wilson liked Sting's songwriting and signed him up for a publishing deal. A record deal would have been nice, but a publishing deal is at least an indication of interest. That's good, isn't it? As it turned out, it wasn't, and eventually it led to lengthy and acrimonious litigation. But that's in the future.

Last Exit also got a handful of London gigs at Dingwalls, the Nashville and the LSE, and three days in a London recording studio, paid for by Virgin.

Phil Sutcliffe followed them everywhere.

'I did a three-page feature. I sold it to *Sounds*, telling them it would be a piece about a northern band coming to London to get their break. I got up very early and went out to South Shields, where the roadie was sticking all the equipment into the transit. Then we drove for ages in the winter.'

The three-page piece, with the title 'Making It', gave their Dingwalls show a rave review and described Sting as having 'commanding stillness. He's fire and ice, transfixing.'

It was incredible publicity for an unknown band and, together with the growing interest from Virgin, put the brass ring within reach.

Things began to move fast.

On 24 September 1976, Curved Air were playing at Newcastle Polytechnic. Phil Sutcliffe, a Curved Air supporter as well as champion of Last Exit, was there.

'I went backstage,' said Phil Sutcliffe, 'and happened on a strange backstage scene. The Social Secretary was being abusive to them. He moaned about paying them £1,000 to their faces. And he got thrown out of the dressing room. They had a code word "alligator", said without any context, and their roadie would throw out whoever was being rude.'

The following day, he met up with Sonja and Stewart and said, 'You might want to go and see this local band who are playing nearby,' because they were interested in new talent.

'They were up for it – I don't know what Stewart was thinking at the time – but he was obviously beginning to think about punk. I don't know where he thought Curved Air was going for him – apart from earning £1,000 a night. Any sensible person could see past that stage.

'They came to the gig at St Mary's, the teaching college in the outskirts of Newcastle, and Last Exit played a very good gig – as usual. They were my favourite band.

'Stewart was interested – I didn't know he was just interested in Sting, because he was always polite to musicians. I introduced him to Sting in the bar and they said hello, but they didn't exchange phone numbers or anything.'

'We both really got Sting,' Sonja said. 'He was very charismatic, even though he was just playing in a college canteen or whatever – there wasn't a big stage or anything. He had the voice, he had the presence, he was the only thing that was really memorable about that band.'

'And that was that,' says Phil. 'And what I remember happening next – Stewart disputes my account, but I'm pretty sure – what I remember is that after Christmas Stewart rang my place, because he had my number, and says, "Sting the singer – I want to get hold of him." So, I did. Stewart says he spoke to my wife and she gave him the number. Another account says I didn't give him the number at all because I didn't want him to break up Last Exit.'

★ ★ ★

A couple of months later, on 23 November, Frances gave birth to Joseph at Newcastle General. Sting, exhausted from a gig the night before, slept through the labour.

He had a son now. Frances' career was London-based. The shit-heap in Heaton wasn't really an option.

'1976 was a crucial year,' Sting said. 'I decided to have this kid, live with this girl, quit my job, move to London. And then I saw the Sex Pistols, had my hair cut, dyed it – it was like an acid trip. It completely turned me around.'

The other members of Last Exit weren't going to London with him.

'By that time it was Terry Ellis and Ronnie Pearson,' Gerry said, 'and they really would not countenance moving down there. They said, "We'll commute," which was never going to happen, and by that time Sting had met Stewart and there was this split focus – which way am I going to go?'

Sting still had Frances pushing him. She told her husband, 'In five years Last Exit will just be the old men the local kids come to for tips on how to play.'

He quit the band and left.

'And, you know, I can't really blame him,' Gerry said. 'Stewart was a real wheeler-dealer, and I was pretty frightened by London... Stewart was established there and just had a mouth like...'

CHAPTER FIVE

THE WORDS ARE BANAL AND THE MUSIC'S FAST

Starting a band in 1977 was a confusing business. The complex problem, endemic to the pop business, of being 'good', when 'good' involves such a number of variables (how many acts can you remember who were just a decent haircut away from stardom), had, in the age of punk, become more complex still. Obviously loud, fast, angry and wasted were important, but how could *your* band stand out from the legions of equally loud, fast, angry and wasted bands.

It helped if you hitched your wagon to a movement of some sort. Punk was a generic catch-all that could contain any number of ideologies, causes, struggles and subcultures. There were many to choose from, all on display at the T-shirt and badge stall down the market (going to Dingwalls in a badgeless jacket or a blank T-shirt was like walking through the Vatican naked).

Anti-nuke ('Protest And Survive'), anti-war ('Bombs, Bullets, Bullshit'), gay lib ('Come Out, Come Out, Whoever You Are'), women's lib ('A Woman Without A Man Is Like A Fish Without A Bicycle'), animal rights ('Meat Is Murder'), anarchy ('No Matter Who You Vote For, The Government Always Wins'), one of the many left factions ('Eat The Rich'), pro-drugs ('I Like The Pope, The Pope Smokes Dope'), various mystic doodaddles left over from the hippy era ('You Are Not Now', 'Don't Hate, Meditate'), and so on, and on and on.

For a band, the two big advantages to allying yourself to a cause were: you'd get gigs (although a lot of them would be benefits, so you wouldn't get paid); and it provided you with a degree of immunity against criticism. Thus, if your band held bona fide 'save the whale' credentials, anybody who didn't cheer you enthusiastically enough would be branded a humpback hater and shunned by decent society. Because (all together, now), if you're not part of the solution, you're part of the problem.

When movements collided, hell broke loose: witness this letter from the pages of the feminist magazine *Spare Rib*:

Dear Spare Rib,
I play rhythm guitar with the Accelerators. On August 2, we played a benefit gig and several of the Merseyside Women's Action Group WAG were present. Some of them persisted in haranguing the drummer's girlfriend because of the sexy clothes she was wearing. He reacted by writing a slogan on his overalls which read 'All women's lib. are cunts'.

In the middle of our first number, one of the WAG walked onto the stage and poured a glass of beer over Brian, his drums, and a plugboard. He hit her once, and Chris, the singer, bundled her offstage. Some of her friends rushed forward, one of them wielding a mike stand. In the brief fracas, [the woman's] face was cut. We later learned that she had to have 20 stitches. My political stand is to play a dirty, noisy, rock'n'roll guitar. But the WAG wants to silence the band I play in. What a great step forward for women's liberation.

Was this really the world in which Stewart wanted to raise a band?

At the start of January 1977, Sting arrived for an 'audition' with Stewart and Henri.

'Yeah, he plays well... Tall, good-looking... You'll see,' Stewart told Henri. 'Okay, he's a bit provincial, and he was playing jazz-rock before. You know these guys, not really into "the look", but we'll soon fix that. He'll be here at three o'clock. We'll play it cool.'

Henri, the better to play it cool, put on dark glasses and black leather drainpipes and tried to look moody and dangerous.

Sting showed up. First glimpse was enough to verify Stewart's claim that he was not into 'the look'. He was accompanied by a baby in a carrycot. He was wearing overalls – dungarees were the standard uniform at the time for social workers at vegetarian craft fairs. History does not record whether his dungies were garnished with an 'Atomkraft? Nej Tak' badge, but chances are they were.

They played, trying out some of Stewart's songs.

Sting passed the audition.

Just as Stewart, by way of an introduction to his plans for the Police, had taken Henri to see the Damned, they dragged Sting off to the Roxy to see Generation X.

Henri could see the new boy wasn't impressed. In Newcastle, Sting had been playing fancy chords and complex rhythms. He'd worked on his technique.

'All that hard work to end up here,' Henri said. 'He was ashamed, and we knew it.'

But the place was packed with paying customers more enthusiastic about Generation X's three-chord thrashes than anybody had ever been about Last Exit's Ebm7b5 harmonic adventures. As Stewart and Miles had already noticed, here, among the safety pins and bin liners, was the land of opportunity. Sting had a baby and rent to pay on the Bayswater basement flat they'd moved in to, and no source of funds other than what he got from signing on at the Lisson Grove dole office every Wednesday and Frances's sometimes substantial, but often precarious, earnings as an actor. He was open to any opportunity going.

At the time he wrote in his diary – later quoted in the High Court when he was contesting his publishing deal with Virgin – 'My tired mind is in turmoil, please God help me.'

And 'What is going to happen to us? I went to the Dole – feel all the usual nausea – the sickening queue.'

And 'Money or the lack of it has raised its ugly head again – Joe is so innocent and vulnerable – God please help us.'

He had a proper northern man's work ethic. Work was work. If he had to thrash about in a punk band to make a living, he would thrash.

All the same, he was congenitally incapable of being bossed around and the differences of opinion with his new bandmates started straight away.

Stewart had been around the music business since he was 15 or 16. He'd roadied for some of the best. He'd played in a headlining band that could make £1,000 a night and had gigged at nearly all the Russell

Group universities, the Roundhouse, Colston Hall Bristol, Free Trade Hall Manchester, Birmingham Town Hall and the Pavilion Theatre Hastings. He'd recorded a proper album at a proper studio with proper sleeve notes that credited him with co-writing three of the 10 songs. His older brother had managed some of the top acts in the business and was currently seeking out many new pies in which to stick his fingers. His other brother was about to take up an influential job with a top talent agency in Macon, Georgia, USA. His dad had overthrown governments. His sister had gone to Vassar. He, Stewart, had invented the Police, he had come up with the name, he had recruited Henri and Sting, he had written the songs. It was his vision.

Sting, on the other hand, was Sting.

In rehearsal, he tried to interest Stewart in some of his own compositions. Henri would hold on to his Jacobacci and try to remain affable while around him the sparks flew. Years later, he wrote it all down.

'Stewart stopped him each time. "Sting, we can't sing a song called 'Don't Give Up Your Daytime Job'! You still don't get it, do you? Write us something along the lines of 'My Job Is A Heap Of Shit And I'm Going To Smash Everything Up'. That we can play." Sting would look at us and I could see he was seething inside.'

Stewart, it has to be remembered, was the American with the can-do attitude who'd never needed a daytime job in his life – unless you count roadieing for Joan Armatrading – and was living rent-free in a Mayfair flat.

In anger, Sting would play at three times the normal speed, Stewart would assault his kit, Henri would try to keep up and, in this way, they achieved a good degree of punkishness.

'I gave Henri private coaching,' Stewart said. 'He used to come over early before Sting to rehearse or he'd stay late and I'd teach him the new songs, because Sting would have flipped if he'd heard Henri saying, "Now what fret do I put my finger on to play that chord?" So, I would teach him the songs first and then pretend to teach him all over again with Sting.'

★ ★ ★

Lawrence Impey, a photographer who'd been at school with Stewart, came over to take some publicity snaps up on the roof of the Mayfair flat.

The threesome tried looking moody with sunglasses. They tried looking cheeky with tongues out. They tried using props – guitars, guns, police hats. They tried most things, but still they looked like three guys pretending to be a band. Maybe it was the clothes. Sting had on a pinstripe jacket and a striped T-shirt. It's not punk, it's not jazz-rock, it's not shabby chic, it's a bloke with no sense of style in an Oxfam shop. His hair looks like it's combed forward to disguise a bald patch. Stewart wears a leather jacket buttoned up to the neck. He looks cold. Henri had a hangover and toothache. He *looks* like a man with a hangover and toothache. They all look ill at ease with each other, with themselves and with the world, which should have been punkish, but wasn't.

★ ★ ★

Before the band had played a gig or released a record, Stewart, just as he'd invented himself a following as Curved Air's drummer with the Weather Master Heads, and the Percussion Services C sticks, was faking a grassroots fanbase.

Late at night, with Paul Mulligan and whoever else was around, he would take to the streets with spray cans.

'We started out with a stencil,' Stewart said, 'but ended up getting more paint on ourselves than on the walls. And the logo just wasn't dominating the canvas with enough pride.' They ditched the stencils and just sprayed 'THE POLICE' freehand wherever a wall could be found.

Passers-by were confused. There had been riots at the 1976 Notting Hill Carnival. The blatantly racist execution of the 'sus' (from 'suspected person') laws, which gave police wide-ranging powers to stop and search, had provoked much anger. 'The Police Are Bastards' seemed a reasonable thing to see painted on a wall. 'The Police Are Doing a Marvellous Job' would have made a sort of sense. 'The Police' with no other comment seemed oddly non-committal.

Paul Mulligan had faith in the band and nurtured ambitions to be a player in the business. He advanced them a loan to finance a record.

★ ★ ★

On 12 February, they went to Pathway, a little 8-track studio in Stoke Newington, north London, because it's where everybody went.

The Damned had recorded 'New Rose' – allegedly (don't start!) the first punk record – at Pathway. At one time or another Elvis Costello,

Lene Lovich, Sham 69, Siouxsie and the Banshees, Madness, Dire Straits and loads of others worked there. It was also where Sting and Last Exit had made their demos for Virgin a couple of months earlier.

The studio was not known for its luxurious appointments. There was no reception area with bowls of chocolate bars on the coffee tables, or restroom where musicians could chill out over a game of pool and drinks from the well-stocked complementary bar; just a studio that you could swing a cat in as long as it didn't have a very long tail, and a control room where you couldn't.

It had a distinctive fuggy smell, which some found comforting and others offensive.

'It was a genuine shithole,' said Barry 'Bazza' Farmer, who'd built the desk and worked the faders. 'You'd be confronted by the smell. It had a problem with damp, and it smelled like an autumn woodland or an old toilet. It would cling to your clothes.'

Stewart, Henri and Sting cut two sides: 'Fall Out' by Stewart, and 'Nothing Achieving' by Stewart and Ian. The enterprise cost £130 of the £150 they'd borrowed from Paul.

A couple of weeks earlier, Henri had been stopped by the police (the real ones) for 'suspicious driving' (in Paul Mulligan's car) and spent a night in the cells. Paul had sorted him out, but the terms of his release demanded that he report to a police station every day at eight in the morning. As a result, he showed up late at the studio, nervous and not at his best.

He fluffed. In the end, Stewart, who'd taught him how to play the songs in the first place, laid down the basic guitar parts and Henri did the solos.

On 'Fall Out', he's chivvied by Sting, yelling, 'Henri', pronounced the French way.

They do the punk thing as best they can. Sting plays a simple eight-to-the-bar duh-duh-duh-duh bassline. Stewart rushes the tempo. The key puts Sting's voice up in the stratosphere – thin and stringy, but possibly still too refined to be genre-appropriate and far more musical than the *Sprechstimme* adopted by a lot of the punk bands. In the last chorus, tune and lyrics are replaced by what sounds like somebody having rough sex with a farm animal.

'Nothing Achieving', the B-side, is a drummer's song, with rhythm changes every other bar and nifty bits where the fills can shine. Sting does another duh-duh bassline and roughens up the voice, but, however much they go for it, it's a hard track to love.

Miles, who was at this point generally unconvinced by his brother's band, nevertheless agreed to put the record out on his newly formed Illegal Records label.

The sleeve used one of Lawrence Impey's photos from the Mayfair roof shoot, set skewed against a bang-on-trend chequerboard background.

Sting spent hours putting the records – they'd had 2,000 pressed – into the sleeves and it was released later in the year, on 19 May.

Stewart worked the phones and tried to drum up interest, but it was an uphill struggle. Every day he'd trek into Miles' office, phone any record shop he could find the number of – 'Hello, is that Fearnley's in Middlesbrough' – and try to hustle them into taking a few copies.

'Meanwhile at the next desk there was Miles' sales girl saying, "Yes, we have the new Chelsea single and Sham 69 and the Fall," and I'd be whispering across, "And who else have you got?"'

Sales were eventually good: they shifted 10,000, but that was two years and a reissue later. They were never remotely close enough for the magic 'Lads, we're number one' phone call to happen. Or even 147.

Hustling actual gigs was even more of a challenge.

'We were very ambitious,' Stewart said. 'Ten per cent more rabid than the other bands. We'd get these calls saying, "The Snivelling Bathrooms can't make it tonight, can you get there by eight o'clock?" And we always did.'

The audience often consisted of 'three girlfriends and maybe about 10 other people'.

Keeping Sting interested kept Stewart busy, too.

'He didn't identify with the group. His attitude was, "Convince me – keep me in the band." So every day I'd phone him and I'd have something to tell him, like, "I've just got the photos back from the session" or "I've just finished the record sleeve – why don't you come over and have a look at it?" or "We've got a gig."'

★ ★ ★

Miles, meanwhile, had been gradually submerging himself in the punk gob-lagoon. He was not a natural fit.

Chris Difford of Squeeze, whom Miles was managing, described him as 'bearing a striking resemblance to John Denver wearing a tweed jacket and grey trousers'.

Miles, however, had made a commitment to punk, and he was ferociously persistent in all his endeavours. To have Miles on your side was like being blessed by the Furies.

It took effort to squeeze money out of any sort of music, and though punk looked like it could turn a fast buck for the right man in the right place, it was never quite the all-consuming, all-threatening craze the headlines made it out to be. Its impact on the charts was certainly limited.

Sex Pistols and the Stranglers both scored regular Top 10 hits, but on the whole punters bought tamer stuff. Paul McCartney's 'Mull Of Kintyre', Baccara's 'Yes Sir, I Can Boogie' and Manhattan Transfer's 'Chanson D'Amour' were the big sellers of 1977, along with Abba's 'Knowing Me, Knowing You' and 'The Name Of The Game', Donna Summer's magnificent 'I Feel Love' and Julie Covington's 'Don't Cry For Me Argentina' from *Evita*.

The Clash made the Top 30 once in the year. The Damned didn't come within spitting distance of the Top 100.

Nevertheless, Miles and Stewart clung to their belief that the future was dirty and noisy. And, besides, Miles couldn't have avoided punk even if he'd wanted to. The bands needed him.

Punk bands, he discovered, didn't care that he had no money. He had other things to offer. He knew stuff they didn't. He'd listen to their music. He'd get them gigs and make sure they got paid. He'd help them make records and sort out ways people could buy them. Once, not very long ago, he'd set up a massive world tour that had ended with Lou Reed locking himself in a toilet. They wanted some of that.

Over the next two years, he was agent, manager, promoter and/or producer for any punk who mattered. He was instrumental in setting up one of the Sex Pistols' tours, he sort of managed the Clash for about three weeks, he brought Debbie Harry and Blondie over for their first UK tour and acted in one capacity or another for Generation X (with Billy Idol), Television, John Cale, Patti Smith and a bunch of others.

By the middle of 1977, his influence was such that, in a *News of the World* shock/horror exposé headlined 'The Punk Rock Exploiters', practically the entire blame for the 'sick', 'dangerous', 'sinister' 'cult' was laid at the door of 'Svengalis like Miles Copeland'.

This, remember, was the bloke who, a couple of years earlier, had been floating on the gentle waves of folk-rock-fusion-prog-hippy-drippydom.

'A lot of people said I wasn't honest in what I was doing,' he said, 'because one day I was in progressive music and the next I was in punk. Well, I believed in what I was doing more than the rest because I had seen the other side. I'd been through the shit of it. Sure, when I first saw the Clash, I thought it was ridiculous, because these guys could hardly play. I took time to adjust my perceptions. But then I got into the excitement of it, which was what I'd been missing. Since when has music ever had anything to do with it? We're in the culture business, the expression business.'

At the beginning of 1977, he'd turned his attention to American punk. People in the know had been paying close attention to the *Max's Kansas City* compilation album, a taster of bands like Wayne County and the Back Street Boys (not *those* ones), the Fast, Cherry Vanilla and her Staten Island Band and Pere Ubu, all of whom had played at Max's Kansas City on Park Avenue South in New York.

Miles had the idea of importing the American bands to the UK and possibly signing some of them to his Illegal Records label. He started with three acts.

Cherry Vanilla had played the title role in Andy Warhol/Anthony Ingrassia's play *Pork* ('the nearest we have yet come to a theatrical emetic', said the *Daily Telegraph*) and worked as a publicist for David Bowie before staking her own claim on pop stardom.

Wayne County had also been in *Pork*, playing a character called Vulva Lips, who took a close interest in the faeces of various species. (One funster described the play as 'expexcremental theatre'.) In 1979, she identified as a woman and changed her name to Jayne County, so we'll settle the pronoun issue by calling her 'she' regardless.

In June 1976, Wayne had been playing CBGB, doing her Patti Smith impersonation when Handsome Dick Manitoba of the Dictators started heckling. The word 'queer' might have been mentioned. Spit might have been ejected.

Anyway, the upshot was that Wayne set about Handsome Dick with a microphone stand, broke his collarbone and was hauled off to spend a night in jail. After that, she spent a lot of time in England.

Her 1977 release, with her band the Electric Chairs, '(If You Don't Want To Fuck Me, Baby) Fuck Off' is as fine an example of that sort of thing as you're likely to find.

The cast of *Pork*, incidentally, while they were over in London in 1971, spent some entertaining hours with David Bowie. Claims have been made that they jived him that he was voodoo like a leper messiah, encouraged him to shave his eyebrows, dye his hair orange, paint his face the lightning way and generally let the children lose it. But the same thing's said about a lot of other moon-age daydreamers.

Johnny Thunders had played with the New York Dolls, the proto-punk band that Malcolm McLaren had provoked, styled and encouraged in New York before doing the same thing in the UK with Sex Pistols. Thunders, along with drummer Jerry Nolan, had left the Dolls in 1975 and formed Johnny Thunders and the Heartbreakers.

Miles saved a few quid on airfares by persuading Cherry Vanilla to travel with a slimmed-down version of her band, leaving the rhythm section behind and just bringing guitarist Louis Lepore and keyboard player Zecca Esquibel. He convinced her that he knew a couple of guys who would fit right in – the two guys being his brother Stewart and Stewart's new pal, Sting. Further savings could be made if the Police, with Henri, played support for Cherry. On tour, Stewart and Sting would get £10 a night each for backing Cherry – although some of the venue managers remember paying them £15. Nobody can remember if they got paid as support band. 'In any case,' Henri said, 'any money I made would have soon ended up as beer.'

For their London opening, Miles booked the three acts into Global Village, a club in Villiers Street under the arches behind Charing Cross Station. It was the place that later became Heaven, the gay paradise. The Global Village's management at the time, two middle-aged gents, discovered that Cherry, Wayne and Johnny were punks, and (having read enough headlines to be afraid) cancelled them.

The margins were tight. Miles needed another London gig, so went to see Andy Czezowski, boss of the Roxy, and after some negotiation (Miles asked for a guarantee of £300 a night, Andy suggested Miles was having a laugh and said he could get the Stranglers for £40), a deal was struck and Andy advertised 'American Week' at the Roxy for the start of March 1977.

Cherry Vanilla was introduced to her new bass player and drummer and remembered the occasion in her autobiography, *Lick Me*.

'We met the Police at a cold damp rehearsal space and got down to business straight away... They were professional and cooperative, though I sensed a bit of condescension or maybe just embarrassment when they had to sing the cock-a-doodle-do choruses on "Little Red Rooster".'

The rest of her band was less welcoming.

'There was definitely some rivalry between them and Louie and Zecca. The Police were, as Miles claimed, excellent musicians, but that didn't stop Louie and Zecca bitching about them, especially Stewart, whose tempos, they both complained, wavered.'

They opened the tour on Tuesday 1 March 1977 at the Alexandria Club in Newport, South Wales. The *South Wales Argus*, in their ad for the gig, included a trigger warning: 'Her songs are highly erotic.'

The same paper also had problems with the name of the support band. 'The *Argus* wouldn't advertise them as the Police, saying that the Chief Constable would be on to them,' says Jonny Perkins, who promoted the gig. 'The *Argus* would only advertise them as "Her Band".'

Rehearsing with Cherry left little time for the Police to run through their own set – an odd mixture of songs that included, as well as the single 'Fall Out', 'Kids To Blame', which was one of Stewart's Curved Air songs; 'Clown's Revenge', one of Sonja's Curved Air songs; and 'Grand Hotel', a Sting/Last Exit song – all given the punk working-over.

'We had one Police rehearsal,' Stewart said. 'And Henri had forgotten all the chords and stuff. Sting was going, "Oh, Jesus Christ!"'

Nevertheless, they completed the set and lived to tell the tale. Cherry seemed to think they did okay.

On the Thursday, they played the 'American Week' gig at the Roxy. The review in *Sounds* gave the Police a favourable mention. 'Their set may have been short, but they packed in as much punch as a thousand two-ton steam-hammers going flat out in the time available to them.'

Johnny Thunders had done the Wednesday at the Roxy, Wayne County did the Friday. All three bands did the business and made enough to cover Miles' overheads.

The Sunday gig, at the Nashville Room in West Kensington, was a bit more shaky.

It was a hardcore punk crowd. Sting, clearly not on message, made no attempt to disguise the band's lack of punk credentials or his dissatisfaction with his lot.

'Okay, we're a punk band and we're going to play some punk now,' he said. 'That means the words are banal and the music's fast. So, here's a punk song for you, you assholes.'

Tuning was never a priority in proper punk circles, but Sting tuned his bass obsessively between numbers. Somebody shouted, 'Get it together.' Sting shouted back, 'Get it together? That's hippy talk. Get it together? You can fuck off.'

Most people who saw the band that night reckoned that, like so many bands of the time, they were a flash in pan. They'd break up soon, possibly within the hour. The odds on this band becoming a world-beater within 18 months would have been incalculable.

They went on the road, in a van with a busted heater that Miles had provided, playing college gigs and the circuit of semi-cabaret clubs, the last resting places of Biba graphics and sophistosexy names – Rebecca's and Barbarella's in Birmingham, Tiffany's in Shrewsbury, the Lafayette in Wolverhampton and Maxim's, Barrow-in-Furness.

John Taylor, later to play bass with Duran Duran, was at the Birmingham University gig and fondly remembered it in his auto-biography *The Pleasure Groove*. He was quick to notice that the Police were not proper punks, but was impressed with Sting's easy manner with the crowd. 'After the second number, he struck up a rapport with the audience of mostly students. A little too familiar, I remember thinking at the time, not knowing then that Sting had been a teacher and spoke "student" way better than he would ever speak "punk".'

John Taylor had taken along his cassette recorder and taped ('no flash photography, no recording devices') both the music and his own heckles.

Sting: We've got the Heartbreakers coming on next.
(Cheer from me and one or two others.)
Sting: They can't play, you know.
Me: Fuck off!
Sting: Who said, 'Fuck off'?
Me: I did.
Sting: It's true. They're great guys but they can't play.
Me: Fuck off, you wanker!
Sting: You'll see. This next song is called 'Fall Out'! 1 2 3 4…

'Everyone is getting along,' Cherry said. 'I like Henri Padovani best. He's got those ugly beautiful looks, like a French film star.'

A hallmark of all these early Police gigs was speed – they played everything as fast as they could without gaps between numbers.

'We had 10 numbers and we played them in exactly 17 minutes,' Henri said. 'The type of gig where each number rolls straight into the next and leaves very little time for the audience to applaud or boo. In any case, this was a good attitude to adopt. All the punk groups did the same. To play and to provoke, that was important. To wait for applause, that was really naff and old fashioned.'

'The first time I saw them with Henri,' says Phil Sutcliffe, 'was at Newcastle Poly on the Cherry Vanilla tour. It was flat-out punk. I didn't think they were good. Not good in the way the Clash were good. It was just fast. It didn't work. Sting couldn't carry on like that.'

★ ★ ★

On the road, the Police did not – at this stage, anyway – fully embrace the rock'n'roll lifestyle. According to Cherry, their high of choice was Benylin cough mixture from Boots. (The recipe did give a halfway decent high before the spoilsports removed some vital ingredient in the 1980s, or maybe they didn't remove a vital ingredient, but users' tolerance rose.)

They couldn't afford hotel rooms, so often had to ask people in the venues if anybody could give them a bed for the night. There was Sting with his cheekbones, Henri with his ugly beautiful French film star looks, and Stewart, the hairy-assed silverback motherfucker banging tree trunks. And they were asking if anybody could give them a bed for the night.

'I imagine,' said Cherry, 'it must have been hard for those guys to avoid certain compromising situations.'

She'd got to know and like Frances and Sonja, so did her best to discourage any of that groupie nonsense or sordid dalliance.

Sting was perhaps the least rock'n'roll of the three. 'Whenever we went on the road,' Cherry said, 'Frances packed him a week's worth of sandwiches and fruit in a box so he wouldn't have to spend money on fish and chips and gyros [kebabs], like the rest of us.'

Later, Cherry summarised the experience in a song called 'Liverpool'.

'Stewart said this is where the Beatles had played / Sting was eating lunch from a box / Everyone was pissed and nobody got laid / We really blew those kids right out of their socks / And we were oh, so cool / Back in Liverpool.'

After they played Middlesbrough on 12 March, the whole band stayed at Sting's parents' house.

'Thank you very much for having us, Mrs Sumner,' conjecture might have Stewart saying.

'You're welcome, lads,' you can imagine Audrey replying. 'Always nice to meet Gordon's friends. Now there's a flask of tea in there for you, two sugars, just the way you like it.'

Rock'n'roll.

★ ★ ★

At the end of March, the tour moved across the Channel for gigs in the Netherlands and France. Cherry was hors de combat by this time, in hospital having an abortion. She's perfectly open about it in her autobiography, but was understandably cross at the time when – so Wayne told her – the Police announced this from the stage.

With Stewart and Sting relieved of their backing band duties, the Police became Wayne's support.

Walt Davidson of the *NME* saw them at the Palais des Glaces in Paris and was less than thrilled:

> You gotta hand it to 'em – the Police tried hard. But I'm afraid I was no more impressed with this outfit than I was on the night they backed Cherry Vanilla at the Nashville. They had a slight advantage in being able to exchange banter with the fans in the local lingo (the lead guitarist is French), and their visuals were undeniably impressive. But all this couldn't make up for a bum sound and incomprehensible lyrics. The audience did allow them the courtesy of one encore.

NME's lack of enthusiasm was widely shared.

The tour had now and then been fun while it lasted – and it lasted well into May – but gigs and record deals did not, as a result, come leaping out of the walls.

Maybe, in an alternative universe, the Police would have broken up there and then. Or Sting would have left. A couple of weeks earlier he'd been offered a job with Billy Ocean who'd just had a number two UK album that had also seen the Top 40 in the US. A sum of £90 a week had been mentioned. Sting needed that money.

Then, in a roundabout way, the future of the Police as an entity was secured by Gong.

★ ★ ★

Gong was a tribe of closely related bands all derived from the ur-Gong 1968 original (sometimes referred to as Protogong). By 1977, scions of ur-Gong had proliferated, including Paragong, Mother Gong, Planet Gong and Pierre Moerlen's Gong.

The band was started in Paris in 1967 by Australian guitarist/poet Daevid Allen, who'd previously been with Soft Machine. It was a couple of years before they started recording and another three before they released their masterwork, the *Radio Gnome Invisible* trilogy – three albums: *Flying Teapot*, *Angel's Egg* and *You* – expounding a philosophy/ mythology/religion/set of curious analogies described in the 1971 manual *The Pocket Guide to the Planet Gong* and featuring a cast of characters that included Zero the Hero, the Cock Pot Pixie and Captain Capricorn.

Urban-spaceman, wibble-wobble, hazy-cosmic-jive, exploding-trouser-circus, hippy Euro-whimsy had never been whimsier.

Gong's personnel was never a John, Paul, George and Ringo certainty. Some say that, at one time or another and in one sense or another, most of us have been in Gong – and if you're thinking, 'I never was', be aware that they may have mastered 'Neuralyzing' technology years before the Men in Black. Or possibly you were in a different body at the time.

Plans had been hatched for a 24-hour Gong tribal powwow at the Hippodrome de Pantin, (aka Le Nouvel Hippodrome and the Hippodrome de Paris), a permanent-fixture circus tent in north-east Paris. As well as playing together, the various members would feature their extra-Gong solo projects and Daevid Allen would premiere a completely new incarnation called Gong-Expresso. The resulting live album would be called *Gong Est Mort, Vive Gong*.

Mike Howlett, bass player and songwriter with Gong between 1973 and 1977, wanted to put together a special band for the Hippodrome show. He had the name – Strontium 90 – and was looking for personnel. He knew Sting through Virgin publishing and recruited him to share the bass and vocal work. At Sting's suggestion, Mike also brought in Stewart on drums. They fixed up an initial rehearsal at Virtual Earth Studios in Swiss Cottage, north-west London.

Mike Howlett had also got hold of the guitar player who'd worked with Soft Machine after Daevid Allen had left. He was a little older than Sting or Stewart and, most lately, had been playing with Kevin Ayers – another Soft Machine alumnus. Stewart already knew him slightly, having met him on the road. They'd talked about guitars.

His name was Andy Summers.

Chapter Six

NOT LONG AFTER THAT, THE BAND BROKE UP

It was quite understandable that Liverpool became a spawning ground for British pop stars. It had no shortage of mean streets in which to spawn them; it was a port into which ships from the US brought the latest rock, roll, rhythm and jazz; and, though generalisations are iniquitous, Liverpudlians are lippy show-offs.

Bournemouth, however, is a less likely – not to say implausible – contender. Mary Shelley, the creator of *Frankenstein*, is buried there, and it has been suggested that the elderly and infirm flock to the town in the hope that some of Dr Frankenstein's magic might restore them to life and health. Maybe it works, and they all look like that because they're undead.

In fact, the stereotype – that Bournemouth is an extended retirement home – hasn't been true for half a century or more. Since the 1950s, it's seen a proliferation of schools teaching English as a foreign language, so you're far more likely to encounter a gaggle of Norwegian teenagers than a whist drive. Even so, it has an indefinable but distinct elderly mien. Hard to say why. Do the waves come in more slowly? Does the air bear the natural smell of Yardley talc and Old Spice aftershave? Are there more ads for denture fixatives in the windows of chemists than you'd find elsewhere?

★ ★ ★

Andy Summers (or Somers, his original name) is from Bournemouth, but wasn't actually born there. He was born in Poulton-le-Fylde, in Lancashire (much nearer Liverpool than Bournemouth).

It was the very last day of 1942. There was a war on. Dad, Maurice, was stationed up that way with the RAF and the family were living in a caravan parked on the River Wyre. Mum, Jean, aka 'Red', worked in a bomb factory.

After the war, the family moved south to Bournemouth. Dad took over the running of a cafe and there was enough money coming in to send Andy, then aged 6, for piano lessons with Mrs Thorne up the road.

His big brother (he had two, plus a sister) was a jazz fan. In the days when the BBC Light Programme devoted several more hours per week to the cinema organ and brass bands than it did to anything swung, jazz fans shunned the BBC in favour of the American Forces Network – AFN. The signal varied in quality, but it was worth persisting, because where else were you going to hear Charlie Parker, Dizzy Gillespie, Chet Baker or John Coltrane – or, for that matter, Muddy Waters, Hank Snow or Charlie Pride?

Andy listened with his brother and absorbed.

The piano lessons lasted for a while, but the story really began when Andy's Uncle Jim gave him a cheap acoustic guitar.

Let us pause there, and – forgetting for a moment the aforementioned importance of uncles in the development of British rock'n'roll – turn our thoughts to the matter of love, and particularly the precious kind of love that can exist between a teenage boy and a guitar.

It is a longing, yearning kind of love. After even a short absence, the poor benighted boy will begin to pine for the object of his affections. He will long to touch its strings, to smell the wood, to stroke a big fat first-position E minor chord, to coax harmonics. Freud would have it that the guitar is – like many such fetish objects – a penis substitute, and he was undoubtedly right, for what does any teenage boy, already in possession of an uncontrollable penis, want more than anything in the world? A second penis, of course. With jumbo frets and big fat humbuckers.

The astonishing rise and rise of the guitar in the post-war years can largely be blamed on cowboys. Singing cowboys – Gene Autry, Tex

Ritter, Roy Rogers – had been a feature of Saturday morning cinema since the 1930s. When they sang, they invariably accompanied themselves on guitar.

All boys who wanted to be cowboys – which, by the 1950s, was all boys – needed a guitar.

When, in 1956, the UK skiffle boom kicked off in earnest, that need became hollering and urgent, and owners of musical instrument shops found themselves having to wipe drool from their windows three or four times a day.

Skiffle was weird – not so much a style of music as a virus that afflicted pretty much every young man (and one or two young women), from the quads and dorms of the great public schools to the slummiest of inner-city slums. It had been building up momentum since 1951, when, at the Festival of Britain, the heir to the throne, Princess Elizabeth, and her husband Prince Philip, attended a jazz concert at which George Melly sang 'Rock Island Line' – a train blues that John Lomax, the American folk-song collector, had recorded at the Arkansas State Prison. It tells the not very stirring tale of a goods-train driver who evades a toll by misrepresenting his cargo.

Three years later, Lonnie Donegan, banjo and guitar player with the Chris Barber Jazz Band, recorded the song with a stripped-down accompaniment – just him on vocal and guitar, Chris Barber on bass and Beryl Bryden on percussive washboard. The track mouldered in Decca's vaults and wasn't released as a single until January 1956, at which time the skiffle virus first began to infect the country.

Like the punk revolution 20 years later, skiffle was essentially 'this is a chord, this is another, this is a third, now form a band' music, with the added advantage that it was cheaper still: no amps, no drum kit; just an acoustic guitar or banjo, a washboard (still a common household appliance back then, at least at your gran's), a broomstick-and-string 'bass' and a checked shirt.

Before long there was an uncountable number – sometimes it must have felt like trillions – of skiffle groups up and down the country singing a repertoire of country and western standards, slave plaints, railroad shuffles, murder ballads and prison moans – songs with sentiments as comprehensible to the average 16-year-old in Acton, Erdington, Ipswich or Taunton as the Latin Bible or logical positivism.

And even though, in the cack-hands of amateurs, the white-hot passion that characterised Lonnie Donegan's delivery was usually replaced by a generalised Boy Scout bonhomie, the music had drive, it had energy.

Skiffle was where the stars of tomorrow learned their trade: Tommy Steele and Lionel Bart were in the Cavemen; Mick Jagger was in the Bucktown Skiffle Group; Cliff Richard was in the Dick Teague Skiffle Group; John Lennon and Paul McCartney were in the Quarrymen; Roger Daltrey was in the Sulgrave Rebels; Barry Gibb was in the Rattlesnakes.

The James Page Skiffle Group appeared on the kids' TV show *All Your Own*.

'What do you want to do when you leave school? Take up skiffle?' asks the show's presenter Huw Wheldon, with a patronising smile.

'No,' says the freshly scrubbed 13-year-old Jimmy Page, 'I want to take up biological research' – as good a euphemism as any for Led Zeppelin's subsequent career.

So, Andy Summers got his first guitar as a 13th birthday present from his Uncle Jim.

A lodger showed him how to tune it and gave him a book of chords. At school, he formed the obligatory skiffle group, like everybody else in the country, and learned to strum the standard repertoire – 'Midnight Special', 'Worried Man Blues' and 'John Henry'.

Then a school friend taught him how to play the intro from Cliff Richard's 'Move It', claimed by some to be the first credible British rock'n'roll record.

After that, like every other junior guitar player in the country, Andy came to regard Hank B. Marvin, the man who played that intro on the record, as a god. When Cliff and Hank came to the Bournemouth Winter Gardens, he waited backstage with all the others – girls for Cliff, boys for Hank – to get his hero's autograph.

Music ruled Andy's world. Music and girls, anyway – the same priorities as Sting – but let's stick with the music for now.

The skiffle chords, the 'Move It' intro, were just a gateway to other highs, and as the cravings grew more intense he began to mainline the serious stuff. He listened to jazz guitarists – Wes Montgomery, Barney Kessel, Kenny Burrell and the like – on the American Forces Network and decided he wanted to play like them. This meant engaging with flat-five substitutions and mixolydian mode. It meant endless hours playing records at half-speed, dropping the stylus on the same groove over and over to learn the solos and figure out how they were constructed. It meant loyally listening to *Guitar Club* with Ken Sykora (the BBC's weekly indulgence of the guitar *aficion*) on the Light Programme every Saturday teatime, even though a lot of it was devoted not to Wes Montgomery or even Hank B. Marvin but to the Spanish stylings of Dorita y Pepe (Dot and Pete from Essex).

Then came the rub. You are never going to sound like Wes Montgomery with the cheap acoustic guitar your Uncle Jim bought you for your birthday.

Andy addressed the problem. God knows how he got hold of the money. In his autobiography, he suggests epic savings from part-time jobs, but it's hard to believe that the generosity of mums, dads and several uncles didn't play a part. Anyway, he got the money, went up to London and bought a Gibson ES-175. Its name gives away the price. When originally produced, it went on the market for $175. Adding import duties, and taking exchange rates and inflation into account, that's a modern equivalent on-the-wall-in-the-Selmer-shop price of ever such a lot.

It was a model that had been around since 1949. With its deep sunburst body (they also do them with a blonde/natural finish which is heartbreakingly beautiful), parallelogram mother-of-pearl inlays on the fingerboard and jaunty, pointy single Florentine cutaway, nothing looks the business and sounds the business like an ES-175. It and the larger Gibson L-5 were the two 'official' jazz guitars. If you wanted anybody to take you seriously as a jazz guitarist, you had to have one or the other. Even today, jazz guitarists who prefer other models and brands usually have an ES-175 at home to whip out if somebody questions their credentials.

In the hands of Jim Hall or Joe Pass, the ES-175 could achieve the sublime. In the hands of a hormone-enslaved adolescent boy with warring priorities, however, it's living on borrowed time.

There is a girl. Andy arranges to meet her in the park. They sit on a bench. He's taken the guitar along with him hoping she'll be impressed both by the instrument's quality and by his knowledge of the mixolydian mode. She isn't. He moves in for the kiss. She ups and hops it. He follows. When he comes back, the guitar is gone.

Luckily, people in Bournemouth insure their belongings. This time, with the insurance money in his fist, he went for a double-cutaway Gibson ES-335. It was a statement of sorts. The ES-175 is definitely a

Andy Summers and Zoot Money outside 'the evil smelling' Flamingo Club, 1964. JEREMY FLETCHER/REDFERNS

'25 pissheads trying to get through to the end of the arrangement.' The Newcastle Big Band (Sting's third on left) in a car park, 1973. MIRRORPIX

Curved Air in 1975. 'I saw Curved Air in Glasgow and would like to know the name of the new drummer.'
GAB ARCHIVE/REDFERNS

Miles Copeland. 'Since when has music had anything to do with it?' RICHARD YOUNG/SHUTTERSTOCK

Sonja Kristina – she moves like smoke across the stage.
ERICA ECHENBERG/REDFERNS

Stewart, Sting and Henri. Stewart invented the Police, he recruited Henri and Sting. It was his vision. Sting, on the other hand, was Sting. PETER BAYLIS/SHUTTERSTOCK

Cherry Vanilla with Sting in the background. 'Whenever we went on the road, Sting's wife Frances packed him a week's worth of sandwiches.' GUS STEWART/REDFERNS

Strontium 90 and '5,000 French hippies in a tent'. The first time Sting and Andy and Stewart (along with Mike Howlett) were on stage together, 28 May 1977. BRIAN COOKE/REDFERNS

Sting, Stewart, Andy and Henri at Mont-de-Marsan's punk festival, 1977. 'It's not fair. Henri always gets the best amp.' DENIS O'REGAN/GETTY IMAGES

'Andy has bulldozed his way into the group,' said Stewart, 'to the benefit of the group.' MIRRORPIX

The band backstage at the Bristol Locarno Ballroom, 1977. Sting: 'I could see that punk was going to develop in some way.' LAWRENCE IMPREY

'We'd get these calls saying, "The Snivelling Bathrooms can't make it tonight, can you get there by eight o'clock?"' LAWRENCE IMPREY

Stewart wearing trousers that are half an inch wider than the regulation punk. MIRRORPIX

'Sting changed when Frances came on the scene.' LAWRENCE IMPREY

On stage at CBGB in New York, 1979. 'Once they hit the stage, their alien blend of soaring tenor vocals and Echoplex pop-reggae went down a storm.' EBET ROBERTS/GETTY IMAGES

The band on tour in Amsterdam, Netherlands, 1979. GIJSBERT HANEKROOT/REDFERNS

The Police drove from the Hammersmith Odeon to the Palais in a US Army M5 half-track armoured personnel carrier, 1979. EVENING STANDARD/HULTON ARCHIVE/GETTY IMAGES

jazz guitar. The ES-335 – though perfectly suitable for jazz – was Chuck Berry's choice, and B. B. King's.

Andy left school as soon as possible and got a job at Minns Music, a shop on Gervis Place (sole area agents for Steinway pianos, 'the choice of artistes throughout the world'). The singer-songwriter Al Stewart (later managed by Miles Copeland) bought his first guitar at Minns. Robert Fripp, later of King Crimson, was a customer, too, but left without buying anything because he was put off by the snotty shop assistant.

Andy had become a frequent visitor at the Blue Note, a jazz club in the Lynton Court Hotel where the Alan Kay Quintet was the resident band. Sometimes Andy asked if he could sit in with them. Alan Kay nearly always said no, but eventually allowed him to play a little when his band took a break.

Andy pushed it. He started bringing in other musicians to play with him, effectively setting up a rival band to Alan's. Alan, knowing when he was beat, let the uppity whippersnapper join his band.

Andy was short of stature (he got that from his mother) and, with his cherubic face and blond curls, he looked all of 12 years old.

'There will be a meeting of the Andy Somers Fan Club after the show...,' Alan used to announce, '... in the telephone kiosk across the road.'

Eventually Andy split with Alan and formed a proper group of his own – initially called the Poll Losers' Trio – with Andy on guitar, Colin Allen on drums and Dave Townsend on bass. When Barry Curtis, a pianist, joined them, they became the Andy Somers Quartet.

Bournemouth was his for the taking. Soon he was gigging all over town at jazz clubs, weddings, bar mitzvahs and hotel ballrooms. They played the Majestic Hotel and Andy and his electric guitar were invited to join the Majestic Dance Orchestra for a while, and there he helped vary the diet of quicksteps and foxtrots with the occasional Shadows number in the hope that the teenagers sitting bored in the audience with their parents might not be quite so bored. Legend has it that he was fired from the Majestic Dance Orchestra for sleeping with the teenage daughter of one of the hotel guests. Another legend says he was replaced in the band by the aforementioned Robert Fripp.

★ ★ ★

It was impossible to be a musician in Bournemouth without eventually running into George Bruno 'Zoot' Money.

Everybody knew Zoot. He was (and still is) a singer/pianist/ Hammond organist who started out vaguely inclined towards jazz (he stole his name from the tenor player Zoot Sims) but was deflected by exposure to Ray Charles and Jerry Lee Lewis into playing rolling, rollicking good-time music with Hammond organ screeches and adventurous sax. Zoot had Italian roots. He knew how to have a good time and was (still is) keen to share it. He'd been gigging around Bournemouth since the mid-1950s – sang and played guitar with various pop groups and played banjo with a trad jazz band.

Then, in 1961, Zoot Money's Big Roll Band made its debut at the Downstairs Club, in the cellar of a greengrocer's shop on Holdenhurst Road. A year later, he acquired a Hammond organ and added a sax player to the line-up.

This band underwent mergers and reshuffles to emerge as the Sands Combo, which became house band at the Pavilion Ballroom. For a time, the support act there was a group led by a certain Tony Blackburn, then a young hopeful singer in a sequinned jacket, later the first DJ ever to be heard on Wonderful Radio 1.

Zoot was unimpressed by the sequinned jacket and would announce them as 'Tony Blackhead and the Pimples'. (When the Radio 1 Roadshow went to the further reaches, fellow DJ John Peel used to keep himself amused on long coach trips by sitting behind Tony Blackburn and trying to figure out how he made his hair do that.)

Zoot had seen Andy playing at the Blue Note. The two bonded and took to spending boozy evenings round at Zoot's flat in Old Christchurch Road, playing Ray Charles records. By 1963, Andy had been recruited into the band – which had reverted (again with reshuffles) to being the Big Roll Band – and the two of them were plotting world domination.

Then Alexis Korner came into their lives.

Alexis Korner was an Austrian/Greek guitar player born in Paris who would, at that time, have been in his mid-thirties. He was already a legend. He'd earned his stripes playing with Chris Barber and Ken Colyer in the post-war British jazz revival that had ultimately spawned Sting's Phoenix Jazzmen and a few hundred soundalikes up and down the country. Then he befriended Cyril Davies, a panel-beater and guitarist who switched to mouth organ after he heard Little Walter.

Alexis was an organiser. With Cyril, he set up the London Blues and Barrelhouse Club in an upstairs room at the Round House pub in Soho (no relation to the Roundhouse in Chalk Farm). Off the back of that, they started an electric band, Blues Incorporated. Since the Round House pub found amplified music hard to take, the club moved base to a vile cellar on Ealing Broadway and was renamed the Ealing Club.

The band's line-up changed almost week by week, and at one time or another featured several Rolling Stones, some Manfred Men and many other stars of the 1960s' blues'n'beat boom.

They released an album, *R&B from the Marquee* – actually recorded at the Decca Studios in West Hampstead. It didn't sell well, and certainly didn't chart, but it led those who bought it straight to the specialist record shops in search of the source: the dirty, gritty world of swooping guitars, searing harmonicas, sodden voices, Blind Boys, Sleepy Johns, Black Cat Bones and Crawling King Snakes. People who, a year before, had not known what a mojo was were now slowly figuring out how to get it working.

Alexis called Zoot and asked whether he would like to come up for London and join Blues Incorporated for a few dates. This was the equivalent of getting a call from Matt Busby to say that Man U were a bit short-handed for the Arsenal match on Saturday and the strip was in the post.

Zoot played the few dates with Alexis, and afterwards decided to stay in London. He asked the rest of the Big Roll Band to join him, saying he'd lined up a couple of gigs at the Six Bells in Chelsea and the Marquee.

Thus it was that, on 1 January 1964, Andy packed up his 335 and moved into a flat on Gunterstone Road, West Kensington, shared with Zoot and Colin Allen, the drummer. He had a tiny room.

'I had a guitar and about 700 LPs stacked along one wall, including a lot of esoteric music that I was interested in – African, Indian and Balinese music – and I had a collection of books on Zen.'

By spring of that year, the Big Roll Band had a regular Monday night gig ('Gentlemen admission 5 shillings, Ladies free') at Soho's Flamingo Club, a place almost as vile as the Ealing Club.

John Mayall described the Flamingo as 'a very dark and evil-smelling basement... It had that seedy sort of atmosphere and there was a lot of pill-popping. You usually had to scrape a couple of people off the floor when you emerged into Soho at dawn.'

A couple of years earlier, it had been a place of high scandal when jazz singer Aloysius 'Lucky' Gordon, former lover of nightclub hostess Christine Keeler, got into a fight with Johnny Edgecombe, Christine Keeler's current lover, which left Gordon needing 17 stitches in his face. A few days later, in a related incident, Edgecombe fired several shots outside the house of society osteopath Stephen Ward. The subsequent police investigation led to revelations about Keeler's relationship with John Profumo, the Secretary of State for War, and Yevgeny Ivanov, the Russian naval attaché. This led to Profumo's resignation from the government and ultimately to the defeat of the Conservatives at the 1964 general election.

Go up the Flamingo, bring down the government. That's hard-core clubbing.

The Flamingo attracted a diverse crowd – posh folk slumming, British West Indians from Brixton and Notting Hill, US military personnel on leave from the airbases and, as the 1960s got going, the cream of mod society. The Big Roll Band, with its repertoire of Ray Charles, James Brown, Jimmy Smith and the like, could have been tailor-made for the place.

The club's manager, Rik Gunnell, was also a booking agent and fed the band gigs all over, sometimes as many as 13 a week. The pay was good, too. On a good night, they could clear £400. And Zoot always gave terrific value for the money. He had a stage presence 'like a psychotic Bud Flanagan' that could turn even the most unpromising assembly into a party. And, after the show, it felt like all the bands and all the punters in London would crowd back to Zoot and Andy's flat, so the party could go on and on and on.

One occasional visitor was Jimi Hendrix. Andy had first encountered Jimi, probably in September 1966, at a club on Cromwell Road in west London and, like Sting, Stewart and most others who had the privilege of seeing Jimi live, was gobsmacked.

'I walked in and there he was on stage playing with Brian Auger. At the time, of course, it was amazing. He had a white Strat and, as I walked in, he had it in his mouth and he had a huge Afro and he had on a sort of buckskin jacket with fringes that went to the floor. Yeah, it was intense.'

★ ★ ★

There was a moment, never exactly dated, when the 1960s turned; when speed and booze were abandoned in favour of weed and acid, and mohair and Mary Quant gave way to kaftans, paisley and crushed velvet.

The Beatles – John and George, anyway – first took acid in the spring of 1965, but it was a good year later before students at top universities started getting hold of it, and probably another year again before supplies got through to Tamworth, King's Lynn and Galashiels.

Andy and Zoot became partial to the occasional trip, and Zoot once spiked his brass section with predictably hilarious consequences. One day, after a particularly heavy trip, he reinvented the band as Dantalian's Chariot (named after the great Duke of Hell who governs the 36 legions of spirit, knows the thoughts of all men and women and who teaches the arts and sciences from a great book he has in his right hand – obviously).

The new band made its first appearance on Saturday 12 August 1967 at the Seventh National Jazz, Pop, Ballads and Blues Festival in Windsor, and two weeks later they played the Festival of the Flower Children at Woburn Abbey. They stood on an all-white stage playing white instruments, dressed in white clothing, turning everybody and everything into a blank screen on which they projected what was believed to be 'the best light show in the country'. It was, as Andy called it, a 'big leap of faith' from good-time blues and barrelhouse to acid rock and psychedelia with half-hour guitar solos and atonal excursions, but it was what people did at the time.

And, on top of that, they started writing their own material.

'I remember sitting around the flat and reading newspapers to find incidents to write songs about,' Andy said. 'We wrote one called "Four Firemen", about some fire disaster.'

Dantalian's Chariot was a big favourite in the places where hippies met – Middle Earth, the Roundhouse, UFO. They released a single, 'Madman Running Through The Fields' exploring the experience of a… madman running through the fields.

It is easy to fool yourself when you're listening to the track that, already in Andy's guitar part, there are hints of things to come: a little electronic tinkering – phasing, perhaps – that gives his characteristic swirly sound, and the faintest whiff in the arpeggios of, say, 'Spirits In The Material World'. It's easy to fool yourself, anyway.

In the middle, it goes spiritual. The tape is played backwards. There is a flute solo. One's only hope is that there is a secret message contained in all this that will immanentise the eschaton. If there is, it hasn't worked yet, but maybe that's because the record never charted.

Their tour schedule took them to the Pavilion Ballroom, their old stomping ground in Bournemouth, complete with the white clothes, white instruments and light show. Peter Viney, a fan, described the light show, eloquently, as 'blobby globules' and provides what is probably the most accurate summary of the crowd's reaction. 'What the fuck,' they apparently asked themselves, 'is this?'

★ ★ ★

Like all bands, Dantalian's Chariot were forced sometimes to tolerate the attentions of groupies. Andy, by all accounts, was very tolerant indeed.

In 1969, one of those he tolerated, Jenny Fabian, wrote a book called *Groupie*. Andy appears in it under the pseudonym 'Davey' and Dantalian's Chariot becomes 'The Transfer Project', but both she and Andy have since been quite open as to the true identity behind the mask.

> he's girlish and his hair curls onto his shoulders. He plays lead and his skinny arms coming out of his tee shirt really turn me on… He came round constantly, even dropping in on the way back from gigs if they passed by before, about half past three in the morning… We didn't go out much… we spent a lot of time in bed.
>
> The more I got into Davey the more I felt I loved him and depended on him. And as this gradually happened, my hangups began to assert themselves. I couldn't believe that he felt the same way about me, and I was terrified he'd find another chick… He never made any bones about being attracted to other chicks.

But surely the killer lines are: 'I was knocked out by the perfection of his genitals. They were compact and beautifully symmetrical, and I reflected that this was the first time I had ever found genitals worth looking at with appreciation.' The book's out of print now, but, at the time of writing, second-hand copies are available for as little as £28. Money well spent.

After EMI dropped them (the band, not Andy's genitals), Dantalian's Chariot signed with the Direction label, a subsidiary of CBS, for a one-album deal. But the band was already falling apart. Though they went down a storm in London, other parts of the country tended to react like Bournemouth and, even in London, the Summer of Love was over.

In September, Tony Blackburn, the man in the sequinned jacket, whose hair was a subject of tireless speculation for John Peel, launched BBC's spanking-new all-pop radio station with the Move's 'Flowers In The Rain', while outside, appropriately, a light drizzle fell on the last remaining scraps of harmony and understanding and the kaftans and paisleys were replaced by worsteds and woollies. Dantalian's Chariot trudged on a little while longer and played some gigs in the Netherlands, Paris and up and down the UK.

One night, coming back from a gig in Newcastle, over the Yorkshire moors in snow, the band's car turned a somersault. Andy came off worst, with a broken nose and an injured back. Still they played on, with Andy's face in plaster (more white for the light show).

Not long after that, the band broke up.

At the Paris gig, Andy had bonded with Robert Wyatt of Soft Machine. When Soft Machine's guitarist, Daevid Allen, went off to form Gong, the Softs worked as a three-piece for a while, then decided they needed a new guitar player. Andy got the job.

Theoretically it should have been a good fit. Andy favoured jazz-rock. Soft Machine essentially favoured jazz-rock, albeit Dada jazz-rock with often a too emphatic stress laid on the Dada. At one gig they did a 40-minute version of a number called 'We Did It Again' which consisted of the phrase 'we did it again' repeated over and over until the audience (it was in Paris) fell into a 'trance-like' state. Luckily, they had the sense not to try that sort of thing at the Pavilion Ballroom, Bournemouth.

Soft Machine were managed by Chas Chandler, the former bass player with the Animals, who went on to manage Jimi Hendrix. Chas had put Soft Machine in as support for Jimi Hendrix's US tour. Andy joined them for the second leg of the tour. It didn't work out. Andy and Kevin Ayers – vocals/bass/guitar – failed to hit it off.

Not long after that, the band broke up.

Meanwhile, Zoot had been playing with Eric Burdon and the re-formed Animals (this was the band's third or fourth incarnation – sometimes it was called the New Animals, and technically it should probably have been called the New New Animals). Zoot and Eric offered Andy a job with the band. They already had a guitar player, John Weider, but John and Andy agreed to alternate between guitar and bass.

'It worked out all right, but Andy was never keen on bands with two guitarists,' Zoot said. 'I remember meeting him shortly after he joined the Police while it was still a four-piece. I could see what was going to happen.'

Andy moved into Eric Burdon's place in Laurel Canyon.

The year before, Eric had released a song called 'Good Times' in which he reflected on all the good times that he'd wasted having good times. He had not, however, as a result, decided to devote the rest of his life working in a leper colony, and remained an enthusiastic waster of good times having good times and an avid user of LSD.

'I dropped acid, man,' said Burdon, 'mainly in LA but everywhere on the planet from then on. It was all over the place. We really did believe we could alter the world on a large scale, but of course all good things end up being bent out of shape and twisted and end up in the wrong hands with the wrong ideals.'

The first gig the new line-up played was at the Newport Pop Festival, in front of 100,000 – Andy's biggest crowd so far.

They recorded a double album, *Love Is*, which consists entirely of covers, massively extended, including a seven-minute version of Ike and Tina Turner's 'River Deep, Mountain High' and a nearly 10-minute version of Traffic's 'Coloured Rain', four minutes of which is Andy's guitar solo, 30 seconds of which, as if to prove his time with Soft Machine wasn't entirely wasted, is the same four notes played over and over.

Side 4 of the album has just one track – a mash-up medley of the Dantalian's Chariot songs.

★ ★ ★

Andy found himself able to tolerate the attentions of American groupies with the same equanimity he'd extended to the British, even though their approach was often more direct and their interest more detailed. As 'Davey' tells Jenny Fabian in *Groupie*,

> The chicks come over after you've played and say, 'Can I kiss you, sir, could I touch you, sir, would you like me to ball you?' It's far more of an occupation with them than it is with English groupies. Have you heard of the Plaster Casters? There are these two chicks who travel all over the country to take moulds of group's rigs. A rig is a penis. They

plate you until you're hard and then thrust it into a container of soft plaster and wait until it sets. It's a bastard getting your hairs unstuck.

Don't even think about it. The market's flooded with fakes.

'Life is a series of natural and spontaneous changes,' said the Chinese philosopher Lao-Tze. 'Don't resist them — that only creates sorrow. Let reality be reality.' It's advice that's particularly pertinent to the working guitar player who one day might encounter groupies who want to put his dick in plaster and the next day comes across Japanese gangsters who want to cut his fingers off.

There are various versions of the Japanese gangster story, some more innocuous than others. The most exciting version goes like this.

Japanese promoters had booked the Animals for a series of concerts, but the appropriate visas were delayed, which meant that the concerts had to be postponed for a couple of months.

When the band arrived, they learned that the number of shows they were scheduled to perform was getting on for twice as many as the number they'd been contracted for. Furthermore, though the contract specified they were supposed to be paid in full, in cash, before they went on stage, only half the money ever appeared.

They understandably rebelled.

Then, one night, while they were on stage, their manager, Kevin Deverich, was kidnapped.

The promoters, you see, weren't genial showbiz entrepreneurs; they were Yakuza, Japanese Mafiosi. They told Kevin they wanted £25,000 compensation for the gigs that had been cancelled and threatened to cut off at least one of his fingers if he didn't cough up (or maybe they threatened to shoot him — the versions vary).

Anyway, the band got out of the country as quickly as possible, leaving their equipment behind.

Andy actually missed out on all of the action because, after the gig, he chose to tolerate the attentions of an American friend and didn't get back to the band's hotel until the following morning, by which time the Animals had already hightailed it to the airport.

Not long after that, the band broke up.

Andy stayed in America. Jobless, he decided it was time he got an education, so signed on at San Fernando State College (now California State University, Northridge) to study music and classical guitar, keeping body and soul together (just) by giving guitar lessons. He shared a house with a young actor called Paul Michael Glaser, who later found fame in the 1970s hit cop series *Starsky and Hutch*.

Just as the romantic lover dreams of 'the one', the romantic guitar obsessive believes there is one guitar that was put on earth just for them – as *they* were put on earth just for *it*.

Some obsessives – though they spend thousands, sometimes millions, in the search, and commission the world's finest luthiers to craft versions of perfection – never find it.

Andy did find it. One of his pupils offered him a battered Fender Telecaster for $200. It was a mongrel of an instrument that had been hacked and messed with over the course of its lifetime. Even its date, 1961, was approximate. Possibly the neck and body had come from different guitars. The neck pickup had been replaced with a Gibson humbucker, and the electronics, switching, bridge and tuners had all been modified.

But he didn't have an electric guitar at the time, so he forked out the $200 and took it home.

Then... 'Something took place on a metaphysical level,' he told *Guitar Player* magazine. 'When you're a guitar player, you pick up a guitar and in two minutes you know whether you're going to like it or not. I couldn't put this one down.'

He had found 'the one'. This was the guitar he used on almost every Police record, the one he could make shimmer and shine, stab and sear. 'It was an absolutely kick-ass guitar.'

He also got married. Robin Lane was a singer-songwriter. Her dad had written 'Everybody Loves Somebody' and was Dean Martin's piano player. Her own career was, however, having trouble getting off the starting blocks.

'While Andy went to school in the Valley and learned to play classical guitar, I would write songs and go to one record company after another trying to get a recording contract. It was always the same, "Well, we already have Joni Mitchell, or we already have Melanie, or we already have Linda Ronstadt." They couldn't seem to think beyond one chick singer per record company.'

In the end, she went to Boston and Andy stayed in Los Angeles. The marriage didn't take, and they divorced after a couple of years.

Just in case you were worried, Robin eventually just about broke through the glass ceiling, went on to make several successful albums, both as a solo artist and as Robin Lane and the Chartbusters. At the time of writing, she's working at the Massachusetts Women's Resource Center, using music therapy to aid survivors of abuse.

★ ★ ★

Andy married again and, in November 1973, came back to the UK with his second wife, Psychology graduate and cellist Kate Lunken, who also became his third wife (they were divorced in 1981 and remarried four years later).

He'd formulated elaborate plans to restart his career, but they didn't work out.

Bournemouth came to his rescue. He ran into Robert Fripp – the man he'd failed to make a sale to at Minns Music, by then at the forefront of the burgeoning prog-rock boom with King Crimson. Fripp was the country's leading exponent of harmonically complex works that vary in time signature between 5/8 and 11/16, while the drums keep up a constant 17/16 and the guitar plays at speeds that make you check your turntable.

Robert put him in touch with Mike Giles, a founder member of King Crimson and a chap Andy knew from the days they'd both smiled and whistled under all difficulties in the Boy Scouts.

Mike, a drummer, had long left King Crimson and was about to go on tour with Neil Sedaka, playing straight 4/4 for a change, on such early 1960s gems as 'Oh! Carol', 'Breaking Up Is Hard To Do' and the faintly worrying 'Happy Birthday Sweet 16'. Sedaka was enjoying something of a renaissance. He'd had a couple of minor UK hits, had just signed with Elton John's Rocket Records and was selling out big venues.

On Mike's invitation, Andy went to see Neil. They got on. Andy was signed up. He got £35 a night – more than most people earned in a week – and a new suit. Neil even subbed him £300 to buy a new amp and never asked for it back.

A live album was made of the Royal Festival Hall gig, with Mike Giles on drums, Andy on guitar, Dave MacRae (later of Pacific Eardrum) on electric piano, Dave's future wife Joy Yates on backing vocals and the massed ranks of the Royal Philharmonic Orchestra spread out behind. It went Top 50.

★ ★ ★

In the November of 1974, Andy did the same sort of duties for David 'Pretty Boy' Essex and braved the 'adulation of the Beatles days as the fans screamed, cried and clutched at their idol'. They had to get the crash barriers out at Preston Guild, it was that bad.

In December, that once-in-a-lifetime opportunity came knocking. Mick Taylor made the surprise announcement that he would be leaving the Rolling Stones. He'd been at a party with his bandmates when he told Mick Jagger that he was quitting and just walked out.

The Stones were about to record a new album in Munich. They needed a replacement guitar player, fast.

Andy was free.

Unfortunately, so was Ronnie Wood.

★ ★ ★

Instead he got a gig with Kevin Coyne. Both Virgin Records and John Peel reckoned that Kevin Coyne would be the next big thing, or at least the next Joe Cocker. Indeed, Peel had been saying this for the past five years, but then he always was a persistent bugger.

Kevin Coyne was a wonderful dark spirit, dressed in curls and blessed with a baby face that was prone to gurning. He was essentially a blues singer, but in an indestructibly English way. Even though he's often been cited as a proto-punk, his songs have nothing to do with the steely anger that drives the best punk. They come from some entirely different part of the human psyche, possibly the same bit that Hieronymus Bosch inhabited. He'd worked for a time in a mental hospital and it showed.

'Good Boy' from *Marjory Razorblade* could be a field recording of a drunk holding a conversation with a trombone in the middle of the A303 at four in the morning. He knows the world is a terrible place, but it's okay, because he has the solution to all the problems: it's arson.

He'd been working with Gordon Smith – described by John Peel as 'the foremost blues guitarist in the world' – but Virgin, perhaps in an attempt to give him a more commercial sound, decided he needed another guitarist, and hired Andy.

As we've already heard, Andy did not play nicely with other guitarists. And the band, as Kevin put it, 'didn't lack for egos'.

'I tried to get on with Andy Summers,' said Gordon Smith, 'but he seemed a bit arrogant. Taking over, telling everybody what to do. The sessions were very tense.'

They were also very drunk. Kevin liked his drink. So did Gordon.

They made an excellent album, *Matching Head and Feet*, featuring both guitarists, then another one, *Heartburn*, with just one guitarist and Andy's friend Zoot Money on keyboards.

'[Kevin] was a punchy little bleeder,' Zoot said. 'He enjoyed the ping-pong match, and everybody had to go through the Kevin Coyne two-in-the-morning rant. He had nerve endings going all the time. He hardly slept.'

Zoot liked a drink himself, but Kevin's consumption was frightening. 'He seemed to think he was superhuman. What starts as social, fans buying you drinks, develops in its own right. You continue after normal people have gone back to work.'

There was a third album. *In Living Black and White*, a live album taken from two concerts with the Andy/Zoot line-up. It gives you a taste of the unhinged poetry with which Kevin Coyne introduced his songs: 'You're not my mother, are you? You're in the dark now and I can't see you. They're put you out. Oh, my mother's eyes, they're wonderful big round things. Like plates. I'd like to tread on them sometimes rather like jellyfish.'

Not long after that, the band broke up.

It was at this time that Andy, through his links with Virgin Records, got the gig playing the orchestral version of Mike Oldfield's 'Tubular Bells' in Newcastle, with Sting and Last Exit playing support. As we already learned a couple of chapters ago, Andy watched a few minutes of Last Exit's set, then wandered off for a cheese roll and a cup of tea.

★ ★ ★

Andy's next gig was with the man he'd had trouble with on the US tour with Soft Machine, Kevin Ayers. Kevin formed a band, which included Andy on guitar and Zoot on keyboards. They went on tour, and the tour took them to Newcastle.

Curved Air happened to be up that way, too, staying at the same hotel. and Andy got talking to the band's drummer, Stewart Copeland – or, rather, Stewart talked and Andy listened.

In his autobiography, *One Train Later*, Andy describes the chat. 'He gives me a long rap on how there is a guitar factory not far from Newcastle and how he has been there and hustled them into giving him a free guitar, even though he is only the drummer in the group and recommends I do the same – it's easy.

Easy, I think, with a mouth like that: they probably gave him the bloody guitar just to get him to shut up and go away!'

CHAPTER SEVEN

THE SECOND INCARNATION

The massed bands of Gong, including Mike Howlett's new band Strontium 90, with Sting, Stewart and Andy, along with 5,000 French hippies, assembled in a circus tent and were treated to elves, witches and alternative realities in their most concentrated form. The idea of a 24-hour experience got truncated to 12 somewhere along the line – three in the afternoon to three in the morning. Fire eaters, trapeze acts and clowns were present. The air people breathed was 40 per cent nitrogen, 10 per cent oxygen and 50 per cent dope. No cops were present. Security was not needed, even backstage. Artistes and punters were one. There was a slight sense of competitiveness about who had the tallest gnome hat, but no trouble, no hassles. Many look back on those times and ask, 'What exactly *is* so funny 'bout peace, love and understanding?'

'Hey, it's a real brown rice scene, man,' Stewart said. 'Far out!'

Among the celestial flutes and whimsical fiddles of the Gong people, Strontium 90's set was unexpected and bracing.

'*Sounds* sent me to Strontium 90, the Gong thing in Paris,' says Phil Sutcliffe. 'I was only interested because Sting and Stewart were there. It went on for hours and hours, so I went out for a salad with Sonja and my girlfriend. And then Strontium 90 came on. It was Mike Howlett, Andy Summers, Sting and Stewart – so, the Police plus Mike Howlett.

I thought it was brilliant. The astonishing thing was that there were two basses, so a really strong bottom line, which made you think, "This is something special." It was much more on the Last Exit end of Sting's repertoire. Sting was really impressed by hearing Andy play, and Stewart was too. He had his eye on the prize.'

The set included two of Sting's more punkish songs – 'Visions Of The Night', which later turned up as the B-side of 'Walking On The Moon' and 'Three O'Clock Shit' – a song about a lonely man and his protest dump on the floor, bits of which (the song, not the stool) were recycled for 'Be My Girl, Sally' on *Outlandos d'Amour* and 'O My God' on *Synchronicity* – which essentially rejigs the lyric without doing it on the floor.

After a sort of follow-up gig in Colmar near the German border, where they supported Dr Feelgood, that was the end of Strontium 90. But a seed had been planted.

Mike Howlett was a proper muso. The music Sting and Stewart had played with him was not necessarily to their taste, but it allowed them to exercise their chops and made them hanker for something a bit cleverer than three-chord punk. Andy had hankerings too. 'The intensity of being with Sting and Stewart – the three of us playing together stays with me,' he wrote in *One Train Later*. 'Being back in the Kevin Ayers band suddenly feels too comfortable, too tame, the old world.'

The bond between Stewart, Andy and Sting went deeper than music. The three shared a steely, last-chance ambition, tinged usefully with arrogance and pig-headedness. Henri had hopes, dreams and schemes, but these three were driven by a force that could frighten gentler souls. Stewart and Miles at one time or another later described it as 'rabid' and, though there's no evidence they ever foamed at the mouth, by God, they could growl.

★ ★ ★

The Police's fortunes – with Henri still on guitar – rose a little. The gigs began to come in more regularly – nothing dramatic, one a week, say – and increasingly they were advertised as 'plus the Police' rather than 'plus support'.

They actually headlined at the Railway Hotel in Putney, and, a greater honour still, at the Roxy.

At the Railway – crucial historical note – Sting wore his flight suit for the very first time. It was given to him by Stewart, who, in turn, had got it from Paul Mulligan. Paul had bought it at an aviation surplus store at Biggin Hill Airport. Sting probably got more use out of that flight suit than many working test pilots.

Andy came to see them at the Marquee on 24 June and jumped on stage to join them for the encore.

Theoretically, Andy was too old for punk. He was older than George Harrison of the Beatles, older than Mick Jagger or Keith Richards of the Rolling Stones, older than Tony Meehan, the Shadows' original drummer who'd scored a number one with 'Apache' in 1960. But punk, it has to be remembered, was a refreshingly age-blind phenomenon. The Stranglers' Hugh Cornwell had previously played bass for Fairport Convention's Richard Thompson back in the 1960s. Jet Black, the Stranglers' drummer, was a successful businessman in his early forties who ran a fleet of ice-cream vans. He'd also had a stint drumming for Julie Andrews' mother (a pianist) back in the 1960s. Dame Vera Lynn, the Forces Sweetheart, could probably have joined a punk band if she'd felt so inclined, and she'd have made a spanking good job of it.

All the same, in relation to Sting, Stewart and Henri, Andy was an éminence grise of rock'n'roll. Their setlist often included a cover of 'It's My Life', the 1965 Animals hit. Andy had played that with the Animals. He'd shared a house with the Animals' lead singer. He knew what he was on about.

His diagnosis of the Police went: 'Sting was larger than life and Stewart was a good drummer, there was no question about that. Sting was able to talk to the audience. He could sing and play bass. I could see the potential in them, but it just wasn't being realised.'

To him the weak link was obvious, and he knew just how to fix it.

The day after the Marquee gig, he rang Sting and told him he thought he should be in the band. Shortly after that, he happened to run into Stewart at Oxford Circus Tube station. It's often been noted that, if he'd taken a later train, he would never have run into Stewart and, if he'd never run into Stewart, the rest of the story might never have happened. Which is why when, in 2006, Andy published his autobiography, he called it *One Train Later*.

He coaxed Stewart into a cafe and told him what he'd told Sting. He should join the Police. Andy already had form for being a one-band, one-guitarist kind of guy. 'I'm ready,' he said, 'but it will be on my terms – in other words, one guitar.'

'It was almost as if he was already a member of the group,' Stewart said, 'and he was giving me a lecture about being late for the bus.'

Stewart warned him that they weren't actually making any money, and they didn't have the luxury of roadies – they lugged their own gear.

'Eventually I told him that Sting's feet smelled really bad…' But 'Andy bulldozed his way into the group – to the benefit of the group. And the credit that I deserve is that I allowed him to fast-talk his way in.'

★ ★ ★

A reminder of the fun they'd had with Andy came when Mike Howlett got Strontium 90 back together – under the new name of the Elevators (sometimes just Elevators and sometimes just Elevator) for two gigs (some remember only one) at Dingwalls and the Nashville Room.

What Sting, Andy and Stewart had in common was a musical sophistication and curiosity that punk could never satisfy. They all heard stuff in their heads – chords that moved in odd ways, melodies that soared, rhythms that gyre and gimble.

Doubts about whether Henri was the right fit for the band had been simmering for a while and, in Sting's case, from the first time the two met. While they were on tour with Cherry Vanilla, they had tried a little poaching.

'Whenever Stewart and Sting got Louie [Lepore – Cherry's guitarist and boyfriend] alone, they were trying to persuade him to leave me and join their band instead,' Cherry wrote. 'Thank God Louie was man enough in that regard to do right by me… Of course, in hindsight, Louie probably wishes he'd taken them up on their offer.'

Replacing Henri was a bigger deal for Stewart than just firing one guitar player and hiring another. Henri had been in the band before Sting. In a sense, he and Henri were the Police. They'd hired Sting.

But Andy hadn't made his approach to Stewart – not at first, anyway. He'd phoned Sting as if it was *his* band.

Andy himself was aware of the dynamic. It was, he said, 'a shift of power'.

Sting saw it, too. 'It was the end of Stewart's band,' Sting said, 'and the only thing that connected us was the name.'

★ ★ ★

They agreed to try things out as a four-piece, debuting at the Music Machine, the huge theatre in Camden Town (later called the Camden Palace, then Koko, but gutted by fire and closed at the time of writing). They shared the bill with the Wasps and the Flicks.

The main auditorium at the Music Machine held about 1,500. A band that does badly in a room over a pub can console themselves with the notion that only 50 people had seen them anyway and they were all drunk. Doing badly in a place you could inflate an airship in is a disaster.

The Police, the four-piece Police, were a disaster. Andy and Henri played as if they were in different bands, with different arrangements and sometimes different chords.

It had become apparent that Henri – who had great 'feel' and terrific attitude – simply did not at the time have the technical proficiency to travel to the places that Andy and Sting wanted to go.

'There was a problem,' Sting said, 'inasmuch as I would write guitar parts and find that Henri couldn't play them.'

'Andy helped produce the sound that Sting wanted,' Henri wrote, 'good love songs and that kind of thing, while I was still more interested in punk.'

★ ★ ★

The climax came, appropriately, in a bullfighting arena.

Les punks had been a thing in France years before the Damned or Pistols had ripped their first T-shirts. Marc Zermati, French punk entrepreneur and founder of Skydog Records, had been *épating les bourgeois* with releases of Iggy, the Flamin' Groovies, MC5 and – just once, Shakin' Stevens – since 1972.

The ripped T-shirts, bondage gear, death make-up, spiked, coloured hair and anatomically suspect piercings were all British (it was a fashion the French could never quite manage without imbuing it with inappropriate chic), but the French could claim the attitude and politics.

Words like 'anarchy' have a different, more concrete meaning in France than in the UK. The Situationists and their guru Guy Debord had excited Malcolm McLaren, but more in the spirit of 'let's mess things up a bit and look at those great graphics'. In Paris, those same Situationists had been a major driving force in the student/worker riots of 1968 that had ground the French economy to a halt and caused the president to flee the country.

Thus, while the British establishment's contempt for punk was based mostly on aesthetics and hygiene, in France, a single misplaced safety pin could have *les flics* breaking out the CS gas.

So, when Marc Zermati wondered if a punk festival might be an adornment to the cultural landscape, he deemed it wise to hold it far away from Paris, deep in the south-west, at the Arènes du Plumaçon in Mont-de-Marsan, where bulls had been tormented for 300 years.

He held his first punk festival there in 1976, when a thousand or so fans had turned up to see Eddie and the Hot Rods, the Pink Fairies and the Damned.

It seemed to go well, and the police didn't close it down, so the following year, Zermati decided to go bigger, better and punkier with the Damned, the Clash, Dr Feelgood, Eddie and the Hot Rods, and Little Bob Story, the French king of dirty rock'n'roll. On the Monday night, Lou Reed, rather than locking himself in the lav, like he had for Miles, emerged and shone.

Somewhere down the bottom of the bill, in letters only slightly bigger than the printer's name, the Police were mentioned.

This time 4,000 turned up.

The musical differences between Sting and punk, exacerbated by Andy's arrival, had become more marked. 'The values I held about musicianship and professionalism were being flouted,' Sting said.

Allan Jones covered the festival for *Melody Maker* and remembers it in his memoir *Can't Stand Up for Falling Down*.

He was surprised to run into Andy. 'What's he doing here? And what's he done to his hair, which is dyed blond and looks like it's been cut by the local council?' (This contradicts the accepted wisdom that Andy didn't dye his hair until some months later, but we'll gloss over that. Maybe he was practising.) 'Turns out,' Allan goes on, 'he's joined a punk band called The Police, which is why most of his former muso chums are no longer talking to him.'

On the bus to France, the differences in lifestyle choice between the Police and the punks became more apparent, too.

Allan sat next to Sting. 'He's wondering now whether he's made the right decision and frets, basically, all the way to Paris while the rest of us abandon ourselves to the beer and sulphate that seems in generous and ample supply.'

While the real punks got pissed, stoned and lit their own farts, Sting sat at the back of the bus reading an improving book.

When the singing started, like a physics teacher forced to accompany Year 9 on a trip to the Science Museum, he looked up and shouted, 'Will you just, please, you know, shut up.'

Meanwhile, Stewart and Henri, with dramatic irony worthy of Shakespeare, made excited plans for the new four-piece Police.

The proper punks were as iffy about the Police as the Police were about the punks.

'We were sort of untouchables as far as they were concerned,' Stewart said. 'I wouldn't have minded being part of the in-crowd but, at the same time, I wasn't going to lose my temper if Dave Vanian [lead singer with the Damned] refused to speak to me one night at the Roxy.'

At the gig, the tension between Henri and Andy found expression in a row about an amp. They travelled, it seemed, without amps – the lesser bands did, anyway – and some sort of selection seems to have been provided at the gig. Henri was at the front of the queue and claimed a classy Hiwatt. Andy moseyed along some time later to find that a poxy little combo was all that was left. He offered the combo to Henri, saying that he, Andy, should have the Hiwatt because he did the solos. His sound mattered. Henri pointed out that if he cared so much about his amp he should have got to the front of the queue earlier. Sting intervened, taking Andy's side. 'He needs a good amp.'

In the end Henri gave in, let Andy have the Hiwatt, walked off in a huff and, after a short negotiation with his pal Henri Paul of the Maniacs, blagged himself a Marshall head with a double stack. Ha!

'It's not fair,' Andy said – or at least Henri says he did – 'Henri always gets the best amp.'

In like manner did Salieri speak of Mozart when Mozart bagsied the fortepiano, lumbering him with a poxy little harpsichord.

★ ★ ★

The festival started at 4 p.m. on the Friday with some lesser-known French bands. The Police went on fifth. They weren't a disaster, but most of the people filing into the arena were there to see the headliners, the Damned and the Clash.

As the Clash went into 'Police And Thieves', Captain Sensible reappeared on stage for punkish japes.

Joe Strummer addressed the audience. 'The Damned just came on stage and put some stink bombs up here because they're fucking jealous. They can just fuck off. And another thing, we all ain't got a sense of smell.'

When security threw the Captain off the stage, he landed with a scaffolding barrier between his legs. An ambulance was called. He seemed comatose, possibly dead, they stretchered him out but, as the ambulance left the arena, he made a miraculous recovery, escaped from the ambulance and leaped over the roofs of parked cars to re-join the fun.

'I like the geezer,' Joe Strummer said. 'I accept that he's got a few screws loose and I like him.'

Meanwhile, Sting had, no doubt, gone back to his improving book.

On the way back, he asked Allan Jones whether he thought he should give up on the band. Because Allan had a terrible hangover and didn't want to prolong the discussion, he told him that, if he was unhappy, he should 'walk away from all of this... knock it on the head, call the whole thing off, pack it in, go back to Newcastle with the wife and kid. You could be back in the classroom by Christmas, leather patches on your tweed jacket, being a much-needed new teacher at an overcrowded comprehensive. Next time I see him, of course, he's a millionaire and the Police are on their way to becoming one of the biggest bands in the world.'

★ ★ ★

John Cale was a Welshman from the valleys, the son of a coal miner. He did well, learned the viola and got into Goldsmith's College in London. After that he immersed himself in the world of the avant-garde, doing stuff with Fluxus, the multinational group of experimental artists, conceptualists and mathematicians. Yoko Ono was for a time associated with Fluxus, as were Christo (who wrapped the Reichstag and the Pont Neuf in fabric) and the proto-minimalist composer La Monte Young.

Cale found his way to New York and, with Lou Reed, started the Velvet Underground, whose first album *The Velvet Underground & Nico*, echoes endlessly in the works of Bowie, every punk band, Pulp, Blur, Grime... keep going, keep going...

By 1976, he was engaged in several solo projects. Miles hired him to produce first a three-track EP, then several album tracks for Squeeze.

'John Cale hated everything we'd written up to that point,' wrote Chris Difford of Squeeze in his memoir *Some Fantastic Place*. 'He just wanted us to be vulgar and rough. So, all our lovely pop songs were put away for another day... he was unremittingly difficult. On our first session, he made us swap instruments, then turned off all the lights in the studio telling us he wasn't going to let us out until we had perfected "Amazing Grace".'

Despite which, it still seemed to someone (possibly Miles) that 'John Cale plus the Police' would be a match made in heaven.

It wasn't. On 10 August 1977, the Police went back to Pathway Studios, the one with the special smell in Stoke Newington, with Bazza once again working the knobs, but this time with revered Velvet Underground legend John Cale producing.

They recorded, or tried to record, two songs: Sting's 'Visions Of The Night', and 'Dead End Job', co-written by Sting and Stewart.

John Cale was, by all accounts, drunk. At times he read the papers and seem to ignore whatever was being played. At other times he'd come into the studio and leap around, wildly and nonsensically enthusiastic. At one point, Andy, mucking about, played the riff from Led Zeppelin's 'Whole Lotta Love'. John went crazy for it. 'We've got to record that,' he said.

He seemed a great deal more keen on Henri's guitar playing than he was on Andy's, and wanted Henri to play the solos. Andy pointed out that *he* played the solos. As a compromise, Mr Cale agreed that Andy should play the solos, but he should play them on *Henri's* guitar. Surprisingly, 'Amazing Grace' was never mentioned.

The overall verdict was that the experience was a waste of everybody's time and money.

★ ★ ★

After the session, Sting drove Henri back to Paul Mulligan's and broached the subject that had to be broached.

From Henri's point of view, Andy had ruined the Police. They'd been a promising punk band with immense potential, then Andy came with his jazz chords and fancy notions and corrupted their punk promise.

Others have agreed. 'From a strict punk point of view,' wrote Henrik Poulsen in *'77: The Year of Punk and New Wave*, 'Henri Padovani was clearly the highest-ranking officer in the Police. Padovani's main guiltiness was that he was hampering the Police's upward mobility in terms of mass acceptance. Was the Police a punk band? If you saw them play at the Roxy in 1977 you would definitely have to say "Yes". If they had only managed their first single and then broke up, they would clearly be regarded as much of a punk band as The Models.'

Sting, of course, didn't quite see it that way.

He and Henri beat about the bush, talking about Henri's ability and Andy's ability and the fact that Andy liked Sting's songs and how Andy's guitar playing suited them better than Henri's straight down the line rock'n'roll style and how Henri had once saved Sting's life (on the way back from a gig in Stafford, Sting had fallen asleep at the wheel and, without Henri's quick thinking, there would now be a hole in the world where lute music should be).

Henri tells the whole story in his autobiography. Eventually he decided to help Sting out.

"'They sent you as the messenger to tell me that the group is finished?"

"'Yeah."'

As far as Henri was concerned, the group *was* finished.

"'You know what? It's OK. No worries, Sting, it was in the cards."

"'I'm so sorry. Stewart and I, we love you."

"'I know."'

'There, it was done. Sting felt better and so did I.'

★ ★ ★

Soon after splitting from the Police, Henri was recruited into a proper punk band, Wayne County's Electric Chairs. He stayed there for two years.

Much, much later, according to Henri, his name cropped up as the answer to a Trivial Pursuit question: 'What was the name of the guitarist who was replaced by Andy Summers in the Police?'

Henri Padovani. Thank you very much. Now, a science question.

★ ★ ★

And thus began, in Sting's words, 'The second incarnation of the group... with Andy's guitar and my songs.'

A week later, Elvis Presley died. Two days after that the Police played their first gig as a three-piece. One could try to make something of that, but it'd be a hiding to nothing.

96

'Elvis was stupid,' Sting said. 'He didn't have any brains, that bloke. That was the problem. Brilliant charisma. Great face. And then he makes *G.I. Blues.*'

The gig was at Rebecca's in Birmingham, where they were contracted to provide an hour's quality poptainment for £75. They went for it, so determined to be an earthquake of punk energy that they took everything at breakneck speed and as a result ripped through their 15-song setlist in 12 minutes. Andy hated it. The crowd loved it. They went berserk. Gratified, the band ran through the entire setlist again, this time padding it with improvisations. The crowd went even more berserk. They played three encores and left the stage triumphant but confused. They definitely had something here, but was it anything they might be interested in, or just an ability to beat an audience repeatedly with a steam hammer until hysteria set in?

Then, nothing for weeks. There was a gig in Scarborough, and others that were promised, advertised, then cancelled. Lawrence Impey, Stewart's photographer friend from his schooldays, sort of managed them for a while, but that petered out. He had managed Squeeze for a while, too, and that had petered out when Miles took over in 1975, enticing the band with a promise of £15 a week each.

Then an Iranian businessman who wanted to get a foot in the door of the music industry appeared and promised the Police fame and riches, but that petered out, too.

They rehearsed endlessly, usually at Manos rehearsal studio up the King's Road, near SEX. They recorded versions of 'Truth Hits' and 'What Can I Do' at Matrix Studio. Sting signed on the dole. They shopped. They ate. They went ice skating. Stewart and Sonja, who'd moved out of the posh Mayfair flat earlier in the year to a place in Fulham, now moved to a place on the Goldhawk Road – the seedier Shepherd's Bush end. August dragged into September, and September into October.

'There were no gigs,' Stewart said. 'The group just disappeared off the scene. People were saying "What happened to the Police?" "Are you still together?"'

The thought must have occurred to them that they should have stayed with Henri.

★ ★ ★

Salvation came from two sources.

Miles had generally been sniffy about his brother's band. As the born-again champion of punk, he knew the Police were only the fake plastic version. He occasionally shoved a bit of work their way if he needed a last-minute fill-in because the proper band hadn't shown up, but generally operated what Stewart described as 'reverse nepotism'.

But, in October, he booked them for a mini-tour of the Netherlands and France, supporting Wayne County and sometimes intersecting with a Damned tour.

'It was a complete fucking nightmare,' Jayne County said in her book, *Man Enough to be a Woman*. 'The Police were the most boring people I have ever met. Polite, charming, professional, but no fun. It was like playing with a bunch of old married men. Sting was so intellectually serious, he never got out of order about anything. Totally businesslike. That's probably why they were so successful!... Sting was always very nice and very polite, and we had to share a dressing room a lot of the time, so I'd get the odd peek at him in the nude, and he did have a nice body. Nothing ever happened but he'd turn around every once in a while and give me a flash.'

The Damned didn't think much of the Police either. One night, at the Melkweg in Amsterdam, Sting knocked on the Damned's dressing room door and asked if they could have a bottle of their wine because they hadn't got any. 'Fuck off,' said Brian James. 'When you're top of the bill you can have as much as you want.' Sting went back to the others empty-handed.

They played the glitzy Nashville in Paris, where the French showbiz elite liked to mingle. This time, cases of Scotch had been provided backstage. While the Police were running through their set, Wayne and her band drank some of the cases and, no doubt hoping to make an impression on the French fashionistas, Wayne glued some plastic forks to her clothes and smeared food on her face before going on stage. A second night at the Nashville was cancelled.

That night, or maybe the next night – or maybe some other night entirely – the legend happened: the one that, according to Police mythology would change the course of history... forever.

It sounds like one of those scenes from a schlocky 1930s musical biopic in which Ira Gershwin turns to George and says, 'Why can't you ever relax? Look it's summertime, the living is easy, the fish are jumping, and the cotton is high,' and George, thus inspired, rushes to the piano to compose a masterpiece. Or when the bailiffs knock on Beethoven's door with the distinctive rhythm that later became the opening of his fifth symphony and Beethoven replies, 'You'll have to knock louder. I'm deaf.'

The Police, having been kicked out of a half-decent hotel because of a Wayne County-related incident, move into a filth-hole around the back of Gare Saint-Lazare. In the foyer of the hotel was a poster advertising the Comédie Française 1976 production of *Cyrano de Bergerac*, the Edmond Rostand play in which a man with the soul of a poet but the nose of an anteater helps his army buddy Christian (a handsome brute) to woo the lady Roxane (with one 'n'), sucking up the irony that he is hopelessly in love with Roxane himself. It all turns out very badly.

Then Sting went for a walk in Paris's red-light district. The phrase 'Roxanne [with two 'n's], you don't have to put on the red light' started bouncing around in his head, and it led the way to Shea Stadium.

★ ★ ★

In the March of 1977, Elvis Costello, another musician who'd surfed into view on the new wave – a term that was increasingly being used as a more inclusive term for 'punk-related things' – had released his first album. *My Aim Is True*, produced by Nick Lowe, had a sleeve featuring the regulation chequerboard graphics, and was recorded at Pathway Studios, so had at least some scraps of punkishness clinging to it. But otherwise it had practically nothing at all in common with the output of the Stranglers or Pistols. These were literate, crafted songs, backed by Clover, a Californian band whose own albums were filed under country-rock between the Byrds and Creedence Clearwater Revival and whose sleeve art sometimes featured shotguns and mules.

My Aim Is True spent five weeks in the UK Top 20.

Track 5, side 1, was a twisted love song called 'Alison'. Released as a single, it never made *Top of the Pops* but later found its way into most of the '500 Greatest Songs of All Time' lists.

For Sting, still labouring under the 'punk or fail' dictum, it brought pause for thought.

'I wrote "Roxanne" when I was in the Police,' Sting said, in a 2009 interview with Elvis Costello. 'It was in the time of punk and all songs had to have titles like "I'm Going To Kill You, You Bitch" so I was reticent about taking it to the band. But then I heard your album and it had this beautiful song on it called "Alison" and it gave me the confidence to take this song with a soppy girl's name to them and say "Elvis has done it so we can too."'

Oddly, many critics have interpreted the 'hidden meaning' of 'Alison', particularly when it comes to lines like 'I think somebody better put out the big light' and 'my aim is true', as being 'I'm going to kill you, you bitch.'

★ ★ ★

The second source of salvation, or at least a bit of cash, came from the German composer Eberhard Schoener.

Schoener was the real deal. He'd played first violin at the Bavarian State Opera and then risen to become the opera's musical supervisor. Later he became an early advocate of Mr Moog's synthesiser and made synth arrangements of Bach and Vivaldi that were similar, but more trance-like and sophisticated, than the *Switched-On Bach* albums by Walter Carlos (now Wendy Carlos).

He'd previously worked on a couple of rock/classical/prog albums with Jon Lord of Deep Purple, the second of which, *Sarabande*, featured Andy Summers on guitar, and he used Andy again on a Krautrock-meets-classical-meets-Gregorian-chant album, released in 1977, called *Trance-Formation*.

(An entirely irrelevant footnote to *Trance-Formation* – one of the tracks, 'Falling In Trance', features a synthesised pulse, developed by Schoener and his technical wizard Robbie Wedel, which they named the 'Black & Decker effect' because, like a Black & Decker advert of the time, it went 'Black & Decker Black & Decker Black & Decker Black & Decker' very fast. Later, Robbie Wedel was called in by producers Giorgio Moroder and Pete Bellotte, working at the Musicland Studios in Munich – a 15-minute drive from Schoener's Bavaria Musikstudios – to help give a track they were working on a futuristic sound. Robbie set up the Moog with arpeggiator and programmed it to do the Black & Decker effect. Moroder and Bellotte loved it. When the track – Donna Summer's 'I Feel Love' – sold a zillion copies worldwide, Schoener sued, trying (and failing) to secure a slice of the royalties. By the time Debbie Harry went 'Black & Decker' on 'Heart Of Glass', he must have started wondering why he bothered.)

Andy managed to get Stewart and Sting included in the Schoener gig and they were joined by Hansi Ströer, a keyboard player, and a children's choir. It was about two weeks' work, rehearsal and performance for the laser show, followed by a couple of days in the studio working on an album *Flashback*, released the following year.

The laser show was, by all accounts, nothing special and the shows were often blighted by power cuts and laser failures, but the Police clearly came up to scratch, because the following year Schoener booked them again. And the year after that.

★ ★ ★

But November and December were, if anything, more barren than September had been. No gigs, no work. Towards Christmas, Stewart decided to reinvent himself as mystery punk-superman Klark Kent, and on the 17 December, with Nigel Gray producing (more of whom in the next chapter), he recorded three tracks (more of which in the next chapter).

Andy spent Christmas with Kate in the US.

Sting was still signing on, living in the Bayswater basement, trying to write songs.

★ ★ ★

At New Year, Stewart brought his hi-fi – louder than most – over to Sting's for a party. With it he brought a 'bunch of Wailers' albums, some Burning Spear, some dub records.'

Jamaican music – reggae, ska, rocksteady and blue beat – had been a feature of British life since at least the early 1960s. In 1965, every kid in every playground was doing Millie Small's 'My Boy Lollipop', and the year before that the Migil Five – white men from London – had appropriated the blue beat for their version of 'Mockin' Bird Hill'. In 1966, the same kids who had sung 'My Boy Lollipop' (the lads, anyway) were now shouting 'Al Capone's Guns Don't H-argue' and worshipping Prince Buster. Two years after that, they were secretly listening to Max Romeo's 'Wet Dream'.

Bob Marley had scored three UK Top 40 hits in 1977. Don Letts, then resident DJ at the Roxy, regularly played Marley, as well as the more refined dub of Lee 'Scratch' Perry.

Reggae had always been something considerably more than a dance beat and, in the UK, in 1976, it took on even greater political weight.

Rock Against Racism was an organisation set up partly in response to the rise and rise of the National Front – the right-wing, anti-immigrant, avowedly racist party of the day that, in 1976, had taken 40 per cent of the vote in the Blackburn by-election. The more immediate catalyst, though, was Eric Clapton's drunken racist rant at a gig in Birmingham, the vicious irony, of course, being that Eric Clapton had learned all he knew from listening to bluesmen and, a couple of years before, had had a hit with a cover of Bob Marley's 'I Shot The Sheriff'.

The organisation blossomed, spawned a magazine and spread to mainland Europe and the US. At RAR concerts and festivals, punk, new wave and reggae shared the same stage and the reggae lilt found its way into punk consciousness. The Clash covered Junior Murvin's 'Police And Thieves'. Elvis Costello brought the beat to 'Watching The Detectives'.

Lilt, it appeared, could be a valid alternative to thrash, just as cool if not cooler, with the added cachet of incontrovertible political okayness.

According to Stewart, Sting hadn't listened to much reggae before – not closely, anyway – but those records, at that New Year's Eve party, opened his ears to the possibility of incorporating those loose-spined rhythms into his own music.

Sudden enthusiasms are often generated by the party spirit, especially if strong drink is taken. They rarely have lasting importance. This was an exception.

Chapter Eight

THE BEST OF TIMES, THE WORST OF TIMES

In 2013, researchers at the University of Canberra figured out that, according to the GPI (Genuine Progress Indicator) – a measure that uses several variables to calculate an index of human happiness – people in the UK were happier in 1978 than they'd ever been before or have been since. Six years later, a team at Warwick University, using the National Valence Index – a measure of subjective well-being – found it to be the unhappiest year the UK has known since 1945.

Literally, it was the best of times, it was the worst of times.

★ ★ ★

Punk was gone. The Sex Pistols disintegrated on their US tour in January. Johnny Rotten reverted to being John Lydon and formed Public Image Ltd, a band whose first album had one foot in punk, another in prog rock, a hand (*Twister*-style) in the European avant-garde tradition and another in dub reggae.

That October, in New York, Sid Vicious, was in deep trouble. 'Sid Vicious,' ran the *New York Times* report, 'bass guitarist of Britain's spitting and stomping Sex Pistols punk rock band, yesterday was arrested and charged with stabbing his sultry blonde girlfriend to death in their room in Manhattan's famed Chelsea Hotel. His face pale and scratched, the dazed looking Vicious muttered curses and "I'll smash your cameras" as he was led from the hotel where the body of Nancy Laura Spungen, 20, was found.' Sid was charged with murder and released into the care of his mother on bail put up by Virgin Records. Next he tried to cut his wrists and spent several weeks in the psychiatric ward at Bellevue Hospital. When he got out of there, he got arrested again for attacking Patti Smith's brother, Todd, with a broken beer bottle. He was hauled off to Riker's Island, where he spent 55 days of cold turkey detox. Released again, with the bail increased, on 1 February 1979, he partied with his new girlfriend. By the following morning, he was dead of an overdose.

★ ★ ★

The sounds of that year, the ones that came from car radios and open windows, were distinctly un-punkish – the Bee Gees and Kate Bush sang in very high voices and Abba in lower ones, Showaddywaddy revived drainpipes and brothel creepers and, endlessly, relentlessly, all that summer and into the autumn, Boney M. told us about 'Russia's famous love machine' and about the brown girl in the ring who looked 'like a sugar in a plum'.

But, among the Heathcliffs and Rasputins, there was still the occasional hit from bands that had emerged from the punk swamp, some of which still trailed varying amounts of punkish algae: among them, Ian Dury (more pub rock than punk), Boomtown Rats, Blondie, Buzzcocks, Elvis Costello, Squeeze, Nick Lowe, the Undertones… and the Police.

A year of the Undertones and Showaddywaddy – the best of times and the worst of times.

★ ★ ★

Nigel Gray was a family doctor, who, when he was at medical school, had been in a band. He'd invested in a couple of tape machines to record demos of his band, then got more interested in recording than playing and bought a second-hand 4-track.

Then, the way these things snowball, he started looking for a studio and found an old village hall. It had an entrance hall, an auditorium, a stage and a bit of backstage space. He and his brother Chris put a partition with a glass panel between the stage and the auditorium. The auditorium became the studio, and the stage the control room. They advertised. Stewart's former boss, Joan Armatrading, used the studio for demos. Mike Batt used it to record bits and bobs for the Wombles.

'Luckily for me the room was big enough to be able to put drums in without them sounding boxy,' he told Jake Brown for his book *Behind the Boards*, 'and it was a little bit too loud, so I put some acoustic tiles on the ceiling I bought cheaply from some guy and the acoustics – just by pure luck – worked perfect for rock bands. It was live enough to be live, but not too live to be difficult to work with. So, drums always sounded good in that room, you didn't have to be a genius to make drums sound good, you just put a microphone in front of them and boom, there you were.'

They upgraded, first to 8-track, then to 'a 16-track Alice desk and an Ampex MM 1000 16-track tape machine'.

It was still primitive – most commercial studios were equipped with 24-track by this time and the Warner Bros studio in North Hollywood had even started mucking about with 32-track digital recording – but it was cheap: £11 an hour, up to £15 an hour when the 16-track was up and running, or £150 for a 12-hour day. A fancy London studio at the time would have cost £40–£50 an hour. Townhouse, the Virgin studio that had just been built in Shepherd's Bush, was charging £85.

So, because Surrey Sound, as the studio was called, was so cheap, and because it was so much bigger than, say, Pathway in Stoke Newington, and because Nigel Gray was easy to get on with, the Police, backed by limited amounts of cash – first from Paul Mulligan and later from Miles – were prepared to undertake the hour-and-a-half drive from central London to Leatherhead, invariably through nightmare traffic, to use it.

Sting's first impressions of the place ran through 'toilet', to 'cruddy, funky place with egg cartoons on the wall'.

Nevertheless, it was here that, on 15 January 1978, that the Police set about making their first album.

★ ★ ★

The punk to-be-or-not-to-be question was still bothering them.

'We were handicapped by punk "rules",' Stewart told *Revolver* magazine years later. 'The trappings of punk were beneficial to us – which is why we succumbed to the straitjacket of the punk hairdo, the punk stance, and other "punkarama".'

The question was whether the songs should go with the hairdo and stance. Sting had sheaves of songs he'd written when he was in Last Exit – some fairly complete, others half-formed melodies and ideas for lyrics. But they, of course, were not punk.

Stewart had songs, too, rich in punkarama, but Sting turned his nose up at them. 'A lot of my songs Sting won't sing,' Stewart said, 'and the songs of mine that he will sing he changes the words. We're very different people with different ways of projecting ourselves, and when he expresses himself in a song, the way I write just doesn't fit him at all.'

They set about recording one of Sting's numbers, 'Next To You'. The arrangement could, at a push, be the Rezillos or the Damned, but the lyric – about the delight and desperation of being in love – was closer to Bobby Vee.

Andy and Stewart both wanted to change the lyric to something more political, more angry, more punk. Andy suggested changing the line, '*All I want to be is next to you*' to something perhaps like, '*I just want to take a gun to you*'. But Sting stood his ground and they stuck with Bobby Vee.

'Though arguments are a feature of our sessions,' Sting said, 'they are always about how a song should go down on tape: this friction is a contributing factor to the tension that is part of the Police sound – it might be the sound of tight compromise.'

It took time, but eventually Stewart and Andy both realised (to their credit) that, much better than anything they were writing at the time, what Sting wrote suited his style, his attitude, his taste and, above all – one of the band's most precious assets – his voice. Perhaps this is what Sting meant by 'tight compromise'.

Sting is on record as saying that the band were never happier than when they were recording that first album and they remained 'insanely optimistic' about their chances, but recording was a herky-jerky process, constantly interrupted by the need to earn a crust. They sometimes pulled all-night sessions, leaving bleary-eyed at six in the morning.

★ ★ ★

Gigs were still few and far between. Often, they were booked and then cancelled. The Rock Garden cancelled them on 30 January. Then the Vortex bailed because the management had gone bust.

Sometimes they'd be asked to fill in when another band cancelled: 'Ladies and gentlemen instead of Cosmic Filth, would you please welcome... the Police.' They would walk on to the sound of the audience walking out.

★ ★ ★

There is a story – entirely irrelevant and probably apocryphal, but good value all the same – about Frank Carson, the old-style comic from Belfast, whose catchphrase, 'It's the way I tell 'em', served him well throughout a long and distinguished career.

Frank, who liked to be busy, was working at a club in Leeds when a message came from another club, just across the way. The headline act billed to perform hadn't shown up. Could Frank fit it in? The money was good, and the timing could just about be managed if he had a car waiting, so he agreed.

He arrived at the second venue bang on time.

'They're a bit rough,' the manager warned him.

'Never bothered me,' Frank said. 'I'll be fine.'

The manager went on stage, 'Ladies and gentlemen. Bit of a change to tonight's entertainment. Instead of the Clash, would you please welcome... Mr Frank Carson.'

★ ★ ★

Even when a gig actually happened with their name on the poster, the Police seldom heard the shouts of acclaim they hoped for. On 20 January, they performed in front of 250 restless punks at the Marquee.

Harry Callaghan reviewed the gig for *Sounds*. 'If you like punk played with the edge of galvanised steel, then you'll probably like the Police.' He clearly didn't like it and left before the end of the set.

The Hope and Anchor in Islington was one of punk's holy places. It had a tiny stage and a low ceiling. The walls and floors were painted red. Some wag said it was like performing inside somebody's mouth.

When it was full, it was grim. Half-full, it was grim and bleak. The audience for the Police, when they played there on 9 February, was about the size of one of the classes Sting used to teach. Frances, Kate and Sonja were there.

Henri showed up, too, but he wasn't impressed. 'They were still singing the same set, the same songs. The style had changed – Andy had bought a bit of professionalism – it was all a bit dispiriting, as if a fire had gone out.'

At night, they still went out with spray cans making sure that every wall in Camden, Islington and Fulham had – in addition to its 'Troops out Now', its fading 'George Davis Is Innocent' and its 'Women's Right to Choose' – a fresh-sprayed, still perplexingly ambiguous 'The Police'.

★ ★ ★

To make ends meet, Sting, meanwhile, had started moonlighting as a model. He had the look and knew how to use it. Like Greta Garbo, Cillian Murphy, Sitting Bull and Cruella de Vil, he had discovered the magical power of cheekbones. 'At the age of about 25, I decided that I could impose beauty on myself,' he said. 'It's a strange thing to talk about. But there is an expression I have. Seductive.'

Frances was close friends with Pippa Markham, formerly an actor who was now working as a talent agent. Pippa scored Sting a couple of adverts.

In dark glasses and sudden movements, he wore his jeans to fit his body and his body under his jeans, got kissed by Dominique Wood of Hot Gossip and went home with a nice cheque in the back pocket of his Brutus denims. And, while he played pinball, several women tried to draw his attention to the fact that Triumph had a bra for the way they are.

Most significantly for the future of the Police, in February 1978 the entire band scored a job playing a pop group in a Wrigley's Spearmint chewing gum ad. It was shot on 15 February at Isleworth Studios and they worked a 15-hour day, starting at 8 a.m., for the 28-second commercial. Stewart noted in his diary that they cut his hair and put 'wanking grease' in it.

The plot involved them (playing a punk band) harassing a rock'n'roll agent until the rock'n'roll agent pulls out his chewing gum, offers it, and thus brings peace and accord. No trace of this ad has ever turned up. Some people have even suggested that it never existed and that those who remember it being shown may be victims of false memory syndrome. But the important fact is that the agency, or the client, or the director, decided that Stewart, Sting and Andy would look more punky if, in addition to applying the 'wanking grease', they all bleached their hair.

Sting went first. Andy and Stewart, rather more reluctantly, followed suit. Andy didn't like it at all.

'The first time I looked in the mirror I had this really brassy orange-looking hair. I looked like an old whore!'

The hair, like Sting's voice, the jumpsuit, Stewart's hi-hat skitters, Andy's shimmering chords and the endless 'eee-oh' became one of the band's trademarks.

In February 1978, though, it seemed less enchanting.

The hair hadn't done their punk cred any good at all. Wags took one look and christened them 'The Bleach Boys'.

'It was pretty grim,' said Andy, 'no work, no money and bright blond hair.'

★ ★ ★

Every chance they got, they braved the A3 to Leatherhead for more recording.

'Roxanne', Sting's song inspired by the *Cyrano de Bergerac* poster and the Parisian sex workers, had been hanging around for months waiting for the right arrangement. Sting had conceived it on a nylon-strung guitar as a Carlos Jobim bossa nova, entirely inappropriate for anything to do with punk, new wave, pop, reggae or rock'n'roll.

They decided to try it with a reggae rhythm, or, as Sting has since pointed out, halfway between reggae and tango.

It is a weird rhythm. James Brown, the Godfather of Soul, laid great stress on the 'one', the first beat of the bar. There's sound reasoning behind this. Without being able to identify the 'one', people can't orient themselves to the beat, and thus can't dance. The Beatles had messed with the 'one' a couple of times – the introductory chords to 'She's A Woman', for instance, give a strong impression of a 'one' and a 'three' that, as soon as the bass comes in, reveal themselves to be a 'two' and a 'four'.

In the verses of 'Roxanne', only Andy is playing the 'one'. Stewart and Sting are bracketing it. It's an unsettling effect. Sometimes it sounds as if Andy is changing chord a beat too early, or maybe a beat too late. Sometimes it sounds as though Sting's vocal has found a strange oriental rhythmic groove. The rhythm glitch is one of the song's hooks. It causes people to prick up their ears and say, 'This is not pop as we know it, and neither is it reggae.' Jazz fans might even refer back to something Mingus or Monk did in 1958, or Joe and Jaco in 1976.

But there was something else there, too. During the weeks and months of rehearsal, a sound had begun to emerge.

Andy, in *One Train Later*, reckons it had a lot to do with an old Echoplex he'd got hold of – 1960s technology that used a tape loop with a movable playback head set at a variable distance from the record head to produce an echo effect. Other adjustments could produce multiple echoes, a shimmering effect that gradually faded away.

In the standard punk band, the – usually heavily distorted – guitar(s) would chunter away remorselessly. Andy, far too tasteful for anything so baseline, took a minimalist approach, finding chords and inversions that let the natural sparkle of his Telecaster, enhanced by the shimmer of the Echoplex, make a mark and hang there for a moment – as it does at the end of each verse in 'Roxanne'. The minimalist approach also left space for bass and drums to make a definite statement rather than (as they did in most bands) just set a groove and keep the beat.

Andy calls the approach 'policification'. 'We can take almost any song and, as we say, "policify" it – even a piece of material by Noël Coward or a folk song from the Scottish Isles. From an instinctive and unselfconscious journey, we discover a sound for which there is no previous formula, a space jam meets reggae meets Bartók collage with blue-eyed soul vocals.'

Andy also brought years of experience to the party.

'The thing Andy provided,' says Phil Sutcliffe, 'was, when someone said, "What we want here is something that does so-and-so," Andy would say, "You could have this," and they would say, "Great," and Andy would say, "Or you could have this," and they would say, "That's great, too." And then Andy would say, "Or how about this?" And they'd say, "That's the one." He'd provide them with maybe 10 alternatives – all good.'

Then there is Sting's voice. Just that one word, 'Roxanne', was enough to convince. 'Roxanne' soars, bends, with longing and purity and, perhaps best of all, the simple joy of achievement that anybody would feel if they could sing 'Roxanne' like Sting sings 'Roxanne'.

It is on this album, and possibly on this track, that Sting found his voice. In the Last Exit recordings and the punk stuff, there is a sense of trapped potential. Maybe he was trying to sound more jazzy, or more punky, or maybe he was just shy. The vocal tract can fall victim to all manner of ungovernable psychological and emotional forces. The move towards reggae might have had something to do with uncaging the power of Sting.

'I was into Bob Marley at the time, singing with that kind of lilt. The melody has a lot of whoops and swoops and then goes into this rock'n'roll chorus. It sounded really odd, but in a nice way. Everyone who heard it said they had heard the constituent parts before but never the hybrid.'

Later he was often accused, notably by Joe Strummer of the Clash, of adopting a Jafaican accent. In a weak defence, he once said: 'With my dialect from Newcastle – it sounds a little Jamaican. I wasn't imitating Bob Marley.'

'With "Roxanne" we compressed the lead vocal a lot, because the melody of "Roxanne" is very like a jazz thing,' said Nigel Gray, 'so every time he sang it, it was different. It is a very improvised vocal, the basic melody was there, but it was just slightly different every time... so we just kept doing takes till we got one he liked. But because we couldn't afford 2-inch tape, we always went over the old ones. We didn't have the facility to keep a lot of takes, because the tape cost more than the studio time.'

As any cheap 'How To' manual will tell you, one of the essential elements of a successful pop song is repetition. 'Roxanne' repeats the word 'Roxanne', on average, once every 7.5 seconds over the length of the song. This can be compared with the Beatles' 'She Loves You' (once every 10.6 seconds for 'She Loves You', but once every 4.7 seconds for 'Yeah'), Abba's 'Waterloo' (a restrained once every 9.5 seconds) and Cream's 'I'm Glad' (in which the word 'Glad' appears, in one context or another, on average once every 2.9 seconds). It's up there with the winners, then. The repetition trick is one that Sting continued to use to great effect in hit after hit.

The acclaim for 'Roxanne' was, and is, not universal.

'Would be a great new wave tune if Sting didn't sing the word "Roxanne" that one way,' says one punter on the RateYourMusic website. 'You know what I'm talking about. You know when you're in an airplane and a baby's crying, and they scream so loud that you can hear the phlegm gurgle in their throats? It sounds like that, and I want to die every time.'

Nevertheless, in 'Roxanne', the Police seemed to resolve one of the great dilemmas facing any pop group, and particularly any pop group at the end of the 1970s. How do you make records that are bubblegummy enough singles to make number one while still retaining that all-important air of credibility that will sell albums to thoughtful men and

111

women who think that cool is paramount and who live in dread that one day a stranger will browse their record collection and find something shameful – *Captain & Tennille's Greatest Hits,* perhaps, or *Paper Lace: Live at Leeds.*

★ ★ ★

One day, Miles came down to the studio to see how his brother's band was getting on. He listened to a few tracks but remained resolutely unimpressed. Nigel suggested that he listen to 'Roxanne'.

In the story – and who doesn't like a good story? – Stewart tried to steer him away from it. 'If you haven't liked what you've heard so far, then this one is even less likely to succeed. It's a love song and no one wants to listen to love songs.'

Nevertheless, Nigel ran the tape and Sting's voice went 'Roxanne', and it didn't make Miles think of the phlegm gurgling in a baby's throat.

'I knew that it was something different,' Miles said. 'So literally, it all came from the first time I listened to that song and realised what it was. None of the others did. I mean, no one in the band thought the song was a game changer at all.'

(Miles didn't always get things right. He told Squeeze that the sublime 'Up The Junction' would never be a single because it didn't have a chorus. It went Top 10 for five weeks, peaking at number two.)

The day after Miles' epiphany, he took the tape into A&M Records and played it to the suits.

They agreed to release 'Roxanne' as a single, with 'Peanuts' on the B-side. At this point it was customary for the manager to blag a massive advance out of the record company. The advance element of the deal is the one the band is usually interested in. This gives them actual money in their hands, now, money they can spend on cars, clubs and cocaine. But, as the name suggests, it is an advance, a loan against future record sales.

Miles wasn't interested in that. 'I said, "No advance, no upfront money, nothing – just give me the highest royalty you can possibly pay and let's go do it."'

The point is, according so Stewart:

How confident are you that you can really do it? If you haven't got that total faith in yourself, maybe you're just going to go for as big a slice of the cake as you can get in one go – namely the advance. Then you'll know that for such a length of time you can have your £50 a week, though eventually of course, it will run out. Where the Clash made their biggest error was in accepting that money from CBS [in January 1977, the Clash had signed to CBS for £100,000]. But their second error was in missing out of their contract a very important clause. Namely, that they retain complete artistic freedom to release whatever they desire, which is something we certainly have.

Whatever, the deal effectively bypassed the possibility that A&M would own anybody's arse.

In another context, Stewart mentions that they did get a smallish £10,000 advance plus a £1,000-a-track budget for the next album, and certainly, some months later, the £10,000 appeared and made all their lives a little easier, enabling Stewart to invest in some new jeans and a couple of albums and Sting to get an MGB sports car.

Trained accountants could probably explain these sorts of anomalies, but the only people who'd be interested would be other trained accountants.

★ ★ ★

When A&M signed the Sex Pistols, Malcolm McLaren had staged the event (actually the real signing had taken place the day before) outside Buckingham Palace. They had just recorded 'God Save The Queen', and the stunt was designed to whip up a press frenzy. The Pistols stumbled out of their limo, looking outrageous and acting drunk. It was rumoured that Sid Vicious's father, who worked as a guard at the Palace, was actually on duty that afternoon but he didn't show up to arrest them or anything.

Shortly after the signing, the band stormed into A&M's office, literally pissed on the furniture and tore the gold records from the walls. A&M ripped up the contracts less than a week after they'd been signed.

So, when the Police appeared, the sighs of relief from the A&M suits must have been audible. Sting, Stewart and Andy were really good about going to the toilet. Sting was a former teacher, Stewart had been to Millfield and Andy was older than Cilla Black.

The band signed the 35-page contract with A&M Records on 31 March and 'Roxanne' was released on 7 April 1978. It got favourable press.

'It's wiry, mainstream rock with plenty of open spaces and one of those high-pitched deliveries. Could even be a minor hit if A&M do the groundwork,' said *Melody Maker*.

'A beautiful entry with a touch of the tangos. The lead singer has the perfect equilibrium of squeaks and rasps in his voice to carry it,' said *Record Mirror*. 'I wish someone would write a song about me... what the hell, go out and buy it immediately.'

The big setback for the single was that the BBC were squeamish about having songs about prostitutes on their playlists.

'There was no talk about fucking in it, it wasn't a smutty song in any sense of the word,' Sting protested later that year. 'It was a real song with a real, felt lyric, and they wouldn't play it on the grounds that it was about a prostitute.'

Often a BBC 'ban' can work in a record's favour. Four years later, Frankie Goes to Hollywood's 'Relax' was doing no business at all until DJ Mike Read refused to play it on Radio 1. Then it went to number one and stayed there for five weeks.

But, even though A&M slapped 'Banned by the BBC' all over the ads, the trick didn't work for 'Roxanne'.

The BBC remained unmoved even when Caroline Stafford, co-writer of this book, spent an entire Sunday running up her uncle Leslie's phone bill, calling the Radio 1 Hotline to get the single put on the 'New Releases Chart List'. Damn you, Simon Bates.

★ ★ ★

Though sales were disappointing, the single did get noticed by rock royalty.

'It was Keith Richards who turned me on to the Police whilst I was travelling with the Rolling Stones in America in 1978,' says Keith Altham, then working as PR for the Stones, later for the Police. 'Every time I passed Keith's room, he would drag me in and ask whether I'd heard his demo disc of "Roxanne" which Andy Summers had sent him. I would reply that he had played it to me yesterday and the day before, and the day before that. "Well come and 'ear it again," leered the Human Riff.'

★ ★ ★

Maybe the single would have been more successful if the band had been around to promote it, but in May they went off to Germany to work again with Eberhard Schoener. A week's rehearsal, a two-week tour and time in the studio playing on his new album – 240 DM plus 40 DM expenses a day (about £60 and £10).

The tour was billed as 'Trance-Formation – Laser in Concert'. The poster showed a circus tent pitched in a sci-fi alien landscape.

The tour started in Göttingen and wound up in Düsseldorf. They did a couple of TV shots, too, in Cologne and Munich.

On the Cologne show, they did 'Only The Wind', a song of Schoener's from the *Flashback* album that would not have been out of place on side 1 of the Beatles' *Abbey Road*. Sting, his peroxide hair longer than usual, sang in an unfeasibly high voice, and Andy played an old-school solo on a black Les Paul.

★ ★ ★

Back in the UK, a low point of sorts was reached when Stewart and Sonja got evicted from their flat on the Goldhawk Road and Sting's dog died. Later in the year, Stewart and Sonja found a flat in Lena Gardens, also in Shepherd's Bush, living upstairs from Usha, daughter of the Maharaja of Burdwan. Sting's dog, on the other hand, stayed dead.

★ ★ ★

'Can't Stand Losing You', the second single release from the projected album, was released on 14 August. It is, in Sting's words, 'a sparse bassline, four in the bar on the guitar; very skeletal arrangement, and again going into a rock'n'roll chorus with lots of eighths. And I did some more of this up-and-down, strange, high-pitched singing. It's pretty juvenile, really. And it's a song about a teenage suicide, which is always a bit of a joke. The lyric probably took me about five minutes.'

The teenage suicide theme once again dished the record's chances of airplay on the BBC. Even if the prodnoses hadn't quite caught the lyric, the cover art would have raised hackles.

The art director, Mike Ross, had arranged for a large block of ice to be delivered to photographer Peter Gravelle's studio. Stewart, with an electrical cord pulled as a noose around his neck, climbed up on to the ice cube, which was standing in front of a two-bar electrical fire. They had about 10 minutes to get the shot right.

The press was not kind.

'Last observed proceeding in the direction of the waste bin. Not worth apprehending,' said *New Musical Express*.

'Having wormed their way into your ear with their careful incorporation of a reggae feel (not rhythm) and vocals carefully arranged to cover their inadequacies, they sling it at you,' said *Sounds*.

Despite which, the single, even on this first release, glimpsed the Top 50, just for one week, before disappearing.

★ ★ ★

Meanwhile, Stewart had the secret project we've already mentioned. It had been brewing for a while.

'We would be together in little bedsit studios,' Sonja said, 'where he'd be sitting with his ReVox, tapping the beat of the song that was in his head... putting the beat down on a cushion. Then he would lay the guitar down... Then he covered himself in green paint and pink film. It was great fun. That was before the Police became really successful... I was watching all of this and that was another magical place to be.'

The name of the green man with pink film who used cushions for drums was Klark Kent. The press release read:

> Kent first appeared in Llandyckkk, a Welsh fishing visit where, in spite of only speaking a New Orleans patois, he became church organist. It was the first in an increasingly bizarre sequence of events that was to culminate in New York at the height of his fame. His personal manners began to excite adverse attention following the unfortunate 'Lasagne Affair' with the beautiful eponymous triplets, who, stricken into sadness after he had rejected their sexual advances, threw themselves holding hands from the top floor of the Mobil Oil Building singing 'Ave Maria', before splashing themselves on to 42nd Street below.

'Don't Care' – a song about a man whose unassailable self-regard makes him indifferent to the approval of others – was one of Stewart's songs rejected by his bandmate(s). Accordingly, he recorded it himself, playing all the instruments, and released it, under the name of Klark Kent, on his own Kryptone label, pressed on green vinyl.

Later in the year, it was re-released by A&M, made number 48 in the Hot 50 and earned Klark a showing on *Top of the Pops*.

As his miming backing band, he recruited Andy, Sting, Miles and drummer/roadie/engineer/friend Kim Turner. Even though the true identity of Klark Kent was the worst-kept secret in pop and Roy Carr had already blown the gaff in *NME*, Stewart wore dark glasses and the others hid their identities with masks – Andy chose Russian premier Leonid Brezhnev, Sting a gorilla.

And that, dear readers, was the Police's first appearance on *Top of the Pops.*

★ ★ ★

Sting had a sideline going, too.

Three years earlier the film of the Who's rock opera *Tommy*, starring Roger Daltrey, Ann-Margret, Oliver Reed and Keith Moon, and featuring cameos from the likes of Elton John and Eric Clapton, took £27 million in the US in the first six months of release. It was director Ken Russell's most commercially successful film.

This made the Who's other rock opera/concept album *Quadrophenia* an exciting property. Its value had been much enhanced by the mod revival that had taken off in 1977, spearheaded by the Jam, whose taste in tonic suits, two-tone shoes and Rickenbacker guitars had renewed the urge to strike a rocker in many old enough to know better.

Franc Roddam had been slated to direct. Phil Daniels had bagged the part of Jimmy, the lead (at one point, Johnny Rotten had been up for the part), and Leslie Ash was playing Steph.

Sting auditioned on 31 August 1978 and landed the part of Ace Face, Jimmy's idol, the coolest mod in the world. The hair, the body, the cheekbones made him a shoo-in. And then, to seal the deal, they put him in a leather overcoat, like a Gestapo officer.

The Police had planned to go to America in early October and had even booked some gigs, but when Sting got the part they had to postpone it.

Tommy was garish surrealism, *Quadrophenia* is nervy realism, an anti-musical, far more akin to British new wave pictures of the early 1960s than, say, *Grease* or *The Rocky Horror Picture Show.*

The glory of the finished film was in stark contrast to the horror of its making. The shoot mostly took place in late summer/early autumn in a year when October night-time temperatures were already down to freezing. It was cold, and Brighton beach was a forbidding location. Between takes, the actors huddled, like penguins, for warmth.

It was scary. Franc Roddam liked to keep things as real as possible. The difference between actors pretending to riot and an actual riot is largely academic. People got hurt.

At one point, Phil Daniels, riding his scooter at Beachy Head, veered a little too close to the edge. Luckily, at that point they were only three days into the shoot, so could have recast without major scheduling problems if he'd gone over.

Another time, again at Beachy Head, the stunt people underestimated the distance a scooter would fly if propelled from a clifftop. Franc Roddam and crew, filming the stunt from a hovering helicopter, nearly made history by dying in the first ever mid-air collision between an aircraft and a Vespa GS Rally.

Sting's main difficulty seems to have been exhaustion. He wasn't a full-time actor. He was the singer and bass player in an up-and-coming pop group. He had commitments.

The band was gigging, not that often, but enough to build a backlog of late nights for Sting when he'd have to be up and on location first thing the following morning. And they were still doing bits and bobs for the album, which had him driving up and down the A23 from Brighton to Leatherhead, dozing at the wheel of his new MGB.

On 2 October, after a hard day's cold, nasty rioting on Brighton beach, he had to rush back to London for the Police's first TV appearance on *The Old Grey Whistle Test*. Knackered, he managed to spray metallic paint into his eyes rather than his hair and was rushed off to a nearby eye hospital. He got back just in time to perform 'Can't Stand Losing You' and 'Next To You' wearing Stewart's dark glasses. It was no way to spend his 27th birthday.

★ ★ ★

It was a year before *Quadrophenia* was premiered, on 16 August 1979. By that time, the Police were big. They had a record riding high in the charts and Sting was no longer 'that bloke out of the Triumph bra advert' but 'that blond god off *Top of the Pops*'. And so, he was no longer a striking accessory with a cameo part, but one of the movie's main attractions.

The critics generally agreed he made a decent fist of it – 'Sting was on screen long enough to make an impact', as one of them put it, 'but not long enough to blow it.'

'Ace is very much part of my own character,' Sting told *NME*. 'I have a very, very strong ego and those scenes – like that in the Brighton dance hall when Jimmy attempts to steal my limelight by dancing on the balcony – well, that look on my face, were that to have been a real situation, would be exactly the same.'

He liked talking about his ego. Throughout the early 1980s, attentive punters took bets on how soon it would crop up in an interview.

'Basically, it's me vs Stewart at times,' he went on. 'We both have these enormous egos – and Andy sort of coasts along over and around the two of us. The safety gauge factor is that Stewart, Andy and I are all too aware of the pitfalls of ego excess and have, whether consciously or subconsciously, "ritualised" the whole process.'

Showaddywaddy rarely talked about the ritualisation of ego excess, either consciously or unconsciously, but then Showaddywaddy never achieved world domination.

Chapter Nine

IT WAS LIKE BEING AT WAR

The Beatles had spearheaded the first 'British invasion' 14 years ago, and still the conquest of America was a rite of passage for a British band – not normally attempted until a firm foothold in the domestic market had been established.

Then the band would do a US gig or two as support for some bigger name. The Who's first US gigs were as support for an American singer, big at the time, called Mitch Ryder – eight days, five shows a day, smashing the gear every show and rebuilding it between. Much later, the Clash made their US debut opening for the Who. Jimi Hendrix opened for the Monkees, Queen for Mott the Hoople, Led Zeppelin for Vanilla Fudge, Metallica for Venom, and so on.

After that, maybe you'd get a US hit, and then, and only then, you might start thinking about putting waterbeds in the private jet.

The Copelands, however, were Americans. For them the US *was* the domestic market.

Ian Copeland was working for Paragon, a huge talent agency based in Macon, Georgia. He knew the business. He figured that a US tour did not have to stadiums or even theatres. Every town had a small club – the equivalent of the 100 in London or Barbarella's in Birmingham. There was no established touring circuit of the small clubs, but there was no reason Ian couldn't invent one. He was a Copeland.

He'd tried the small-club idea with Squeeze earlier in the year – a three-month tour of places like the Rat Club in Boston, Flaming Sally's in Macon and Bottom's Up in Baton Rouge. The tour didn't move empires, but it did build a useful word-of-mouth following. They got some press; they sold a few records.

The key thing with such a tour was to keep the overheads down. In this respect, the Police had a big advantage over Squeeze. They were a three-piece; Squeeze, a five-piece. Even if you're eating at McDonald's, those two extra Filets-O-Fish per night over three months could cut profit margins to the bone and God help us all if they started on the Fantas.

'Miles and I figured that if anyone could turn America on to new music, the Police could,' said Ian, 'and if we cracked the American market, more bands would have the chance to do the same. In the bigger picture, it was a way of saving the music business from the stagnation that had set in, a way to revive the excitement that once defined rock'n'roll.'

He lashed together a 25-day, 23-gig tour.

'I concentrated on the major cities in the north-east and nearby, but in order to fill up the Mondays and Tuesdays, the most difficult nights to fill, and to pay for the hotels every night along the way, I was forced to find dates in some very peculiar places.'

★ ★ ★

Stewart and Miles were already in the US, visiting their dad. Andy and Sting travelled from the UK on the no-frills Laker Skytrain, the Ryanair of the 1970s, carrying their guitars as hand luggage.

Ian and Kim Turner picked them up at the airport in a Ford Econoline van that he had loaded up with backline equipment from Manny's music shop and drove them straight to the first gig at CBGB.

CBGB, the storefront club in East Village, was already a legend. Patti Smith, Wayne County, Television, the Ramones, Blondie and Talking Heads had all found a home at CBGB. In 1977, the Damned played there. A couple of days before the Police came, Elvis Costello had shown up and sung a couple of songs with Richard Hell's Voidoids.

'Where CBGBs is, it isn't one of the best streets,' Sting said. 'I thought, "Man, this is incredible, it's like Hades!" And the club is even worse.'

They played two sets, Sting in his flying suit, the first at midnight, the second at 2.30 in the morning. Still running on UK time, to Sting and Andy this was the equivalent of 5 a.m. and 9.30 p.m.

It was a Friday. The place wasn't packed. Nevertheless, the band was juiced on adrenaline and went for it. By the end of the first set, the audience was howling for more.

'Stewart and I had a fight in the dressing room after the show,' Sting said. 'I thought he was speeding up, he said that I was slowing down. We were strangling each other and then we heard the calls for an encore. We stopped strangling each other, did an encore and then came back, had another fight and then back for another encore.'

Like Stewart says, 'We don't do passive aggressive. We go straight to aggressive.'

Jim Green was there for *Trouser Press*, the New York fanzine that championed the British new wave.

'They're from Britain – so big deal. And they all have bleached blond hair – swell. But jeez, if you listen – hey, this is hot stuff! The bassist is jumping around in a boiler suit and he's singing in this neat, kinda high-pitched voice – and the drummer's bashing away so hard he's gonna bust those drumheads. And there's a twinky little guitarist in striped tee and leather jacket, standing there with a look of distraction on his face, kinda like a child whose face momentarily looks old when deep in concentration.'

And thus it began: 25 gruelling days, thousands of miles, on $20 a day each to cover expenses.

'It was like being at war,' Sting said. 'We were out there fighting a war. And we won.'

★ ★ ★

They went down to Philadelphia for a gig at Grendel's Lair, then doubled back up to the Last Chance Saloon, Poughkeepsie, New York, where the audience consisted of six people (not counting the two who took a quick look, then left before they had to pay, but including bar staff and other club personnel).

'We'll introduce ourselves, if you introduce yourselves,' said Sting.

The audience obliged. They were Paul, Larry, Mike, Jane, Lee and Stan.

Nevertheless, the Police, pros to the last, did a show that would have set Shea Stadium alight.

Afterwards Mike, one of the club's owners, helped them lug their gear to the van. The take on the door had, of course, been pathetic, so, feeling sorry for them, Mike gave them a few extra dollars from his own pocket.

'We stuck together,' Sting said, 'and we stuck it out.'

They played Syracuse, Connecticut, and on to four nights at the Rat, Boston. Faint rumours began to circulate that here was something worth knowing about.

Carter Alan, then working at WMRB, the campus radio station at MIT, was there on the last night.

There was a definite buzz around the Police, passed on by friends who had gone to one of the first three nights... Nobody had the album yet, so nearly all the material was unknown. It didn't matter... The ladies noted, in particular, that the three band members were quite easy on the eyes, certainly that cute lead singer, a blond Adonis in the flesh... He announced, 'There should be more dancing'... People shrugged off their reticence, leaned into the music and got involved. In less than a dozen songs, the band owned the room. Everyone was moving, even the bartenders.

Representatives from the US arm of A&M Records heard the rumours and began showing up and sending word back to base.

Jerry Moss, co-founder with Herb Alpert of A&M and a music industry god, decided he wanted to release the album in the US early in the next year.

The American Dream that Miles, Ian and Stewart had told Sting and Andy about was all coming true.

Swissvale, Pennsylvania; Buffalo, New York; up to Toronto, Canada; Detroit, Michigan; Cleveland, Ohio; Dayton, Ohio; Johnstown, Pennsylvania, where they played in a little log cabin tucked away at the summit of a ski slope; Washington, DC; back to Grendel's Lair in Philadelphia; and to where they started – CBGB.

And in between they spoke volubly to any local radio DJ who'd let them and gave long, long interviews to journalists.

'Miles and Ian,' said Sting, 'had made a plan of campaign but we were the troops who went out there and gave our blood and guts, staying in grotty motels and driving round in the wagon.'

John Pidgeon, from *Melody Maker*, came with them in the van for the last leg of the tour. 'The Police are not punk,' he wrote. 'The Police are not disco. The Police are not heavy metal. The Police are not power pop. The Police are just the best rock and roll band I've seen in years.'

The tour came to an end on 15 November. Andy flew home just in time for the birth of his daughter, Layla, on the 19th.

'The most important thing', Andy said when they returned, 'was that we played continuously for nearly four weeks. We'd never done that before. It really pulled us together. And there was a reaction, too. That's what you need – unless you get a response – what's the point?'

★ ★ ★

They were still in the US when the album, called *Outlandos d'Amour* (Bandits of Love? Gangsters of Love?), was released in the UK.

The album had been tinkered with off and on throughout the year – an overdub here, a remix there.

Sounds said, 'The Police have finally come up with a distinctive and mostly enjoyable first album.' And, 'These guys have got ideas and a future.'

Paul Morley in *NME* described Sting as 'dishy model, actor and diffident bassist, a natural but dutiful singer and a tame but negative composer.' He went on: 'the album's ten well designed songs are neat but strained and tend to run into each other'.

Smash Hits said, 'Loud and energetic rock'n'roll but short and catchy tunes (remember tunes?) with great playing and tight, interesting arrangements.'

It was advertised. A&M took out a full page in the *NME*. But, still, initial sales were slow (but watch how they pick up in the next chapter).

★ ★ ★

The third single of the year, 'So Lonely', released the day after the album, didn't see much business either.

It was, in Sting's words, '"No Woman, No Cry" sped up with a slightly different melody. Those chords, classic, aren't they? C, G, A minor, F.'

'This was white reggae,' says Phil Sutcliffe. '"So Lonely" was obsessive, angry and intense – all elements of the punk rush. It was an example of Sting writing songs in two halves. So, you'd have a punk-rush chorus and then you'd slow down and think about this with a reggae beat. Stewart was always good at the reggae beat and Andy was just floating over the top.'

Reviews for the single were grudging.

'Repeated airplays'd give you time to get over Sting's horrid castrato wailings,' said *Sounds*.

'[Quite] a lively knees-up, especially when the chorus gains speed,' said *NME* in an unintended slight to Stewart's timekeeping skills.

★ ★ ★

Rumours and reviews of the American tour had filtered back to the UK. The gig diary began to fill.

A few days after they returned, they headlined at the Electric Ballroom in Camden, where Sting stripped for the people, finishing in just his socks and underpants.

★ ★ ★

At the end of the year, they joined a tour as support for Alberto y Lost Trios Paranoias, a comedy/rock band from Manchester that had been around since 1973 and had better claim than most to the 'proto-punk' label. (The band's name, for younger readers, is a mauling of 'Alberto y Los Trios Paraguayos', a South American quartet who had a couple of harp'n'poncho hits in the early 1960s but are now mostly remembered as the people who had their name mauled by Alberto y Lost Trios Paranoias.)

The Albertos dealt in musically accomplished pitch-perfect parody ('Anadin' actually sounds more like an authentic Lou Reed track than Lou Reed doing 'Heroin', and 'Mandrax Sunset Variations 1, 2 and 3' would have fitted right in at Strontium 90's Gong Festival). A couple of months earlier, their 'Heads Down No Nonsense Mindless Boogie', which they did better than Status Quo ever could have, stormed into the lower reaches of the Top 50 for a week and dominated the number 51 spot for another two. They'd also branched out into theatre and their play *Sleak* (sometimes called *Snuff Rock*), about a band that tops itself the better to enhance the evening's entertainment, played at the Royal Court in London and transferred to New York (not quite Broadway, but in that general direction).

They were big on the higher education circuit. This meant bigger venues than most of the clubs the Police played: Barbarella's in Birmingham held about 300, the Leeds University refectory a couple of thousand, and a lot of those 2,000 would have at least two Bs and a C in core subjects.

So, although it seemed like an unlikely match, hitching the Police's wagon to the Albertos would bring them a bigger audience – and a better-educated one, possibly, who knows? – more appreciative of the polyrhythms and forgiving of the unpunkiness.

Miles seemed keen to get his band on the tour, anyway. Jimmy Hibbert, one of the singers with the Albertos, suspects that he may even have slipped Blackhills Enterprises (the Albertos' management) a couple of quid to seal the deal.

'And when we first saw these three platinum blonds,' Jimmy says, 'we thought it doesn't really fit with the Albertos but we were faced with a fait accompli.'

The doubts remained, particularly when the Police turned out to have a good bit more pizzazz than a headlining act likes to see in the support.

Indeed, according to Andy, at Bath University, the Police whooped the arses of the Albertos. 'The place erupted,' Andy remembered. 'Total mayhem. Girls throwing their knickers on stage. The poor Albertos were standing on the side of the stage with white faces muttering "Bastards!" That's when we knew something was happening. I remember going home and telling Kate, "You wouldn't believe it. A total riot."'

Jimmy doesn't remember it quite like that, but standing on the side of the stage muttering 'Bastards' rings a bell. When they came off stage, Les Prior (another singer with the Albertos) was waiting in the wings.

'Oh, so that's your game, is it?' Les said. 'Going down well.'

Les Prior would introduce them. 'I want you to put your hands together now. I'm going to bring on not one ordinary man, but three ordinary men.'

Jimmy got on with Sting. Jimmy's a very nice chap, from Henley-on-Thames with a BA (Hons) in Drama from Manchester University. Why wouldn't Sting get on with him?

'Stewart wasn't keen on us at all,' Jimmy says. 'He was a bit grumpy. I think he thought that the Police shouldn't be supporting this band that didn't take anything seriously, and also because I got on well with Sting, and at that time he wasn't getting on well with Sting. There was a lot of fighting – regular fist fights, not play fighting. Andy would stand to one side and shake his head.'

Possibly some of Stewart's grumpiness was brought on by the living conditions.

'In Edinburgh, we [the Albertos] were staying in a boarding house,' Jimmy says. 'It was a very ropey old boarding house, but the Police were very envious because they were still sleeping in the transit van.'

Some of the venues weren't to Stewart's taste, either.

At North Staffs Poly, they 'didn't have a stage, so they had to put all the tables together in the refectory and the band had to stand on the tables and perform. Dodgy when Sting was doing all his jumping around.'

And when Stewart was trying to keep his bass drum anchored while beating the shit out of the rest of his kit.

One day, Stewart gave Simon White, one of the guitar players, a drum lesson. 'Think of your French teacher and then go... Wham! and hit every drum that you can reach within a five-mile radius as hard as you can.'

Later, as we'll discover, Stewart replaced the French teacher with Sting, and wrote aides-memoires on his tom-toms the better to personalise the whamming. But the Police were playing to bigger crowds, girls were throwing knickers, word of mouth was spreading.

Phil Sutcliffe caught them on the Albertos tour when it came to Newcastle on 8 November. 'They had a truly musical connection with the audience,' he wrote. 'Sting got them chanting the "yeahs!" in the dry, hypnotic "Hole In My Life". Then he had everyone clapping the double beats on the encore of "Can't Stand Losing You". Small details, maybe, but they make the difference between sycophants and participants.

'The Police gave it everything, then bounded away so frolicsome, it looked as though they would gladly have stayed for another hour. Their next headlining tour should be an event.'

CHAPTER TEN

CLEANING THE TOILETS

There was a general election in 1979. Margaret Thatcher became prime minister, largely by pulling in support from traditional Labour voting groups – most notably, the C1s, the skilled working class like Sting's people – and from young people. In the five years since the 1974 general election, support among 18- to 24-year-olds for the Conservative Party had practically doubled.

The appeal to the C1s is not hard to see. The Conservatives had sold themselves as the party of aspiration. In her election manifesto, Thatcher promised to 'restore incentives so that hard work pays, success is rewarded, and genuine new jobs are created'. Virtue, diligence and industry, in other words, would lead to glory. Her message was, in effect, a British version of the American dream that Miles II so firmly believed in – that through hard work and enterprise anyone can own a private jet, buy a small Caribbean island and become president (or, in the Brit version, own an Indesit twin tub, buy a bungalow in Perranporth and become regional sales manager).

The young vote is a little harder to explain, although it might, according to many commentators, have had something to do with punk. It has to be remembered that punks were not of one political hue. While many marched with Rock Against Racism, the Anti-Nazi League, Gay

Liberation and Women's Liberation, many others (maybe most) had little or no ideological focus.

'The punk thing wasn't really built on anything,' said Jimmy Pursey of Sham 69. 'It wasn't built on a structure. It was built on just the fact that we wanted change and, whatever that change is, we're the essence of it.'

Margaret Thatcher promised change. She was most definitely not an anarchist, and neither was she (although many will tell you different) the Antichrist, but she sometimes came across as something of the disrupter, possibly as fond of argy-bargy as any lagered-up Sham 69 fan down the Palais or the pub. Or she might just have seemed that way to a Sham 69 fan, but you have to bear in mind that there was a lot of bad smack knocking around at the time.

Anyway, she won the election. The Genuine Progress Indicator immediately plunged, inflation soared and, over the next couple of years, unemployment doubled. But the lady, apparently, was not for turning.

★ ★ ★

In the year of Thatcher's first triumph, Stewart, Sting and Andy did their best to prove that 'hard work pays, and success is rewarded'.

One thing you could never fault about the Police – and one that would most certainly have endeared them to Mrs Thatcher – was their work ethic. They were gluttons for it. Even – especially – Miles.

Kim Turner said that one of the reasons why Miles succeeded was that he was willing to do *anything*. If the toilets needed cleaning in the building (Dryden Chambers), he would do it himself. Later on, he would have the money to pay somebody else to do it, but until then he'd roll his sleeves up.

It has been pointed out that every star finds success in showbusiness by an entirely different route. Thus, the answer to the question 'What route is it best to take to find success in showbusiness?' can only be 'All of them', and then some that nobody ever thought of before. And that's what the Police did.

★ ★ ★

Just before the end of 1978, Stewart, as if the Police and the Klark Kent project weren't enough to keep him busy, was moonlighting with another band.

Brian James, the former guitar player/singer/songwriter with the Damned, was the man who, when the Damned were on tour with the Police and Sting had knocked on their dressing-room door begging a bottle of wine, had replied, 'Fuck off.'

James, now parted from the Damned, was managed by Miles, and Miles had booked him in to support Squeeze at the Electric Ballroom in Camden. James didn't have a band, but Miles said he'd find one, which, on the posters, he billed under the placeholder name 'The Brian James All-Stars'. Then he roped in Stewart on drums, Kim Turner, the Police's tour manager and miracle worker, on bass, and Alan Lee Shaw, previously of the Maniacs on guitar.

They played good-time punk. To get everyone in the appropriate mood, Stewart turned up at the first rehearsal equipped with a cardboard box filled with the wines and spirits that A&M had given him for Christmas.

Sting and Andy came to the gig, then got up on stage and took over with a short four-song set.

'Stewart was very much a centre-stage and force-of-nature type of drummer,' Alan Lee Shaw said, 'technically gifted with great feel. It was a real pleasure to work with someone so good… I remember having a brief chat with Sting after the show and you could feel things were about to happen for them.'

★ ★ ★

On 2 January, the Police left for Munich to embark on another Eberhard Schoener tour – a week's rehearsal and three weeks on the road.

During the very limited downtime, Sting found opportunities to get pissed and to write their first two number one hits. 'I was drunk in a hotel room in Munich,' Sting said, 'slumped on the bed with the whirling pits, when this riff came into my head.

'I got up and started walking round the room singing, "Walking round the room, ya ya, walking round the room." That was all. In the cool light of morning I remembered what happened and I wrote the riff down. But "Walking Round The Room" was a stupid title, so I thought of something even more stupid, which was "Walking On The Moon".'

Then, on the tour bus between Düsseldorf and Hamburg, another riff came into his head. That one turned out to be 'Message In A Bottle'.

When Lennon and McCartney realised how much money their songs were making, they took to meeting up and saying, 'Let's write a swimming pool.' In the space of a week or so, Sting had written a couple of fully equipped leisure centres with state-of-the-art gyms, Olympic-sized pools and helipads on the roof.

They flew back from Germany on 3 February.

★ ★ ★

Sting found himself with a couple of days off, so fitted in another movie.

Radio On was a British road movie directed by Chris Petit and using a hits-of-the-day soundtrack from David Bowie (it opens, magnificently, with 'Heroes'), Kraftwerk, Robert Fripp, Ian Dury, Wreckless Eric, Lene Lovich, the Rumour and Devo.

Sting plays a petrol pump attendant, called 'Just Like Eddie', who lives in a caravan, plastered with Eddie Cochran memorabilia, round the back of the garage. He plays a Gretsch guitar (just like Eddie) and tells the hero how, when Eddie was killed in a car crash, near Chippenham in Wiltshire, the first man on the scene was a young police cadet who later went on to become Dave Dee (of Dave Dee, Dozy, Beaky, Mick & Tich).

The part was originally no more than a cough and a spit, but then...

'It was the idea of the cameraman and sound engineer that Sting should sing "Three Steps To Heaven" by the petrol pumps,' says Chris Petit, 'and I remember thinking, "What a terrible idea." Then I thought, "If it makes them happy, then let's shoot it and I can always drop it later." The second day was particularly cold and miserable, and I could see the idea meant a lot to them and it was too freezing cold for me to bother to disagree with them.'

So, Sting stands there by the petrol pump, with his Gretsch guitar and sings a couple of choruses of Eddie Cochran's 'Three Steps To Heaven'.

He got about £20 for that. He was lucky. The art director doesn't remember getting paid at all.

★ ★ ★

On 6 February, they were in Newcastle performing 'Roxanne' and 'Can't Stand Losing You' for the Tyne Tees TV programme *Alright Now*.

Then gigging all over the place, then on 13 February, they were back at Surrey Sound with Nigel Gray to start work on the two new songs Sting had written and another nine they'd need for their second album.

The usual routine with most bands is that they get together at school, they do shitty gigs for three or four years, they fire the drummer, they get a deal, make the single and then make the album, which, often as not, is a bunch of songs they've played a thousand times on stage. Then comes the second album and 'second album syndrome' kicks in. Having blown everything they had on the first album, there's nothing left. They have to start from scratch.

The Police were working backwards. When they made their first album, they barely knew each other, and musically were still in the experimental stage. Are we punk, are we reggae? Should Sting try a Jamaican accent? What's Andy up to – can we use that? Who writes the songs around here?

For the second album, they were in better shape.

'This time the material wasn't rehearsed but the band was,' Sting said. 'We knew each other's styles because we'd been playing together constantly for eight months, which we hadn't been doing when we recorded the first album.'

And there was no shortage of material.

According to Andy, Sting had 'a whole book full of lyrics. He had this giant book – a big, thick, hardbound book – with pages that had lyrics all the way through it. He didn't come into the Police and start writing songs – he had been writing them for years.'

A&M, who had great hopes for the new album, were against them using Surrey Sound. Too downmarket. They thought they'd do a lot better in one of the flash London studios – Townhouse or Olympic, maybe.

But the Police wanted to work with Nigel again and, besides, he'd upgraded to 24-track by this time, which gave them the opportunity for endless overdubs and alternative takes.

The drum part on 'Message In A Bottle', for instance – the one that Andy always claimed was Stewart's 'finest drum track' – was assembled 'from about six different parts'.

And, besides, Surrey Sound was familiar. It was within their comfort zone, which was never particularly comfortable at the best of times. The tensions, the fights, the difficulties had become routine.

One of the staff at the studio described Sting as being 'intense, keyed up, dictatorial'.

There was a lot of 'playfighting' between Stewart and Sting – bear hugs, arm wrestling. It usually had an edge.

'Was Sting a scumbag? No. Did I think Sting was a scumbag? Yes,' Stewart said of those times. 'If I wanted to reduce Sting to a screaming maniac, all I had to do was call one of his songs a pop tune. It worked every time.'

★ ★ ★

Meanwhile, over the other side of the Atlantic, their star was rising.

At the end of February, 'Roxanne' had entered the Billboard Hot 100. Rod Stewart was at number one with 'Do Ya Think I'm Sexy'. Dire Straits' 'Sultans Of Swing', another track that had been hanging around for a year or so without doing any business, was in there, too, at number 29 and climbing.

Airplay had a lot to do with the success of 'Roxanne'. At that time, college radio was becoming more and more important in America. Some of the college stations even showed up on the national ratings. Thanks, in some measure, to A&M's careful plugging, the college stations picked up on the Police early, and that resulted in the band getting plays on the more major stations.

'Americans have been listening to all this shit on the radio, and along come the Police,' Miles said. 'It's got to be refreshing for them. We've been working a year to crack this place and now we're doing it.'

★ ★ ★

To maintain the momentum, Miles and Ian had booked them a second tour, so, on 27 February, leaving the album half done, they left for Los Angeles.

They arrived at a tricky time. Punk had given British bands a bad name.

In the previous year, the Sex Pistols had insulted audiences, sprayed them with gob, blood and other fluids, and earned themselves a reputation as the rudest, laziest, most unreliable band anyone had ever seen. Then they'd broken up.

The Stranglers, too, on their 1978 tour, had offended American sensibilities.

'We were provocative everywhere we went,' said J. J. Burnel. 'We thought that it would bring out the best and worst in people. Those that desired to be offended were shocked. Others viewed it in the slightly humorous and tongue-in-cheek way it was meant to be. It was more of a game than anything...'

He liked to tell audiences, 'We know that you hate us, but you don't hate us as much as we hate you.'

In Michigan, there were demonstrations against the Stranglers' misogynistic lyrics.

'It doesn't take much for some people to be shocked,' said J. J. 'The Sisterhood were demonstrating outside the gig in East Lansing and we got attacked. Hugh and I tried bundling one of the girls onto our bus, but we got seriously battered over the heads with their placards.'

As a result of such capers, venues and promoters were understandably wary of anything that came from the UK, unless it was called Elton.

'The Stranglers really fucked it up for the new bands over here,' said Miles. 'I had to tell these people the band wouldn't wreck their theatres.'

'Most promoters [in the States],' said Ian Copeland in his autobiography *Wild Thing*, 'were leery of getting involved with the punk or new wave scene. They were afraid of punk crowds or what they had heard of them.'

Not being punk enough, which a year or so previously had seemed a distinct drawback, was now, in the US anyway, working to the Police's advantage.

It had been the same story 15 years earlier, when mums and dads had preferred the nice clean Beatles to the dirty Rolling Stones because at least the mop tops looked as if they were enjoying themselves. The Stones always looked as if they had indigestion. A smile costs nothing and it was, of course, smiling that had kept them so cheerful in the Blitz.

The Police always looked as if they were enjoying themselves on stage, too. They laughed. They danced. They bantered with the audience. And, as they'd proved on their first US tour, they turned up on time and provided rattling good entertainment for as long as they were booked for, with an encore or two if that was what the audience required. They looked like they showered and brushed their teeth regularly. They didn't spurt blood into people's faces and, as far as anybody knew, hadn't killed anybody at all.

They were also – it has to be said about their appeal in a country where racism has bitten deep into the collective unconscious –

unspeakably Aryan. And, when Sting took off his shirt, which he did at the drop of an eyelash, you could see he kept himself in good shape. Nothing skinny or pasty about him. If they'd had a few more like him 10 years earlier, Vietnam would now be the 51st state.

That song he sang was, admittedly, about a prostitute, but – and remember evangelical Christianity runs deep in that same collective unconscious – the man in the song is, like Jesus, saving the poor fallen woman from her life of black sin, Hallelujah, Praise the Lord and pass me another snake to fondle.

Thus, America felt able to take the Police, even though they'd been touched by the stain of punk, into their hearts.

Ian found that promoters and club owners who'd booked them on the first tour – even people who'd lost money on them – were keen to book them again. Bigger venues, too, were willing to take a punt.

They did 37 shows in 39 days, covering more than 7,000 miles, starting with three nights at the Whisky a Go Go in Los Angeles and finishing at the Walnut Street Theatre in Philadelphia. Again, they flew cheapo-cheapo on the Laker Skytrain and stayed in grim motels with nickel-in-the-slot vibrating beds and *Psycho* showers.

'The Whisky was packed with satisfied customers making a fair attempt at dancing along,' wrote *Sounds* journalist Sylvie Simmons, who caught the third night of the tour, 'with the very theatrical Mr Sting (look-at-me-I'm-evil stance, jutting out his chin, throwing back his shoulders) thrashing out some of the best basslines the Whisky sound system has transmitted. You've got to hand it to them, the Police aren't a one-dimensional pogo band. Each song smacks of various influences and to their credit they make them mesh together and come out with something that stands out from the crowd.'

As the tour progressed, the band was 'constantly ill with colds, viruses and sore throats that pass between us like a game of ping-pong', Andy wrote. 'We try to sleep during the ride to the next gig by taking over-the-counter sedatives and wake up a few hundred miles later hungover and groggy from the sleep that is no sleep.'

A few gigs had to be cancelled when the viruses vanquished Sting's throat, but otherwise they gave good value.

On 8 March, in Houston, a local radio station staged a Roxanne competition. Local girls, dressed as prostitutes, paraded in front of the band, who were invited to rank them in order (presumably) of sluttiness.

The band had the good grace to be embarrassed, but nonetheless went through with it. Job description.

The day after the gigs at the Bottom Line in New York (Robert Fripp and Daryl Hall were in the audience, along with many rock journalists, bussed in by Miles), Miles set up a photo opportunity for the band at the NYPD precinct in Harlem. The band were posed locked in a cell. One of the detectives joked to his colleagues, 'How does it feel locking up a bunch of white guys for a change.'

The tour wound up in Philadelphia on 9 April, and the following day they flew home.

Miles and Ian liked to keep things moving. Kim Turner, doing the driving, left the van at the airport when the band left, so that Squeeze, due in on the next flight, could take it over – the seats still warm, the viruses still playing ping-pong.

A 'Roxanne' lookalike competition organised by the local radio station KLOL at the Old Texas Opry House, 1980.
MICHAEL HART

Sting as Ace Face in *Quadrophenia*, the coolest Mod in the world. MOVIESTORE COLLECTION LTD/ALAMY

King of the World... Sting in New York. Stewart already felt 'that we were Aztec sun princes and any day soon our hearts would be cut out'. MIRRORPIX

The very theatrical Mr Sting (look-at-me-I'm-evil stance, jutting out his chin, throwing back his shoulders) on stage in America, 1980. MIRRORPIX

'That Gordon dikra, such a nice boy. And what a voice, baap re.'

On stage, South America leg of the world tour, 1980. MIRRORPIX

Argentina, 1980. 'What the fuck are we doing here?' asked Andy. MIRRORPIX

Sting and his band returning triumphantly to Newcastle for a gig at the City Hall, 1980. MIRRORPIX

Sting, the tax exile, in Ireland, 1980. MIRRORPIX

Andy, the tax exile, in Ireland, 1980. MIRRORPIX

The Police on stage in New York during the *Zenyatta* tour, 1980. 'The last album,' Andy admitted, 'was a bit of a cock-up.' MIRRORPIX

Japan, 1981. 'At least we'll be able to find some interesting ethnic music to rip off.'
KOH HASEBE/SHINKO MUSIC/GETTY IMAGES

Sting on stage at Madison Square Garden, 1981. 'We're here for the next ten years now.'
EBET ROBERTS/GETTY IMAGES

Behind the mixing desk at the Montserrat recording studio, 1981. 'It was very horrible. Our marriages were breaking up, yet we had to make another record.' LYNN GOLDSMITH/CORBIS/VCG VIA GETTY IMAGES

Andy alone in his big empty house after his marriage break-up. MIRRORPIX

Sting and Alexei Sayle backstage at *The Secret Policeman's Other Ball* at the Albany Empire, Deptford. ADRIAN BOOT

Read those drums. Stewart's message to Sting. LYNN GOLDSMITH/CORBIS/VCG VIA GETTY IMAGES

'By the beginning of 1982 there was speculation in the press about the band being constantly at each other's throats.' LYNN GOLDSMITH/CORBIS/VCG VIA GETTY IMAGES

CHAPTER ELEVEN

'NEXT YEAR I'LL BE RICH, AND THAT'S WHEN THE ROT WILL SET IN'

They left America with 'Roxanne' in the US Top 40. It peaked, a week later at number 32.

And, the day after they landed, the Police, without a thought for jet lag, played the Nashville in Fulham, then Holland, Paris and Slough.

Meanwhile, spurred on by its success in the US, A&M re-released 'Roxanne' in the UK – and it led to the Police's first appearance on *Top of the Pops* (other than as the masked musicians with Klark Kent).

By this time, *Top of the Pops* had been running for 15 years. It had always been regarded as irredeemably BBC, which meant irredeemably naff. When it started, in 1964, it was seen as an inept rip-off of ITV's *Ready Steady Go!*, but where *Ready Steady Go!* appeared to be set in a basement dive just off Carnaby Street, *Top of the Pops* looked like a church hall youth club in Maidstone. Where *Ready Steady Go!* had Cathy McGowan, who was gauche and easily flustered but 20 years old, *Top of the Pops*, in the early days, had Pete Murray, David Jacobs, Alan Freeman and Jimmy Savile, all of whom were pushing 40. Nevertheless, *Ready*

Steady Go! withered while *Top of the Pops* endured to become a fixture in the BBC schedule as secure as the Shipping Forecast.

And, though nobody with any pretence at cred, cool or musical integrity (whatever that means) would admit to watching it, they all did, and its effect on record sales was terrifying.

There was a chicken-and-egg angle to it. An appearance on *Top of the Pops* pretty much guaranteed the record would chart, but, since the show gave little airtime to new releases, it was unlikely you'd get an appearance if the record wasn't already in the Top 40.

There were other problems, too. How could any band with pretensions of musical integrity (whatever that means) appear on a show where your suffering-wrought work of genius would be sandwiched between, say, 'Save Your Kisses For Me' and 'Agadoo'? The Clash refused to do it. Until they did. The Stranglers demonstrated their contempt by putting more effort into wafting the dry ice off stage than into their miming. Years later, Oasis thought they'd subvert the whole thing by having one brother miming to the other brother's voice. Questions were not asked in Parliament.

And the idea that it was all a bit shit was very much confirmed by the bands who actually did it. BBC Television Centre, up Wood Lane in Shepherd's Bush, was never palatial. Sometimes they tarted the place up a bit by stapling some orange hessian to a bit of pegboard and hanging it on a wall, but otherwise it could have been a dole office.

And the mood backstage on *Top of the Pops* was akin to a busy day at A&E.

'I'd never imagined Marc Bolan having to get up at eight in the morning go to a dingy studio with people sweeping up from *Blue Peter* the day before,' said Johnny Marr of the Smiths, remembering their *Top of the Pops* debut in 1983, 'and sit around for 11 hours waiting for his turn.'

The Police were excused waiting and indeed bypassed the whole grim escapade. They had a tour schedule to stick to. The only way *Top of the Pops* could have them was by pre-recording their segment. So, they were shown miming 'Roxanne', at the Fulcrum Centre in Slough, where they happened to be gigging, a week or so before the transmission. But somehow the BBC technicians still made the place look like your auntie's living room.

Stewart set up his drums so that he could play standing up at the front of the stage. Sting ostentatiously ignored his mic and smacked his bass. Ha, take that, miming.

The programme was aired on 3 May, and the Police appeared in company with Banana Splits (people in animal costumes wearing red helmets who sang 'Tra-la-la'), Wings, the Undertones and Abba.

Whatever, it did the business. By the next Monday, 'Roxanne' had leaped 15 places in the charts and the week after it jumped another 15 to peak at number 12.

By that time, the Police were well into their third US tour – indeed, they left the country the day after the Fulcrum gig, just two weeks after they'd landed from the second tour.

'Once you've cracked the States,' J. J. Burnel said, 'you've got your pension sorted.'

The Police, this time, did 25 gigs in not many more days, but there was a clear possibility that one last push would bring undreamed-of fame, fortune and power. And get their pensions sorted.

★ ★ ★

Fashion, a Birmingham band, also managed by Miles (or 'that pompous American arse', as they liked to call him) was flown out to support them on some of the gigs.

They'd supported the Police before, without finding much comfort in the experience. In his memoir *Stairway to Nowhere*, Luke James (who, under the name of Luke Sky, fronted the band) recalls a gig at King's College in London.

'Our dressing room had the usual cracked sink, tarnished mirror and toilet stall with no door, so we found our way to the Police's dressing room which was much bigger. It was swirling with people... and had a table loaded with wine. Stewart was very welcoming – he was dressed in a schoolboy's jacket with a $100 bill stuck in the top pocket. Andy stuck his nose in the air. When I ask him "What do you play?" he answers "Brilliantly," and turns and walks away.'

After their set, while the Police were on stage, Fashion staged a raid on their dressing room to filch food and booze, but Kim Turner had taken the precaution of locking it.

(An interesting detail, revealed by Luke James, is that one of the key differences between university gigs and club and pub gigs in the UK at the time was that institutes of higher education often provided sandwiches even when it wasn't a contractual obligation.)

Anyway, in New York, Miles booked the Police and Fashion into the Iroquois Hotel on West 44th Street.

In 1911, nearly 70 years earlier, the hotel was notorious as the site of a sensational murder, when Paul Geidel, a bellhop, chloroformed and robbed a guest, and then, maybe because he didn't trust chloroform, suffocated him. Geidel served 68 years in stir – according to the *Guinness World Records*, the longest sentence ever.

The Iroquois – now place of boutique luxury – at the time looked as if nothing had changed much since Geidel's day: ancient furniture, leaking sofas, fag burns on the bedside tables. But the Iroquois did not turn punks away and thus became the place where British rock bands on limited budgets could grab maybe half an hour of drug-induced sleep. It was where the Clash wrote 'Rock The Casbah'.

The Iroquois set the standard and, as the tour progressed, the shabby food and junk motels started taking their toll.

Peter Bilt, guitarist with Pearl Harbor and the Explosions, who opened for them here and there, remembered seeing them get off the tour bus in Santa Cruz, California. 'They had that grey pallor,' he said, 'that only comes from months on the road. It was unmistakable.'

One gig was cancelled when Sting came down with something.

In Tulsa, on 10 May, Stewart had a cough and a fever so bad he was taken to the ER (A&E). They diagnosed bronchitis and dosed him up. But he got back on stage that night and soldiered on.

On 25 May, they played the last gig of the tour in Chicago and flew straight to Munich to record a TV special with Eberhard Schoener. Their work on that finished on 30 May.

On 31 May, they played the 2,600-seat Apollo, Glasgow. Every seat was sold. By this time, they were in a state of, as Stewart put it, 'permanent stupor'. Nevertheless, they were a triumph. The audience sang along with every song, even the little poem Andy did in a Yorkshire accent in the middle of 'Be My Girl, Sally' about having sex with a blow-up doll.

Afterwards, they were mobbed.

'It took three attempts to leave the Glasgow Apollo,' Sting said, 'three charges involving police, bouncers, everybody. It was like a rugby scrum. The car was chased through the street with girls banging on the roof.'

The next day they moved on to the Edinburgh Odeon. Originally, they'd been booked to play Tiffany's in Edinburgh, a much smaller venue, but the buzz was growing.

They'd hired a PR man.

Keith Altham, who'd started his career as a cub reporter on *Fabulous* magazine and by 1962 was known as 'Fab's Keith', had since done PR for Townshend, Bolan, Morrison, Jagger – you name 'em and he'd either got their name in the paper or kept it out, depending on the circumstances.

As he tells in his memoir, *The PR Strikes Back*, he sussed out the lie of the land on his first meeting with Sting.

> There was already something contradictory about Sting's image, when he arrived in my office in Old Compton Street on his push bike as a not so young punk with the Police – blond spiky hair, ripped tee shirt plus combat boots. Sting was charm personified, but I couldn't help recalling Peter Pan's advice – never smile at a crocodile.
>
> It was apparent to me from our first meeting that Sting wasn't just hungry for success – he was ravenous. Nothing was going to stop him succeeding and although the predominant impression was charm on two wheels there was a strong ruthless streak. He was unstoppable. If he had gone public, I would have taken out shares in him there and then.

But, after a few weeks, 'I could not put up with any more GBH of the ears from Miles,' he writes:

> who seemed under the impression that 'Manners' was an English butler and 'Etiquette' was a French table napkin as he bellowed his weekly instructions down the phone like an enraged rhino.
>
> 'Godammit, Altham, why isn't Sting more famous than Elvis yet? Why have you not got us the front page of *Time* Magazine. Why aren't Andy and Stewart getting as much space as your other clients like The Who or The Stones? Why are you not working, quicker, cheaper, faster, longer and why are you still allowing the sun to set in the west when Sting is in the east?'

Keith had a word with Sting. Sting was sympathetic.

'"Leave it to me," Sting said. And Miles simply went away for a number of years.'

Once it had been Stewart's band with brother Miles, the manager, calling the shots. But now, it seemed, the power was most definitely shifting. The Copelands weren't the only ones who knew how to overthrow governments. Or, as Altham put it, 'Never smile at a crocodile.'

Sting, who'd previously been too busy singing to put anybody down, was getting himself organised. Partly as a tax wheeze (common enough in showbusiness), he and Frances become co-directors of Steerpike Ltd 'to carry on business as theatrical and entertainment agents and to enter into contracts for the appearances of groups bands singers orchestras artist dancers actresses and actors in clubs licensed premises theatres halls places of entertainment and sporting and athletic events'.

At the same time, the Police formed Roxanne Music, a repository for their A&M money.

Sting was still tied into the Virgin publishing contract he'd signed while he was in Last Exit that gave Virgin a very sizeable chunk of his songwriting royalties. He issued a writ claiming the firm had made 'fraudulent use of a dominant position' in their dealings with 'Mr Sumner'. He claimed damages and a reversion of all copyrights.

Virgin offered to improve the deal to a 75–25 split in Sting's favour, but Miles refused, because Virgin stipulated that they wanted the contract extended. Richard Branson, boss of Virgin, tried to bypass Miles and sent one of his legal men to speak to Sting. Sting lost his temper and threw him out. The dispute went on for three years, ending very publicly in court.

Sting, Frances and Joe were still living in their two-bedroomed basement Bayswater flat, but good times were just around the corner.

'Can't Stand Losing You' was reissued hot on the heels of 'Roxanne'.

'Not so much a reissue,' *Smash Hits* said, 'more a reminder from A&M that it's still available and as they don't seem ready to release a new Police single just yet, they'd be grateful if you'd go out and buy this one again.' It was, according to the same mag, 'a cut that scars the thin line between anguish and anger, please investigate it now. Play it loud and marvel at how it slices through gristle to your gut.'

On 12 July, the Police aired the song on *Top of the Pops* (straight after a Tom Baker *Doctor Who* episode written by Douglas Adams, who later wrote *The Hitchhiker's Guide to the Galaxy*, and before a David Attenborough programme about foxes – they knew how to make telly back then). They were there for real this time, at the studios, but found it – like many others – a joyless experience. Siouxsie and the Banshees were among the other acts appearing that week. Stewart found no camaraderie on set.

'That whole thing is such a drag, basically because I actually happen to really dig Siouxsie and the Banshees and, when we've encountered each other at *Top of the Pops*, my first reaction is to go over and say, "Hey I really liked your music."

'But they always behave so ultra-cool as if to actually confer with us would be tantamount to some grand display of heresy on their part. The same with Johnny Rotten and Public Image.'

Nevertheless, *Top of the Pops* worked its magic again. By the end of the month, 'Can't Stand Losing You' was at number two, being cruelly denied the top spot by the Boomtown Rats' 'I Don't Like Mondays'.

It was the year in which the sales of single records in the UK reached their all-time peak. Getting a record to number one – or even number two – meant selling a lot more units than ever before, or ever since.

And, to seal the deal. *Outlandos d'Amour*, the album, had entered the UK album charts on 21 April and was slowly climbing, eventually to spend 39 weeks in the Top 20, peaking at number 6. In the US, it was already at number 26 and would peak at 23.

The Police had two hit singles and a hit album in the UK. They had chart presence in the US. They packed 2,000-seat venues. Fans chased their limo down the road. It could only be a matter of time before tipper trucks filled with money would be queuing at their front doors.

'Yeah,' Stewart said. 'It's looking pretty clean and green for us.'

'Next year I'll be rich,' Sting said, 'and that's when the rot will set in.'

★ ★ ★

The work did not let up. In June they played practically every night somewhere or other – Birmingham, Newcastle, Bristol, Berlin, Hamburg, Stockholm.

They played the huge Pinkpop Festival at the Burgemeester Damen Sportpark in Holland, alongside Elvis Costello, Dire Straits, Rush (Canada's finest proggers) and reggae star Peter Tosh. The Dutch police estimated that 75,000 people attended. John Peel presented the acts and was so impressed by the Police that he asked them to record a session for his Radio 1 show later that month.

Initially, John's producer John Walters wasn't keen.

'I'd seen the Police in a pub and turned them down as far too retro – they were clearly going back to playing proper tunes and singing proper songs – and, although they had a following, I thought, "No." Then Peel was knocked out by them at a Dutch festival (they played particularly well, said Peel) and we got them in. They did a good session, but if you follow the philosophy of the programme, they shouldn't have been on: they summed up conformity, whereas punk was all about nonconformity.'

Still, Mr Peel had his way, and the Police were summoned to the BBC Maida Vale studio for a four-song session. The Peel accolade made many who, like John Walters, had been thinking 'No' change their opinion to 'Hmmnn'.

On 24 August, they brushed shoulders with Mr Peel again when he introduced them on the first day of the Reading Festival. He mentioned that he'd seen them at Pinkpop and claimed, 'They blew everyone off the stage.'

Some 21,000 people were at Reading that year to see them presented with a Gold Disc for *Outlandos*. The hard-core punks sneered. 'What kind of losers get Gold Discs?'

It was the biggest crowd they'd ever played to. Sting, veteran of miners' clubs and classrooms, soon had them clapping, chanting and singing to order.

Superfan David Brown, 19, got hit by a falling beer bottle. He was rushed to the emergency tent, had stitches and still got back in time to witness the absolute triumph of 'Can't Stand Losing You'.

Andy, as he came off stage, encountered Lemmy from Motörhead.

'Who smells of roses, then?' Lemmy said.

Hamburg, Munich, Wiesbaden, Voorburg, Derby, Blackburn, Birmingham, Southampton.

At the New Theatre, Oxford, the show was interrupted by a gang of 30 or so skinheads who pogoed while shouting 'Sieg Heil'.

Sting had the chutzpah to invite them on stage to sing along and he won their confidence to the extent that, when he told them to fuck off, they left without killing anybody.

On their way to play Swansea, the Police stopped off at a Little Chef on the M4 and sat at a window seat from where they had a good view of their car on fire.

Fashion, supporting, were nervous. A Frank Carson moment was looming, 'Ladies and gentlemen, topping the bill instead of the Police, please welcome to the stage – Fashion!'

Luckily, the Police showed up just as the axe was about to fall.

★ ★ ★

In between all the fire and fury, Stewart managed to fit in some Klark Kent sessions and, somehow, they also finished the album.

It was called *Reggatta de Blanc* – which could be fake foreign for 'White Reggae', 'Festival Of The Blondes', 'White Boat Race' (as in rhyming slang for 'face'), or an interesting starter made of fromage frais, celeriac and butter beans.

It was released on 2 October 1979, by which time 'Message In A Bottle', the first single from the album, released a couple of weeks earlier, was already causing excitement.

'That was where it all clicked,' Sting said. 'There was so much happening in my writing and singing, Stewart's and Andy's playing, and suddenly it all meshed together. We had reggae influences in our vocabulary, and they became synthesised into our infrastructure until it was utterly part of our sound and you couldn't really call it reggae any more. It was just the way we played.'

The pressure even to pretend to be a punk band, or indeed any other sort of band, was off. They had played together for thousands of hours. They had figured out what each of them could contribute and what the audience would react to. They knew the sonic palette they were working with. They had not only found, but comfortably settled into, a collective identity.

On the whole, the critics agreed that the album (give or take the odd jokey interpolations from Stewart and Andy) was an astonishing accomplishment, poised, professional and polished, and it would undoubtedly sell by the truckload.

'Those first four tracks ought to be enough to convince even cloth-eared sceptics that the Police are about to be the biggest trio since Cream,' said John Pidgeon in *Melody Maker*. 'Whatever the current competition, it's impossible to imagine anyone combining the strength of those songs with the power of their performance.'

But, for many, even in the post-punk world, 'poised, professional and polished' were not necessarily things to boast about. There was a suspicion that there was some vital ingredient missing.

'The group once again exhibits the same high-standard, crafty superciliousness that marred *Outlandos d'Amour*,' said Debra Rae Cohen in *Rolling Stone*. And 'Sting's spliff-and-swagger reggae vocals often sound bloodless and condescending, checking off rather than embodying emotions.'

It was a theme that Garry Bushell warmed to in *Sounds*. 'Nothing: I've played this disc several times now and all that's left at the end is a big fat zero in the reaction stakes, tinged with boredom and nagging feelings of bewilderment.' He found Sting's vocals 'trying and unattractive' and said, 'the Police operate in that area paralleling the early sixties white reshaping of R&B – the late seventies white remoulding of reggae, an area fruitfully developed by the Clash, the Ruts and the Members. And the difference between those and the Police can be summed up in one word: passion.'

Bushell bracketed the Police in the bland stakes with Dire Straits, another band that had vaguely emerged from the punk melee and whose records were selling like Coca-Cola on both sides of the Atlantic.

It was, of course, inevitable that those who had fallen so deeply in love with punk (and indeed reggae) should feel this sense of betrayal. Punk was all about passion. Sometimes, certainly in live gigs, even the three chords were jettisoned in favour of a fuzzbox, a scream and garments rent in anguish. Sensibilities attuned to such extremes would find anticlimax in anything short of trench warfare.

Nobody took any notice of the critics anyway. 'Once the punters took their fingers out of their ears and listened to the music,' John Pidgeon wrote, 'they made up their own minds about the Police.' And, having made up their own minds, in Our Price, HMV and Tower Records, they elbowed each other at the checkouts in their eagerness to have more Police in their lives.

The riff from 'Message In A Bottle' is one of those that invariably brought audiences to their feet after – what? – the first two notes, maybe three. At the time, many accused the Police of nicking the riff from Blue Öyster Cult's '(Don't Fear) The Reaper', but those critics know nothing. The 'Message' riff is melodically and harmonically more complex, more sophisticated and more better. Its place in the Top 10 riffs of all time is well deserved.

Top of the Pops ran a video of the band miming to the track in a dressing room, intercut with slo-mo concert footage. Stewart uses a chair for drums. He loons. Andy looks endearingly bewildered. Sting looks vaguely threatening. All three are clearly sex fodder on which teenage fantasies (of both sexes) can gorge. The record went to number one by the end of the month and stayed there for three weeks.

'Message In A Bottle' also received the ultimate accolade of being sung in playgrounds all over the country, the lyric only very slightly adapted to become 'Massage In A Brothel'.

Reggatta de Blanc, the album, went straight into the album chart at number one, held the position for four weeks, then hung around the higher reaches, Top 10 or near as dammit, for the next six months. In the USA, it went to number 25 in the Billboard 200.

The second single, 'Walking On The Moon', the one that Sting wrote drunk in Germany, was released on 4 November, and, again, went to number one. Just for a week, though. The following week it was displaced by Pink Floyd's 'Another Brick In The Wall'.

A third single from the album, 'Bring On The Night', was released in France, Germany and the USA. It went to number six in France, but was a disappointment elsewhere.

And, somewhere in between, Miles the chancer snuck out a re-release of 'Fall Out', still on the Illegal Records label. It made number 47 in the UK. It didn't matter. They had had two number one singles and a number one album, and Sting's film *Quadrophenia* was out and packing them in at the picture houses.

'I felt like God,' Sting said, 'and I loved it.'

★ ★ ★

They had a fan club now, just like they were Cliff Richard or the Bay City Rollers. Outlandos, as it was called, was formed on 10 October and announced with more exclamation marks than are consistent with an education to GCSE level...

The birth of our club and what a day! Not only is 'Message in a Bottle' No 1 in the top Twenty Charts for the third week running but the new album REGGATTA DE BLANC has entered the LP charts at No 1!!!!

What a double event! We are all very excited and wish Andy, Sting and Stewart were here to join in our celebrations.

It has taken us a week or so to get the club organized and operating because of all the extra work including the event of Sting's birthday, which brought in hundreds of gorgeous birthday cards. We are saving everything for his return as we are also doing with the interesting letters addressed to The Police...

Being so busy meant they missed most of the fun. They missed the glory of being number one, they missed the fan club and the exclamation marks.

They were back in the US, amidst the leaking sofas of the Iroquois Hotel.

Kim Turner was interviewing roadies, including Danny Quatrochi, who went on to become Sting's bass roadie and a trusted friend. The lift at the Iroquois was broken, so Danny's initiation was to carry three boxes of T-shirts and a 4x12 Marshall cabinet down 11 flights of stairs. Miraculously, he passed.

They were supported again by Fashion and Luke James in *Stairway to Nowhere* provides further insight into the dynamic of the Police at this stage of their career.

While they were in New York, according to Luke, Andy blew $3,000 on a guitar from Manny's. Stewart, not to be outdone, bought an expensive Super 8 film camera. He decided to make a thriller, called *Nat Hunt*, and gave everyone parts – including the members of Fashion – but resolutely refused to let Sting be in it. Stewart said he was fed up of hearing about Sting's fabled acting prowess.

Luke says Sting took it badly, and 'went off for a bit of a sulk with a Nabokov novel'.

As the tour got going, pranks were played. One night, Sting came on stage during Fashion's set, armed with a stepladder and set it up next to Luke while he was in mid-song. Luke is 6'10" tall. Sting climbed the stepladder and emptied a box of cornflakes over Luke's head. Luke, resilient, pretended to ignore it and kept singing.

(Sting sometimes dedicated 'I Can't Stand Losing You' to Luke, referring to the line, 'Your brother's gonna kill me and he's six feet ten'.)

But a lot of the gigs were no fun at all.

According to Luke:

- At Cain's Ballroom in Tulsa, Oklahoma, they played (like Spinal Tap) behind a chicken-wire grille to deflect the beer bottles.
- At the Hullabaloo in Rensselaer, New York, they had to share a dressing room with the owner's pet leopard. But at least it was chained to the wall.
- At the 1,000-seat Bama Theatre, in Tuscaloosa, Alabama, they played in front of an estimated 100 people. Although some suspect the estimate might have erred on the generous side.
- At the Gusman Hall, in Miami, Florida, they had to cancel the second show because so few tickets had been sold.

Sting complained to Miles about the disappointing sales. Back in the UK, 'Message In A Bottle' was number one, and here they were still on the chicken-wire and leopard-in-the-dressing-room circuit. Miles soothed Sting by promising to throw more money at promotion.

After the Gusman Hall gig, they became resident band, for two nights, at the Tomorrowland Terrace, Disney World, the happiest but not necessarily most rock'n'roll place in the world. They'd baulked at this one. Then Miles had mentioned a fee of $8,000. The contract did not specify Tinkerbell costumes.

At the other end of the scale of strange, they played one night in front of 500 inmates at Terminal Island prison in San Pedro, Los Angeles, and afterwards donated $5,000 worth of instruments and equipment to the inmates (although one wonders whether this is just a roundabout way of saying that they fled the place leaving their gear behind). And, at the Kennedy Space Center, they made their video of 'Walking On The Moon', shown on *Top of the Pops* on 29 November. Stewart got to play drums on a Saturn V rocket.

★ ★ ★

And so it went, on and on, back in the UK in December, then Paris, Aachen, Bremen, Düsseldorf, Leeds, Chester, on and on.

★ ★ ★

They ended the decade in triumph.

On 18 December, just before Christmas, Miles booked them into two gigs on the same night: the first, at the Hammersmith Odeon (at the time of writing called the Eventim Apollo, but it changes its sponsor and name every other week); the second, just the other side of the roundabout at the Hammersmith Palais (demolished in 2012).

The first show started at 6 p.m., the second at 10 p.m.

To transport them from one to the other, Miles, possibly using some of the money he'd promised to throw at promotion, provided a US army M5 half-track armoured personnel carrier. They travelled slowly, waving like royalty, reaching down and shaking hands.

The crowds turned out in force, parting like the Red Sea as they approached to let the 'Three Kings of Pop' pass, then falling in behind, following yonder stars.

Four nights later, at the Lewisham Odeon, they did a benefit, with Joe Jackson and Squeeze. The tickets were not for sale. To get in, you had to bring a toy for the orphans.

God bless us, everyone, and God bless Mr Andy and Mr Sting and Mr Stewart.

Chapter Twelve

THE BOMBAY TIME & TALENTS CLUB

Being a rock star on tour can kill you in several ways. The time you spend in cars, buses and planes means your chances of a Buddy Holly/Eddie Cochran/Otis Redding end are higher than the average commuter. The lack of sleep, the need to be on every night – and most of the day for interviews and photo sessions – and the need somehow to come down after the onstage adrenaline rush, make drink and drugs useful helpmates. Then they become a necessity, then the reason you're living, and then the cause of death.

The magic number, 27, is well known – the age at which Jimi Hendrix, Janis Joplin, Brian Jones, Kurt Cobain, Jim Morrison and Amy Winehouse shuffled off. If you can survive that, it's likely you'll make it to be a 40-year-old smackhead, or even a 45-year-old acid casualty, subject to frequent attacks by the lobster-people, or maybe, if you're really lucky, a skeletal 75-year-old with expensive teeth and somebody else's liver.

And we haven't even started on gun-related incidents and sexually transmitted diseases.

The Police could handle it all better than most. This was partly because, as Jayne County said, they were, 'the most boring people I have ever met. Polite, charming, professional, but no fun.'

The Police did, of course, eventually progress from the Benylin they'd favoured when they were on the road with Cherry Vanilla to more effective and expensive ways of dealing with chesty coughs and other ailments.

'What kind of drugs were you taking?' Adrian Deevoy asked Sting in a 1993 interview for Q magazine.

'Normal drugs,' Sting said. 'Cocaine. We went through a cocaine stage which was totally stupid. It exaggerated everything. Total paranoia. It is the most mindless, pathetic drug. Why anyone would want to take it, I don't know. I guess you take it as a sort of reward: we've made it now, we can take some coke! God's way of telling you you've got too much money.'

Anyway, by the time the really heavy tours came along, they'd all passed their 27th birthdays, or near as dammit. In fact, Andy celebrated his 27th in 1969, when Jimi, Janis, Kurt, Jim and Amy were all still alive.

They were not starry-eyed kids. They'd all been around the business for long enough to know what the job entailed. They were ambitious. They were prepared to put in the hours, to do what was needed – the gigs, the interviews, the signings, the photo sessions. They didn't always do it with perfect good grace. The outbursts of ruthless acrimony, mostly against each other, became more frequent as time went on, but still they showed, they did what they had to, they hit their marks, they signed, they smiled, they posed as required.

Miles, one of the smartest managers the business has ever known, had the whole phenomenon summarised in one of the statements he liked to trot out whenever a journalist was in earshot.

'The Police,' he said, 'have come through with a new formula of music. They've synthesised a new blend of musical forces – punk rock, combined with the musicianship of the previous age, combined with the reggae beat. Plus, they realise it's a business and they are willing to accommodate the business requirements. So, they just have a beautiful blend of all these things that are necessary.'

'The average Police fan is spending money on me,' Sting told the NME, 'he believes in me and he expects something from me, and I feel a responsibility to that kid, I don't want to serve him up the same old shit.'

They gave good interview. They weren't much cop at the witty, whacky one-liners with which the Beatles used to keep the press at bay, but they all enjoyed shooting their mouths off and they were smart enough to keep it coherent. Whereas, with other acts, the journalists would slave over a hot Olivetti trying to turn the sledgehammer grunts of a hitmaking moron into passable prose, the Police did the work for them. Edit the transcript, five or six sentences to join it all up, bit of description, 1,200 words, thank you very much.

They played very nicely with photographers, too. 'It's very rare to see a bad Police picture,' David Hepworth observed in *Smash Hits*.

'We're professionals and it's part of our job,' Sting told him. 'Our bodies are for sale as much as the music. It's not that we enjoy it – it's just that we know that we have to do it.'

The *Smash Hits* interview was one in which Sting comes across as absolutely self-aware and in control. He talks – as he so often did – about his ego, puts forward the (debatable) theory that a big ego (he describes his as 'huge') means there's more to absorb the constant adulation without becoming a 'raving arsehole' – as if egos are like sponges: small ones get saturated with bits of praise and the owners fall quickly into raving arseholedom, while big ones can take loads before succumbing.

More modestly, he's conscious that his success might owe as much to genes as to accomplishment. 'I have this (vocal) range because my doctor looked at my throat the other day and he said it was amazing, because the high end's tiny and the low end's huge. That's purely a biological accident. See, I've got the films I've had because I've got this pair of cheekbones. It's not really you – it's what surrounds you.'

The wives joined them whenever they could spare time from their own careers and commitments.

Sting claimed that he and Frances were 'both jealous as hell and utterly monogamous'. They were both brought up Catholic. They knew about sin.

When Andy Hudson, Last Exit's manager, had once suggested to Frances that Sting, when on the road, might now and then succumb to temptation, Frances had replied, with near papal certainty, 'That will never happen.'

'I'm courted constantly,' Sting said. 'But I never trust the reason behind it. I do not give myself easily. I won't jeopardise my position for a quick fuck.'

Stewart, on the other hand, knew he was 'a natural born flirt. And that can get me into trouble... the main point is that Sonja knows I'll be back whatever happened.'

Whatever.

★ ★ ★

The three heroes, with their crew, and their two tons of equipment, continued their progress around the world: Buffalo, Cleveland, Memphis (where they visited Elvis's birthplace at Tupelo), Ann Arbor, Granite City, New Orleans, Denver, Salt Lake City, Seattle, Vancouver, over the Pacific to Honolulu.

The gig at Norman, Oklahoma, was cancelled because Stewart had hurt his ankle. Somewhere along the line they fitted in a TV special. And then there was, wherever they went, the constant barrage: 'Is Sting your real name?' 'What exactly did the message in the bottle say?' 'What qualities do you most look for in a girlfriend?' and 'Andy, over here', 'Could my friend and I have a photo with you?' or 'Would you sign my tongue?'

Then on to Japan.

'Most groups wait until their career is over before they go outside the States and Europe,' Miles said, speaking like a walking, talking press release again. 'I say the energy of the Police is now. Let's take them to the rest of the world when they are at their most impressive. Let's have the whole world selling for us for the next 10 years!'

They were already, as they say, big in Japan. The press queued for access. One day, the band spent four hours giving interviews to Japanese magazines.

The BBC made a documentary called *Police in the East* directed by Derek Burbidge, who made a lot of their music videos. It was presented by the Radio 1 DJ Annie Nightingale.

It's mostly the band in concert playing the hits, intercut with them doing some Monkees-style looning around. They dress up in local costumes, mug for the camera and strike poses, but you can see they're tired and they're not naturally gifted looners.

'Andy Summers is the reincarnation of Harpo Marx,' Annie Nightingale suggests. He isn't.

The film does provide some fascinating insights into the lives of Japanese groupies and particularly one who follows the band from gig to gig, booking herself into the hotels they're staying in. How does she know what hotels they're staying in? A friend, whose identity she will not reveal, has access to such secrets. She gets the money from her father, who thinks she's sightseeing. It's not revealed whether she was actually having sex with one of the band, but, since a woman that resourceful has to be the head of a major corporation these days, it's probably best not to dig too deep.

In Hong Kong, they played to 500 people in a club with essentially no stage and fans literally in their faces.

Annie Nightingale was supposed to interrupt the set and present them with the British Rock and Pop Best Album award for *Reggatta de Blanc*. British TV would be recording the shenanigans via a satellite link for later transmission as part of the ceremony. It was arranged with the band that she'd come on during 'Walking On The Moon' and they'd pretend to be surprised. As it turned out, the signal that the satellite was ready didn't come. The Police stretched out 'Walking On The Moon' until it could be stretched no further, then left the stage. So, Annie had to present the award in the dressing room after the show instead. The band tries quite hard to look surprised.

After Hong Kong, they flew to Christchurch in New Zealand. Customs found a half-smoked spliff in Stewart's luggage, so they insisted on searching every suitcase, flight case, pocket and hat. This was irksome, particularly for the roadies, but at least nobody went to prison.

Halfway through the concert at Christchurch, Sting fell prey to laryngitis, which endured, causing the rest of the Australasian leg of the tour to be cancelled. They gratefully took their ease for a while. Kate came out with the baby, and Frances with little Joe.

★ ★ ★

Then came India.

Western pop had made only limited leeway in the subcontinent. The Beatles, even though they studied meditation in India and George played sitar, never actually played there. The Stones had never played India. David Bowie had never played India. The Beach Boys had never played India. Queen had never played India. Abba never played India. Elvis played his last show ever in Indianapolis, but that's different.

(On the subject of Abba in the subcontinent, by the way, it might interest you to know that, in 1981, Salma and Sabina Agha, Pakistan-born sisters, made a stir with their album of Abba songs in Hindi. 'Mitha Maze Dar' – their version of 'Dancing Queen' – beats the pants off the original.)

For Miles, setting up the gig was seen almost as his duty as an agent of cultural imperialism. 'It's obviously a good thing for the Police to play the Third World,' he said, 'because it gets to the youth of those countries, people who will one day be running them. And if they are Western-orientated because they like Western music, then it's good from our governments' point of view. I happen to believe in the old values of the West. I believe in free enterprise capitalism. I'm not saying we are perfect, but we are definitely better.'

With Margaret Thatcher in Number 10 and Ronald Reagan well on the way to swiping the White House from Jimmy Carter, free enterprise capitalism was on the ascendant, and Miles was bang on message.

And, being a Political Science graduate, Miles can't have been unaware that he was echoing Cecil Rhodes, champion of the worst excesses of British colonialism, who wrote, 'I contend that we [the British] are the finest race in the world and that the more of the world we inhabit the better it is for the human race.'

'The thing you have to understand about Miles,' Sting told the NME, 'is that he has this very laissez-faire rightist attitude in which he sees rock'n'roll as bringing freedom to all these obscure places we've gone and played in. As far as I'm concerned, though, the reason we've done them is because being a world-class group shouldn't just be restricted to being big in the Western world – the popular conception of it. It should mean you're a force everywhere.'

Journalist Allan Jones, covering the India gig, overheard Miles saying, 'We figured that sooner or later, some decadent, greedy, capitalist, Western rock'n'roll band was going to move in and exploit the shit out of them [the population of India], and we simultaneously agreed it might as well be us rather than the Jam, the Boomtown Rats or a fink like Elvis Costello.'

Anyway, whatever its imperialist, decadent, greedy, capitalist overtones or undertones, the tour was generating massive coverage in the European and American media.

'Here's the other great reality of business,' Miles said.

The media needs something to write about. Every day, fucking *Melody Maker* or *NME* (or whatever the newspaper is) gets a photograph of a group. There they are in their spandex trousers, long hair with a guitar. Same fucking photograph I saw 50 times in the last three weeks. What makes them different?

All of a sudden, they get a picture of these three guys by the Taj Mahal in fucking India, all dressed up as maharajas, looking like they're out of their fucking minds. What the fuck is that!? All of a sudden they listen to the music, they see these guys, it looks glamorous.

Sting was definitely with Miles on strategies for winning over the press. Phil Sutcliffe remembers him explaining how he'd won over Paul Morley – then an influential journo on the *NME*. Paul had never been big on the Police.

'The way Sting did it,' Phil said, 'was just saying, "Would you like to come to India, Paul?" So, Paul went and did a massive article.'

★ ★ ★

The set-up in Bombay (now called Mumbai) was refreshingly parochial.

The Bombay Time & Talents Club had been, according to one of its leading lights, 'in existence for the last 46 years. We are a band of ladies all working entirely for charity giving our time, energy and talents. This is the very first time we are involved in presenting, I'm very proud to say, one of the world's greatest or maybe *the* greatest pop/rock group.'

It was, according to Sting, 'The greatest gig of my life… They'd never seen a rock concert, so there was no element of ritual, no preconceptions.'

They played a 5,000-seat open-air arena. Ticket sales raised about £5,000 for a children's charity. Outside, another crowd, about the same size as the one inside, tried to storm the gates. They got shirty. The cops had their hands full controlling them, so, after they'd let the bona fide ticket holders in, they gave up, left the gates open and it became a free-for-all free concert, just like Woodstock.

The audience included a fair sprinkling of British and American hippies, veterans of the great hippy trail, who'd most probably come through Chicken Street in Kabul 10 years earlier hoping to make it to Kovalam beach, then got stuck in Bombay. But there were also the ladies of the Time & Talents Club, the chief of police, civic dignitaries and folk of every class and caste. There were complaints from the seated ticket holders that the standing freeloaders were obstructing their view. Sting suggested they should all get up and dance. They did. At the end, there was another little riot. The cops staged a baton charge. It was all strangely reminiscent of the night the Stranglers played the Finsbury Park Empire.

'It was an incredible gig,' Sting said. 'Emotional beyond belief.'

On, then, to Cairo. This was where – as has already been told in Chapter 2 – the band's gear was held up at customs and Miles phoned a chap he'd known since he was a kid, Hassan Tuhami, deputy prime minister of Egypt and President Sadat's closest confidant, to see what could be done. The gear was released.

On the way to the hotel from the airport, they encountered demonstrations by Islamic radicals, protesting about the Shah of Iran, who'd just been deposed in Iran and had fled to Egypt, where he was welcomed by President Sadat.

Stewart looked out on the demonstrations, turned to Allan Jones, the embedded reporter, and said, 'I can't believe we've come all this way only to be upstaged by the fucking Shah. Sting's going to be seriously pissed, man.'

The Cairo gig was small fry compared with the one in Bombay. They played Ewart Hall at the American University – a grand place where the university's commencement ceremonies were held. The words 'Let Knowledge Grow from More to More, but More of Reverence in Us Dwell' were inscribed in big letters over the stage, reminding everybody why they were really there. Could have been a college gig anywhere in the world, from Nottingham to Newark.

The audience again included a lot of Brits and Yanks, and 'smart-suited Egyptian teenies brought up on Demis Roussos'.

The *Egyptian Mail* was not impressed by any of it, claiming Sting 'has all the sex appeal of a hover fly.

'About an hour after the concert began, bouncers had been withdrawn, but more people filtered out than in. Meanwhile an enthusiastic following at the front, turned punk for the night, jumped up and down with vigour. But it wasn't enough to persuade the Police to give more than one encore.'

Greece had become another rock'n'roll desert. The Rolling Stones had played Athens in 1967, but shortly afterwards there'd been a coup and the military regime that seized control preferred brass bands and folk tunes about fluttering rose petals in the Aegean to anything about gin-soaked barroom queens in Memphis.

But things had loosened up a lot since 1974, and in 1980 the rather more liberal New Democracy party won an election.

The Police, then, were the first UK or US band to play Athens for 13 years. The authorities were nervous. Coachloads of cops were turned out, as well as bouncers who prowled the auditorium like testy gangsters hoping to give their new brass knuckles a trial run.

The mostly male crowd were clearly eager to get out of their seats, to cheer, dance, scream and wave, but their excitement was tempered by fear of reprisal from the scowling heavies.

Outside, just as had happened in India, people without tickets turned tricky. The cops drew their batons. Heads got broken. The message the concert delivered about the nature of free-market capitalism could have been interpreted in several different ways.

★ ★ ★

Then it was back to what they'd hoped would be more humdrum venues – Brussels and the like.

However, at the PalaLido, the big basketball stadium in Milan (now the Allianz Cloud), thousands of fans forced the fire doors and invaded. Polizia in riot gear followed. Allan Jones, still travelling with the band, described hitting the deck in the dressing room as the police drew their side-arms and began firing over the heads of the invaders. He records the ensuing dialogue in his memoir *Can't Stand Up for Falling Down*:

'Fuck me,' Sting cries. 'They're shooting people now.'
Tear gas canisters are let off inside the stadium. Miles remembers the film crew that is travelling with them.
'Just remember, this is all great for the movie.'
'Oh, I will remember that when they rush the stage,' says Sting.
'I don't know why you're so worried.'
'I'm worried,' Sting replies, 'because I've got to go out there to face that mob. While you sit in here and count the money.'

And on to France, Germany, Spain.

There was more trouble in Hanover. They were knackered, did about 50 minutes and left the stage without explanation. The audience chucked bottles. A shot was fired. The Polizei arrived to disperse the crowd. The Police had had enough, cancelled their next gig and went back to the UK.

CHAPTER THIRTEEN

ANKLE DEEP IN MILTON KEYNES

At the beginning of 1980, 'So Lonely' had been reissued. On the first release, in November 1978, it had not charted. Now it went to number six.

Sales were no doubt boosted by the song being featured on *Top of the Pops* with Legs & Co., the heirs to Pan's People, dancing to it.

They appear to be in some sort of wide-bore central-heating conduit. They are dressed in Capri pants, white stiletto heels and jackets. During the first chorus, they take off the jackets. During the second verse, they put them back on again, only to take them off again in the third chorus. They keep doing this.

Jim Davidson was on ITV.

The record might also have had a boost, or otherwise, because of a mishearing of the lyric. Many thought it was about the TV presenter Sue Lawley, putting it up there with other top misheard lyrics of all time like Desmond Dekker's 'My Ears Are Alight', the Eurythmics' 'Sweet Dreams Are Made Of Cheese' and Dire Straits' 'Money For Nothing, Chips For Free'.

★ ★ ★

In June, since there had been no product out there for a while, Miles put out a six-single box set called *The Police: Six Pack* all pressed on blue vinyl and consisting of 'Roxanne'/'Peanuts', 'So Lonely'/'No Time This Time', 'Can't Stand Losing You'/'Dead End Job', 'Message In A Bottle'/'Landlord', 'Walking On The Moon'/'Visions Of The Night', and 'The Bed's Too Big Without You'/'Truth Hits Everybody'.

Some of them were re-releases of re-releases. The only new material was the mono mix of 'The Bed's Too Big Without You'.

The band had unanimously opposed the project – 'The last thing we need is a third release of "Roxanne",' Stewart had said. But Miles had gone ahead anyway.

Nevertheless, the fanbase was either obsessively completist, rich, loyal – or all three – and bought enough copies to send the box set to number 17 in the singles chart.

It was the kind of trick that had been virtually unknown since the early 1960s, when anything, in any length or format, that the Beatles put out tended to show up in the singles chart.

Money was pouring in and Miles did his best to make sure they got what was theirs.

'Miles thinks that anybody who makes money out of us is stealing from the group,' Stewart said. 'If Miles sees someone selling chewing gum outside one of our gigs, he thinks they are exploiting us.'

★ ★ ★

In the first budget after the 1979 election, Margaret Thatcher's government had cut the top rate of income tax from 83 to 60 per cent. But it was still 60 per cent, and when Miles said, 'Everybody wants to make money out of the Police,' this was just the sort of thing he was talking about.

The Tom and Jerry relationship between the entertainment industry and the Inland Revenue was well established on both sides of the Atlantic.

Bruce Springsteen never paid tax, on the grounds that nobody from New Jersey ever did. When the Revenue men caught up with him, they ripped the bones from his back and left him, at the age of 30, with just $20,000 to his name.

The comedian Ken Dodd kept a third of a million pounds in cash in his attic for fear the taxman would get hold of it. Thanks to him, we know that a suitcase containing £100,000 weighs much less than you might think.

UK tax on foreign earnings could be avoided if you lived in the UK for less than three months of the year. The Police's touring schedule meant they were close to this already, but, to expedite matters further, Sting and Andy both found properties in Ireland that, at least for the taxman's benefit, they could call home. Stewart, an American citizen, had no need of such subterfuge.

Andy paid £40,000 for a four-storey Georgian house, overlooking the harbour in Kinsale, County Cork, on the south-east coast. He didn't like it. It was too cold, too quiet, too boring, and the shops had nothing worth buying. The locals didn't like him, either. They sprayed rude things on his walls and put nails under the wheels of his Audi. Irish exile, he later reckoned, was at least partly to blame for the eventual break-up of his marriage.

Sting bought a £60,000 picturesque pile in Roundstone Bay in County Galway on the west coast and devoted himself to writing songs, nipping over to Keystone Studios in Dublin now and then to make demos.

Sting, whose politics were considerably to the left of Miles's, decided not to let tax avoidance trouble his conscience. 'In the few months we're in England this year, we're going to play for charity. We can play a festival and make £50,000 in half an hour. That's why I don't feel any qualms or uneasiness about becoming what other people describe as a tax exile.' In another interview, he presented tax avoidance as a form of political protest. 'I believe strongly that money is freedom and power, but, to Thatcher, people without money can go to the wall. She's not building more schools or feeding the kids who attend them, she's building sites for American nuclear warheads and sending working-class kids to get killed in Belfast. I'm not paying for it if I can help it. We made about £150,000 from our gigs in England in 1980 and that will all go to youth organisations.'

★ ★ ★

While Sting and Andy cooled their heels in Ireland, Stewart went to Surrey Studios with Nigel Gray and shape-shifted into Klark Kent. They recorded enough material for an eight-song, 10-inch LP.

A&M released it on green vinyl for £3.99.

Smash Hits complained about the terrible surface noise and said, 'The songs belong to the "Fall Out" mould, energetic, utterly straightforward and reasonably tuneful, if a bit lacking in the lyrical department – while the excellent musicianship is relaxed and inventive, not unlike the Police (surprise surprise) on their day off. An enjoyable sideshow (7 out of 10).'

The album spawned two singles: 'Rich In A Ditch', which sounds like an unholy union of the Police and the Dave Clark Five; and 'Away From Home' ('A raucous schoolboy chant set to a swaggering bumbling out-of-bounds beat'). The charts took no notice.

Stewart told Phil Sutcliffe that Klark was now a big movie star in the Middle East as well as the founder/leader of the Church of Kinetic Ritual. He also described the process by which the roar of the crowd during Police concerts could endow him, Stewart Copeland, with genuine Klark Kent superpowers.

'Think of me on stage magnified 10 times by the PA, another 10 times by their imaginations: I feel larger than life. I can perform feats of stamina and strength that shouldn't be possible for a weedy person such as myself. It's a congregational experience as the Kinetic Ritualists have it.'

Sutcliffe remarked that Klark Kent was possibly more like Stewart Copeland than Stewart Copeland was.

'You've touched on something very profound there,' Stewart said. 'The point is that Klark Kent is more like everybody than anybody is.'

★ ★ ★

For tax reasons, it was also advisable for Andy and Sting to make their next album anywhere but the UK, so, along with Nigel Gray, they moved operations to Wisseloord Studios, a state-of-the-art facility built two years earlier by the Philips company in Hilversum, Netherlands.

In those days, it was a three-studio complex. Mike Batt, composer of 'Bright Eyes' and 'Remember You're A Womble', was in one of the other studios, also for tax reasons, recording his album *Waves*. He was living in a caravan on the site.

Telly Savalas, aka Kojak, TV's favourite bald, lollipop-addicted cop, was in another studio, showing off his versatility on an ee-zee listening album called *Sweet Surprise*.

It rained incessantly.

The pressure was on. The entire record industry had been in trouble for a couple of years and A&M were suffering along with the rest. Although there'd been a boom in record sales the previous year, they were falling fast. Home taping really was killing music.

The A&M execs knew that a new Police album could do a lot to restore their fortunes.

'While we were in the States last year,' Stewart said, 'A&M fired 180 people. So many people earn a crust from my activities. Occasionally, I get vertigo.'

'The bedrock of this whole corporate structure is songs,' Sting said. 'I've gotta go and write a song; otherwise this whole thing is going to collapse.'

'We're like a chain of shops. The Police are the Marks & Spencer of pop.'

'Making records is really hard, you know,' Stewart told *Melody Maker*. 'The first two records were like a challenge. It was the beginning of an adventure. Now that we've kinda conquered the world, they're more of a responsibility. The album has to be out by 19 September. Everything is planned around that date. Like Miles says, it's a military operation. That's a very heavy pressure.'

'For *Outlandos* they had a lot of songs that Sting had written and they had played on the stage,' Nigel Gray said. 'For *Reggatta*, Sting could delve back into his past to get more songs for them to adapt. But by *Zenyatta* the only material they had was what they'd been able to write in their month off.'

'We were a bit fucked up emotionally,' Andy said. 'On the point of a possible break-up, in fact.'

'There was a lot of depression in the studio,' Stewart said. 'There were record executives hanging around the studio and stuff: all making us very aware by their presence that we had to deliver an important piece of product.'

'There was a sense of urgency and quite a lot of drugs,' Andy said. 'None of us had to go into rehab or anything, it didn't get too bad, we were just experimenting. But we should have been concentrating on the music. We didn't like each other much at this point. There were three big egos pulling in different directions.'

The often-told story of Andy's instrumental track, 'Behind My Camel', gives some indication of the mood.

It is a strange and repetitive piece, not much more than a riff played by a heavily effected guitar. Sting and Stewart both hated it. Sting refused even to play on it – 'He's not a team player' – so Andy had to overdub the bass as well as the guitar parts.

'I hated that song so much,' Sting said, 'that one day, when I was in the studio, I found the tape lying on the table. So, I took it around the back of the studio and actually buried it in the garden.'

But it was unearthed, made it onto the album and won a Grammy for Best Rock Instrumental Performance.

Stewart got two tracks on the album. 'As hard done by as I ever felt in this band, I could always take comfort in the fact that Andy got shafted even worse than I did.'

Halfway through the recording process, they had to down tools to go and do a couple of gigs: the first at the Milton Keynes Bowl on 2 July, in front of 25,000 punters ankle-deep in mud; the second at Leixlip Castle in County Kildare, Ireland, the day after.

Neither were much fun.

At Milton Keynes, Miles insisted that all the press photographers sign a contract handing over the copyright of photos to the band. The press took their revenge.

'They left me utterly cold,' said the *NME*. 'During leisurely, strung-out tunes I could feel my concentration wandering, shortly followed by my feet. It was no place for the undevoted.'

At Leixlip, somebody threw a bottle during a long rendition of 'Roxanne' and cut Stewart's leg. Sting called him out. 'Bring me that tosser with the ginger hair!' he screamed into the crowd (not the most useful form of identification in Ireland). 'Wait till I get him backstage.'

However, it's an ill wind, for it was here that Stewart met the beautiful Marina Guinness – daughter of Desmond Guinness, who owned Leixlip Castle, and granddaughter of the infamous Diana Mitford – and, although he didn't find out about it for another four years, fathered a son, Patrick.

Then it was back to Holland for some more, by now increasingly frantic, recording. They kept going until 4 a.m. on the morning of 9 July. At 8 a.m., they had to leave for a gig in Le Touquet, in France. The day after, it was Werchter in Belgium... and on and on.

And, even then, the album wasn't finished.

'In Holland,' Nigel Gray said, 'everything sounded enormous, but when I took the tapes back to England, they sounded woolly and boring. So, we had to remix the album. By then we had run out of time and we ended up mixing five tracks in five hours, which was crazy.'

Despite which, nobody was prepared to be overgenerous when it came to paying Nigel for his devotion. Phil Sutcliffe and Hugh Fielder's 1981 book *L'Historia Bandido* gives a full account of the story.

On the previous two albums, Nigel had worked for a fixed fee. Now he thought, with much justification, he deserved a cut, a percentage, a point or two.

When he asked, Miles 'went berserk' and offered him a flat 10 grand. He was even more pissed off when 'the band didn't have the guts to say, "Look, we owe the guy a point, give it to him."'

In the end Nigel settled for a flat payment of £35,000. A point or two would have earned him several multiples of that amount.

'Miles is a wonderful human being,' Stewart once said. 'Or, rather, he is wonderful, but I'm not sure he's a human being. He might be a robot dropped in by strategic air command at the end of the war.'

★ ★ ★

The album was released on 3 October 1980. The title, *Zenyatta Mondatta,* is either nonsense syllables, like the other titles, or is Sanskrit for 'Top Of The World' (Sanskrit scholars might choose to question this).

It was welcomed with mixed reviews.

Rolling Stone described it at 'near-perfect pop'.

'Once you skim off the hits, you're left with uninspired though well-crafted filler,' said Andy Shernoff in *Creem*.

'An intriguing album of rather reserved musicianship and considerably less obvious song writing,' said David Hepworth in *Smash Hits*.

'About half the tracks are excellent, but many of the other tracks, like the instrumental "Behind My Camel", sound like weak fillers,' said the *Guardian*.

Breaking with every precedent, neither Andy, nor Stewart nor Sting rushed to defend *Zenyatta*.

'The last album,' said Andy, when interviewed the following year, 'was a bit of a cock-up.'

Nevertheless, it went straight in at number one, stayed there for four weeks, then hung around the Top 10 for another nine weeks. It made number five in the US.

Eventually the 'cock-up' went platinum in the UK and double platinum in the US.

Two tracks from the album were released as singles.

'Don't Stand So Close To Me', the song about illicit love between teacher and pupil, was inspired partly (but not closely) by Sting's experience in secondary schools while he was doing teaching practice, and partly by *Lolita*, the novel by Vladimir Nabokov. Sting's use of 'cough' to rhyme with 'Nabokov' is often cited as the worst rhyme in pop song history, but it's a close-run field.

The tune, by Sting's own admission, was 'inspired' by the riff from Buffalo Springfield's 'Rock And Roll Woman'.

Released in September, 'Don't Stand So Close To Me' went straight to number one, and stayed there for four weeks.

'De Do Do Do, De Da Da Da' was apparently inspired partly by Joe's baby babblings, and partly by the great nonsense lyrics of all time, like 'Tutti Frutti', 'Do Wah Diddy Diddy' and 'Da Do Ron Ron'.

It's about the moment when love grows so intense that words prove inadequate and babble takes over.

'When their eloquence escapes me, their logic ties me up and rapes me' is another contender for the 'cough'/'Nabokov', 'there'/'chair', 'yacht'/ 'apricot' award ('there'/'chair' is from Neil Diamond's 'I Am... I Said' and 'yacht'/'apricot' Carly Simon's 'You're So Vain' in case you were struggling).

It was released in mid-December, possibly as a contender for the Christmas number one spot. In fact, as things turned out, this was an honour that should have gone, if there were any justice in the world, to John Lennon, who was murdered on 8 December that year. But then the St Winifred's School Choir singing 'There's No One Quite Like Grandma' snuck out of nowhere and stole a march on both Police and Lennon, which caused many people to lose faith in the entire gubbins.

Munich, Essen, Winnipeg, Regina, Calgary, Vancouver, Seattle, Portland, Oakland...

In Arizona, they were accused of playing the Devil's music, just like Elvis and the Beatles had been all those years ago.

Albuquerque, Austin, Dallas, Cullen, Minneapolis, Madison, Chicago, Detroit...

The ego problems, particularly the attention given to Sting, now and then rankled.

'It works like this,' Stewart said. 'A journalist comes on the road with the band to write a feature. I talk to him for hours, Andy talks to him for hours and Sting never says a word – except that just once he walks through the room where I'm busy bending the guy's ear and he says, "Where's the toilet?" And that's the headline.'

And sometimes Andy and Sting hankered for a less overt drummer.

'On stage, he's not that responsible a performer,' Sting said. 'He gives everything too much and too often... It comes back to the rivalry between me and Stewart. He's at the back and he wants to be at the front. What's so fascinating about him is that he's a lead guitarist in the guise of a drummer. And I'm, of course, a lead guitarist with a bass.'

★ ★ ★

Back in the UK, Frances was having trouble with *Macbeth*.

Peter O'Toole decided he wanted to essay the role and approached the Old Vic theatre.

O'Toole, star of *Lawrence of Arabia*, *How to Steal a Million*, *Becket*, *The Lion in Winter* and *The Ruling Class*, a man with so many awards on his shelves that the scrap value alone could have provided for a comfortable retirement, was welcomed by the Old Vic with open arms. He asked for, and got, an unusual degree of artistic freedom.

One of his ideas was that the scenery should be inflatable, the advantage of which would be that if the production ever went on tour, the entire set could be packed in the boot of a car.

He happened to be the director of a company developing such state-of-the-art inflatable technology. They were also working on a tiny lighting rig 'using small but very powerful lamps made of Campbell's soup tins, which can be operated from a transistorised panel on someone's lap, sitting in the stalls'.

O'Toole said he was happy to finance a full demonstration out of his own pocket and Timothy West, then co-director of the Old Vic, agreed.

'The Irish designer arrived,' West said, 'and installed himself in rehearsal room B with an enormous pack of black dustbin bags and some tins of adhesive, saying he required nothing from us except a bottle of Powers whiskey to be left outside his door every morning.'

Days passed. Eventually the set was assembled on stage. Timothy West and other members of the theatre staff arrived for a demonstration.

There was a whining noise.

'Air compressor,' O'Toole said. 'We can deal with that.'

'The curtain rose,' West said, 'to reveal a dimly lit collection of black plastic phalluses swaying in the wind. The general effect was of a blustery day during a refuse collection strike.'

Then there was a smell of burning.

The inflatable set idea was abandoned.

Frances was cast as Lady Macbeth – a glowing tribute to her reputation and talent that turned out to be a poisoned chalice.

For some reason, Princess Margaret, the Queen's sister, attended a run-through. She wondered whether there should be more blood. Accordingly, on the first night, Brian Blessed, playing Banquo, was drenched in the stuff. It left puddles on the stage. If he turned round quickly, it would shower the front row of the stalls.

There were other calamities, too. People bumped into the scenery. During a sword fight, one of the swords got bent, like Tom's in Tom and Jerry's *The Two Mouseketeers*. People laughed. Most people agreed that Peter O'Toole was, throughout every performance, out of his brain on drink.

When Michael Billington, the *Guardian*'s esteemed drama critic, retired in 2019, he was asked what, during his long career, was the worst production he'd ever had to witness. Without a moment's thought, he replied: 'Peter O'Toole's *Macbeth* at the Old Vic in 1980.'

Frances came out of it with dignity intact – just about. Some of the reviews even praised her performance. But every other aspect of the production was slammed.

One of the witches was played by a 26-year-old actor called Trudie Styler. She and Peter O'Toole, 20 years her senior, had an affair. When it all went wrong, Trudie turned to her friend Frances for comfort.

★ ★ ★

Boston, Washington, Owings Mills (Maryland), Atlanta (Georgia), St Petersburg, Florida...

At Passaic, New Jersey, there was a bomb threat and the audience was asked to check under their seats.

XTC supported them some of the way.

'We all shared the proverbial bus,' Andy Partridge, XTC's frontman said. 'Even off stage, Sting was the tough guy: he used to humiliate you at backgammon and come up with surreal words in Scrabble – "iqba" – that he dared you to challenge. He was an odd mix, half school bully and half crippled by shyness. He could freeze you out with that leonine stare or come across as an affable, fun-loving bloke. I'll say this for him – in the right mood, he could give a stunning performance as your best mate. I actually liked him.'

Possibly the take-away message from this account is that Jayne County was right. This is a band that played Scrabble on the tour bus.

In Sunrise, Florida, Nigel Gray met up with the band to record Sting's vocals for the Spanish and Japanese versions of 'De Do Do Do, De Da Da Da' (linguists might like to note that 'De Do Do Do, De Da Da Da' in Japanese is 'A Do Do Do, A Da Da Da').

Then to South America.

They had wanted to cancel the South American leg of the tour. Sting had been ill. But the Argentinian promoter somehow persuaded them to come and the gigs were rescheduled.

Argentina was not a nice place to be. The president at the time was Jorge Videla, who ruled primarily by death squad, torturing and killing an estimated 30,000 citizens during his five years in office. A favoured form of execution was taking planeloads of people out over the Atlantic and pushing them out. He also stole babies.

On 15 December, the Police played Club Atlético Obras Sanitarias, a sports hall in Buenos Aires.

Like Athens, the place was crawling with Polícia and security looking for heads to break. At one point, an excited young woman left her seat and tried to rush the stage. A cop grabbed her and set about her, so Andy came to the front of the stage and kicked the cop in the face. The crowd loved that. They rose to their feet and cheered.

But the cops gathered, mob-handed, at the sides of the stage. They had guns.

Between songs, the roadies passed messages to the band: 'They're going to arrest Andy.' 'Six months in prison at least.'

When they finished the show and came off stage, the cop Andy had kicked was waiting. The promoter had magicked a lawyer from somewhere.

'You have to go down to this guy, crawl, nip it in the bud,' the lawyer told Andy.

Andy did as he was bidden. He apologised profusely and was photographed for the local press doing so.

Charges were not pressed.

Then, to cap it all, on a beach in Rio they had all their stuff nicked, and a couple of days after that they played Tooting bloody Common in South London. In a tent. Three days before Christmas. In the bleak midwinter. Tooting bloody Common. I ask you.

CHAPTER FOURTEEN

I USED TO BE A GLORIOUS AMATEUR

'Just because the Police have played in India is no reason to turn their Tooting Bec tent concert into a simulacrum of the Black Hole of Calcutta,' said the *NME* in an excoriating condemnation of the Tooting venture. 'It was hell in there, so over-packed was it!'

The *NME* blamed the band for cramming 5,000 fans into a circus tent in the depths of winter, charging them £5 a head and then turning up an hour late. They blamed the band for making that crowd wait outside for 45 bloody minutes in the freezing bloody rain. They blamed the band for the cost of refreshments (tea at 70p a cup, beer at £1 a pint) and for the cost of the merch (a Police sweatshirt was £7). In those days you could buy a three-piece suit for £7 at Mister Byrite.

It was an age when bands and promoters took it into their heads that a gig – and particularly a gig in a tent – should be treated as a circus. Some bands hired jugglers and fire-eaters, either as support act or to stand at the side of the stage juggling and eating fire. Others hired stand-up comedians. The jugglers weren't so bad, because it didn't matter if nobody looked or listened, but stand-up comedians are pointless if nobody takes any notice.

For their 1972 tour, Mott the Hoople had both – jugglers and a comedian – the latter being comedy legend Max Wall ('I've had a difficult life: I lost both parents at the age of eight. What a card game that was').

They almost got away with it, but when Ian Dury hired the same Max Wall for a gig at the Hammersmith Odeon in 1978, it didn't go well. An unruly crowd heckled poor Max (he was 72 at the time) and threw things. Possibly they'd have offered physical injury if Ian had not come on stage and saved him.

And yet the myth that a rock'n'roll audience would appreciate an old-school comic persisted.

Another comedy legend, Tommy Cooper, a proper national treasure, got the Tooting gig. Tommy's schtick was inept conjuring with unruly props interrupted by Christmas cracker one-liners. ('I went to Blackpool and knocked on the door of the first boarding house I came to. A woman stuck her head out the window. She said, "What do you want?" I said, "I'd like to stay here." She said, "All right, stay there."')

The fans – cold, unhappy, belligerent – were mystified. Tommy was mystified and (according to several observers) drunk. The fans would have been drunk, too, if they could have afforded £1 a pint.

They shouted, 'We want the Police. We want the Police,' and pelted Tommy with plastic cups and the fluorescent necklaces they'd just bought for an outrageous 50p.

Sting had to intervene the same as Ian Dury had at the Hammersmith Odeon. He came on stage and, in his best schoolteacher manner, told the crowd that the Police would not play unless Tommy was given the respect he deserved. This calmed them down long enough for Tommy to say, 'I went to the doctor's the other day. I said, "Doctor, I've got wind." He gave me a kite. Thank you very much. You've been a lovely audience,' and to get off.

Eventually the Police came on and, despite the weather, the prices and the shaky support, Sting underwent the by-now-customary shirt removal and the band got three encores.

★ ★ ★

He had moved to a new house.

Frognal, Hampstead, was deep in London's culture ghetto. The house he bought there had once belonged to Tamara Karsavina, prima ballerina with the Ballets Russes. Next door had been the home of E. V. Knox, essayist, poet and former editor of *Punch* magazine. Kathleen Ferrier, the contralto, had lived up the road and, during the war, Charles de Gaulle had lived for two years at number 99.

'I don't feel I belong here any more than I used to belong in Wallsend,' Sting said.

★ ★ ★

'My philosophy of life is that if we make up our mind what we are going to make of our lives, then work hard toward that goal, we never lose – somehow we win out,' said Ronald Reagan, echoing Margaret Thatcher's promise to make sure 'that hard work pays, success is rewarded'. At the beginning of 1981, Reagan became the 40th president of the USA. He was an old-time movie actor who never quite made the first rank and had subsequently gone into politics. When he became governor of California in 1967, Sam Goldwyn, the veteran Hollywood producer, said, 'No, no, no. Jimmy Stewart for governor. Ronald Reagan for governor's best friend.'

He was, by one associate's estimate, 'an amiable dunce', but he, like Thatcher, was a champion of free-market capitalism, favouring low taxes, low subsidies for the poor, huddled and tempest-tossed, and seeing himself as defender of the world against the evils of communism. 'We must not break faith,' he said, 'with those who are risking their lives – on every continent from Afghanistan to Nicaragua – to defy Soviet-supported aggression and secure rights which have been ours from birth.' In pursuing this belief, he did much to address Miles Copeland Sr's complaint that America 'isn't overthrowing enough anti-American governments or assassinating enough anti-American leaders'.

Perhaps emboldened by Reagan's go-get-'em-isms, Miles developed a new strategy for America tours – go short, but go BIG.

He lined up Madison Square Garden in New York and the Memorial Sports Arena in Los Angeles for Police concerts. The band weren't sure that this was a wise move. Their American audience, the one they were used to, lived in joints that smelled of beer and taco chips.

For both artiste and punter, the difference between club and stadium is more than a matter of scale. The club provides an intense physical experience, a build of excitement that starts with the buzz of the PA and the clatter of the drummer adjusting cymbals, and builds (when the band knows its stuff) to a visceral intensity that (when the band really knows its stuff) can keep you high for a couple of days or the rest of your life. The division between band and punter dissolves and you're all in this together, one orgiastic mass of swaying humanity, soaked in beer and sweat. Whatever the band is providing – sex, aggression, fun – is immediate and real.

The stadium gig is a formal religious celebration, a gathering of the tribe to give thanks and to celebrate their belief. Though the orgiastic element is still there, it's ritualised. The band orchestrate it but cannot be part of it. They are the priest-gods, the objects of veneration. When a band makes the move from club to stadium, they become a different order of being.

To convince them that they could make the transition, a couple of months earlier the New York promoter Ron Delsener had taken Sting, Stewart and Andy, along with Ian Copeland, to Madison Square Garden to see Mr Bruce Springsteen. The Boss.

All Bruce's albums since *Born to Run* had gone Top 5 and, in the previous year, *The River* had gone to number one. But he'd never quite cracked the singles market. To date, 'Hungry Heart' had been his only Top 10 hit.

But, with the E Street Band, he was the best live act going and could sell out a stadium faster and more reliably than any of your johnny-come-lately stars on 45.

Bruce gave good concert.

On the streets of a runaway American dream he'd holler and sweat, then Clarence blew, then the teenage tramps in skin-tight pants did the E Street dance and everything was all right.

On the night the Police went to see them, Bruce and the band played for nearly three hours – 35 numbers, starting with 'Born To Run'.

He pulled a young fan out of the front row and danced with her on 'Sherry Darling', just like he did three years later in the video of 'Dancing In The Dark'.

The audience got to sing the first and last verse and chorus of 'Hungry Heart'; and 20,000 people watched, listened, loved and knew more joy than they could ever remember.

'I could see from Sting's face that our show was on,' Ian wrote. 'Sting saw Bruce take that huge venue and turn it into a club atmosphere, and he rose to the challenge to do the same.'

The Police at Madison Square Garden gig was announced. Tickets sold out in four days (or a couple of hours, depending on who you believe). They stayed, not in a crappy motel with no name, but in the St Regis overlooking Fifth Avenue, and they were driven to the venue, not in a Ford Econoline van, but in a powder-blue Cadillac limousine.

★ ★ ★

On the night, Jools Holland announced them as 'those tall blond gods'. All the same, they needed to earn their right to be there, and for the first few numbers seemed to have trouble connecting with the audience. Then, during 'De Do Do Do, De Da Da Da', somebody lobbed a bottle on the stage and it went through the head of Stewart's bass drum. Roadies rushed on stage to effect repairs, but Sting, realising the hiatus could cost them the rest of the show, announced, 'A real supergroup would go off at this point. But we're just assholes, so I guess we'll stay.' And, with that, to the accompaniment only of his own bass, performed (as he always did in such circumstances, and had done for years) a version of the 'Yellow Rose Of Texas', remembered, one assumes, from his primary school days when *Davy Crockett* and *The Man from Laramie* were both current in the cinema and in the hit parade ('Oh, the Yellow Rose of Texas, and the man from Laramie / invited Davy Crockett to have a cup of tea / the tea was so delicious that they had another cup / and then left Davy Crockett to do the washing-up').

That got them. Putty in his hands.

John Stevens, a photographer, was in the pit.

'You know,' he told the *NME*. 'I've seen Springsteen, another very good crowd manipulator, from that same pit. And you soon see that in order to reach those people right up at the back of the auditorium, he's hamming it up and faking it quite a bit. But Sting wasn't doing that – he didn't seem at all contrived.'

He was, in other words, a natural.

The following night, they did the newly opened Ritz Theatre on East 11th Street, a fancy place with state-of-the-art 30-foot video screens. But, having conquered Madison Square Garden, it was hard to be arsed for a mere 3,000-capacity joint.

'I wasn't doing very well last night, was I?' Sting told Phil Sutcliffe the following morning. 'I didn't want to pretend I was enjoying myself. And

177

the more the audience didn't seem to notice that, the more annoyed I got. Very selfish. A shameful performance by me.'

He blamed it on fatigue, tired body, tired voice. Already he was pining for the old days.

Phil was interviewing each of them – one by one, never together – for *L'Historia Bandido*, the book he wrote with Hugh Fielder that was published later in the year. He also tried to get an interview with Miles Sr and rang him. From a phone box in the UK. Putting 10p pieces in the slot.

'We would really like to do a proper interview with you, sir.'

'Are Miles and Stewart getting a piece of this book?'

'No, it's not an official biography. The band just agreed to talk to us.'

'Well, I'm not speaking to you, then. Goodbye.'

It should be noted that, according to Phil, if Miles and Stewart had been getting even a sizeable piece of the book, it would perhaps have bought them a pint of milk and a Mars Bar.

★ ★ ★

They played New Orleans, then moved up to the Memorial Sports Arena in Los Angeles. Andy, in his autobiography *One Train Later*, tells us that the band prepared for the show by dosing themselves with nose candy.

As a result, tunes were played at breakneck tempos that rendered some of them unrecognisable. And maybe the technical crew had access to the band's stash, because the sound was hell, too.

'The disappointment of Thursday's show,' said Robert Hilburn in the *Los Angeles Times*, 'is that the Police seemed so intent on overwhelming the audience with its energy that it sacrificed the nuances that give its music at least some character.'

The crowd didn't seem to notice, though, or if they noticed they didn't mind. The ritual was the ritual. Sting – according to the *LA Times*, anyway – addled them with sex.

He 'came on stage wearing an open kimono over his white undershirt and jeans and was shrouded suggestively in the dimmest of bedroom lighting. When the kimono finally came off, Sting's body appeared as elegantly structured as his face as he twisted and turned his way around the stage, offering some of the flashiest springs into the air since the early Peter Townshend.'

The reviewer concluded: 'The Police should be able to sell out two or three nights at the Sports Arena next time.'

Perhaps to show that, despite their status, they were still down with the kids, or perhaps in an effort to recreate the buzz the band felt when they were a club band, Miles and Kim Turner added a previously unannounced show at the Variety Arts Theatre in Los Angeles. The $11 tickets were available only from the theatre. And it was decreed that the only way you could get into the gig was to be blond: even Jerry Moss, the head of A&M, had to do fake blond. Sting, Stewart and Andy played their encore wearing black wigs.

Then on to Honolulu, Japan ('At least we'll be able to find some interesting ethnic music to rip off' – Sting), Wellington and Auckland in New Zealand, then Australia, where they played to 25,000 at the Sydney Showground.

Karen Hughes, in the *Australian*, like so many others, found herself pining for the old pre-stadium Police – the Police of their previous Australian visit, a few months earlier. 'Then they were the Penthouse Punks, who had just made it to the top of the charts with their unique sound and not a little image manipulation.' Now, she said, they were a product. In those good old days of last year, they worked on sheer bravado. Now they strutted with the entitlement of the rich and famous. The audience had changed, too. They wanted the product working through the hits with carefully orchestrated climaxes and shirt removals.

Pre-teen girls were 'fainting by the second. Or at least pretending to faint once they realised that this meant being carried backstage in the arms of a big burly bodyguard at which time the swooning level became more frequent. I spied one who, limp in the arms of a bouncer, suddenly came to life with a big smile and cheery wave as she sailed past the front of the stage within touching distance of a most amused Sting.'

The Australian leg of the tour finished in Perth on 26 February. The following day, by the hotel pool, Sting ran into Willie Nelson, the country and western god who'd written 'Crazy' for Patsy Cline. They chatted. Sting congratulated Willie on his Grammy award. Then he ran into jazz piano legend Oscar Peterson. Unfortunately, Oscar had never heard of Sting or the Police, but this didn't change the fact that Sting was now the kind of person who rubbed shoulders with these kinds of people by hotel swimming pools, and if he ran into the Pope, the Pope might say, 'Hi, Sting,' and they'd chat about the doctrine of transubstantiation, and, as they chatted, the Queen might pass by, and the

Queen might turn to Prince Philip and ask, 'Who's that bloke chatting with Sting?'

They were supposed to go on to Germany and Scandinavia, but the gigs were cancelled.

Rumours began to circulate that the band was on the verge of splitting.

The Outlandos official fan club newsletter for March smacked down the rumours in no uncertain terms: 'the band decided that considering the number of things planned for the year ahead and the physical state of their health at that time it would be pointless to continue with the tour of Germany and Scandinavia – especially as the album was no longer new. They do promise to visit these countries as soon as they hit the road again.'

★ ★ ★

Sting arrived at Heathrow at around four in the afternoon, took a taxi home, kissed his wife and baby, had a cup of tea, got in the car and drove to Nottingham, where he started rehearsals for a BBC film, co-starring Hywel Bennett, called *Artemis 81*.

Andy and Stewart, in a move that could not have endeared them to their wives and children, went straight from Australia to Bali to further their collective interest in photography.

Here, just as Sting had run into Willie and Oscar, Andy ran into the *Blues Brothers* actor John Belushi, who was so far out of it he never did return and was found, almost exactly one year later, speedballed to death in a bungalow at Chateau Marmont in Los Angeles.

Andy and John found a restaurant in Bali that served magic mushroom omelettes. Nobody knows what happened after that.

Back in London, Andy told journalists that he planned to produce a photography book and Stewart announced he wanted to get good at making movies and he'd started work on a documentary called *So What* about the punk explosion in England. The film enjoyed a limited release in 1982.

Stewart and Andy both got involved in music projects outside the Police – Andy with his old Bournemouth mucker Robert Fripp, and Stewart with Brian James.

★ ★ ★

All three were adamant that they wanted to branch out and start doing things other than just being a megastar supergroup roaming the world conquering countries and continents.

'I used to be a glorious amateur and loved every minute of it,' Sting said. 'My whole week was centred on waiting for Wednesday night, when my old band Last Exit played the Gosforth Hotel in Newcastle. But now it's such a pain to get through a show – actual physical pain in my throat, I mean. You can hear it.

'I can remember pretty well every night of the first tour; which gigs had tricky stairs to negotiate with the gear; what was said in the dressing room; which encores we did. But a stadium just looks like a stadium.'

★ ★ ★

Stewart, too, was unsure about the elevation to the rock'n'roll priesthood. 'It's almost impossible for us to blow people's minds any more. We don't freak people out. We need to turn on new people, to change new minds, start new hysteria and there's nowhere left to go.'

★ ★ ★

So, apart from a quick trip to Bremen at the end of March for a TV show, they engaged in no Police-related activities for a couple of months.

Meanwhile, glory and accolades continued to shower from the heavens. Their single 'Don't Stand So Close To Me' reached the Top 10 in America, and the following year they'd got a Grammy for it, and another one in the Rock Instrumental Performance category for 'Behind My Camel', Andy's track that Sting had tried, literally, to bury.

Zenyatta Mondatta went to number one in the UK and ended up spending an incredible three years in the UK charts. It went at least Top 10 everywhere else in the pop-buying world.

'Yeah, we're still going up,' said Andy. 'I would like us to get into a position where we can keep the group, work when we want to work, enjoy making records together, but do lots of outside things – so that being in the group isn't the be-all and end-all. We don't want to be one of those groups that makes another record or makes another tour of America, 'cause we all have a lot more going than that.'

Slowly, in May, things began to get back into gear. On 4 May, Sting went off to Paris to start recording demos for the next album. He'd been in the west of Ireland, writing hard.

Two years earlier, when Mark Williams of *Melody Maker* had asked Sting how long he thought the band would last, he'd replied, 'Three albums. I think there are few groups worth more than three albums. Listen to their first three: fresh and new. Then listen to the numbers four to ten and you can tell they are just going through the options of being rock stars.'

The Police had done their three. The new one would be number four.

Three albums ago they had developed a mode of expression that, for better or worse, defined them. It had arrived as an answer to the question 'If we're not a punk band, what are we?' And that answer, which Andy had called 'policification', was a melding of talents, tastes and styles, the best of three musical brains. Reggae, rock, skitter, shimmer and swoop had served them well, but it had clearly come to the end of its usefulness. Something new was needed.

Other bands, the ones that started at school, grow together. The Beatles – the unavoidable comparison – started out excited about simple rhymes and the novelty of the major sixth chord, then embarked with George Martin on a collective journey of discovery, each introducing his new finds into the mix. If you bend the string far enough, you can get an entirely different note! What happens if we turn the tape backwards? Hey, everybody, look at my new sitar! Every album was a snapshot of where they'd got to.

Sting, Andy and Stewart didn't come together as semi-amateurs learning their craft. They'd done most of the learning before they met. There was no journey of discovery – just a blending of what was. Policification was one result of that blend. There might have been others, but the strain of working them out would most likely have ended in a messy murder trial. And, even if they'd been able to work one out, there was no guarantee it would have been successful. Many roads lead to free jazz.

Somebody was going to have to take a very definite and positive lead.

★ ★ ★

Sting already had a name for the album, *Ghost in the Machine*, which he had taken from Arthur Koestler's 1967 book about the human mind and its appetite for self-destruction.

'The book talks about how the modern brain of Homo Sapiens is grafted onto older and more primitive prototypes, and how in certain situations these reptilian modes of thinking can rise up and overcome our higher modes of logic and reason,' Sting wrote, looking back on the album in his 2007 book, *Lyrics by Sting*. 'I tried, as far as it was possible in a collection of pop songs, to deal with some of these issues.'

There are other undercurrents in the lyrics – themes of love, guilt and betrayal.

In the same book, Sting mentions that Trudie Styler, Frances's friend who'd played a witch in *Macbeth*, then had an affair with Peter O'Toole, 'helped me with the French and a lot of the passion' contained in 'Hungry For You', a song that speaks, in French, of the singer's love for '*ma belle traîtresse*' ('my beautiful traitor') and lingers on the lines about thwarted desire and longing.

★ ★ ★

He was exploring new musical directions, too. 'Spirits In The Material World' was written on 'one of those Casio keyboards. I just tap, tap, tap and there it was, just by accident. That was the first time I'd ever touched a synthesiser.'

This was a confession that, in the synth-drenched aural landscape of 1981, seemed almost inconceivable.

July's number one, 'Tainted Love', featured only the voice of Marc Almond and the multilayered synths of David Ball. Gary Numan's sell-out concerts at Wembley were awash with oscillators and it was a Roland RD-800 that made the Human League go 'duh' with such authority.

★ ★ ★

When Sting was done with his Casio, the band assembled at Surrey Sound for an afternoon's pre-recording, then decamped to Super Bear Studios in Nice for some more.

On 16 June, they all flew to New York, where Andy went out on the town with John Belushi, and the day after that they flew to Antigua, where they picked up another plane to the Caribbean island of Montserrat.

CHAPTER FIFTEEN

THOUGHTFUL POP FOR NOW PEOPLE

The notion that it was beneficial for a band to go off into the country and get their shit together had been around for a while. It was a hippy thing: communal living and big doses of nature (trees, birds, lakes and mountains, but not drizzle or sleet) were both good for spiritual growth and therefore enhanced creativity, which meant better albums, which meant more hits.

The band Traffic, soon after they formed, retreated to a farmhouse in rural Berkshire that had neither running water nor electricity. It was the perfect idyll for five minutes or so. Then somebody said, 'Where do we plug the amps in?' and a generator had to be sent for.

The Rolling Stones' album *Exile on Main Street* was largely recorded at Nellcôte, the house that Keith Richards had rented in Villefranche-sur-Mer in the South of France. Visitors during the recording process included some of the world's most experienced drug users and for a time it must have seemed that Nellcôte was, all by itself, keeping the economies of Laos and Colombia afloat.

But there was always a danger, with a band living hugger-mugger in the middle of nowhere with often no responsible adults around to exercise the restraining hand, that chaos and madness would descend, that somebody might decide they were invisible and walk naked through the nearest town, or begin to harbour a grudge against elm trees and acquire explosives.

Even greater was the danger, when they were recording at a studio in the middle of nowhere, that the drummer might, in the middle of the night, wipe all the guitar parts from the master tapes and replace them with ambient sound, or the bass player would try to bury an entire song in the garden.

It was in the spirit of 'going off into the country and getting your shit together' that the Ward brothers opened Rockfield Studios in rural Monmouthshire and Richard Branson opened the Manor in Oxfordshire. Then George Martin, the Beatles' producer, took the whole thing to some sort of extreme when he opened AIR Studios, in Montserrat.

It's a tiny volcanic island, a British overseas territory in the Lesser Antilles, 16 kilometres by 11, favoured in early colonial times by the Irish, with the result that Irish was the main language there until the middle of the 19th century. The giant ditch frog survives there, as does the galliwasp, a kind of lizard.

George Martin went to Montserrat on holiday, fell in love with the place and decided to build a state-of-the-art studio there, better equipped, and certainly more salubriously positioned, than anything in London, Los Angeles or New York. The 30-acre site featured, as well as the studio, living accommodation, a pool, a games room, all just 10 minutes from a beach where speedboats and water skis were on hand for those Young Ones moments.

It became a sort of reward for bands who'd spent their formative years playing Tiffany's and Jake's Beer Cellar and recording in pegboard and electrocution studios off the Goldhawk Road. The sun would shine, bananaquits would share their breakfast, they'd spend all day by the pool and in the evenings sit with rum punch and look out to sea waiting for the green flash. And, in between times, they'd make a record.

The arispopracy loved Montserrat: Dire Straits, Elton, the Stones, Duran Duran, Ultravox, Clapton, Lou Reed, Black Sabbath all did time there. It was an opportunity to work, rest and play. To chill.

Unfortunately, the Police weren't good at chilling. When they were recording, they rarely strayed beyond cantankerous.

Stewart described a typical Police recording session on Montserrat as 'one of us overdubbing in the studio, one of us off by the pool, and the third sitting by the mixing desk being abusive, insulting and inflammatory. Which, as it turns out, gets the job done.'

Hugh Padgham, who'd made hits for Elton, Phil Collins, Mott the Hoople and lots of other people, had been flown in to produce. After a few days he resigned, unwilling to take the aggro. He was prevailed upon to stay, but the squabbling continued.

Sting had fixed ideas. He had demoed the songs with drum machine, piano, bass and guitar, and needed to be persuaded that his arrangements were not perfect. He wanted to play saxophone on some of the tracks – he'd been practising since January – and to import a keyboard player, Jean Roussel.

Andy and Stewart had doubts. Saxophones and keyboards were not Police things. They had developed as a trio. That was how they worked best.

'Every Little Thing She Does Is Magic' was a particular sticking point. Andy and Stewart didn't want to do it at all. It was too poppy.

Sting dug his heels in. 'I was saying, "But listen, it's a hit." We tried to do it from scratch as the Police, but it didn't have the same energy as the demo. After a degree of hair-pulling and torturing on my part, I got the band to play over the top of my demo.'

Andy wasn't happy at all. 'As the guitar player, I was saying, "What the fuck is this? This is not the Police sound."'

Stewart wasn't happy, either. 'I remember saying, "Okay, put up Sting's original demo and I'll show you how crummy it is." So, Sting stood over me and waved me through all the changes. I did just one take, and that became the record. Then Andy did the same thing on the guitar. We just faced the music, bit the bullet, and used Sting's arrangements and demo. Damn.'

Sting decided he didn't want Andy to play at all on 'Spirits In The Material World'. He wanted synth – no guitar. After a degree of verbal violence, a compromise was reached to use synth and guitar. Then Sting took control of the mix and Andy's guitar part all but disappeared.

The icing on the cake came when Sting vehemently opposed A&M's idea to release Andy's composition 'Omegaman' as the first single to be taken from the album. Sting won and 'Invisible Sun' was released instead.

It was 'very horrible, very dark', Andy said. 'Our marriages were breaking up. The Police's marriage was breaking up and yet we had to make another record.'

Andy's wife Kate phoned him while he was out there to tell him she wanted a divorce. In later interviews, he attributed the estrangement of her affections to his love of groupies and long absences from home.

'You can imagine the position we were in,' he said. 'We were like the three most desirable men in the world, so what's a guy going to do?'

'The band was just fucking gigantic,' Andy said in an interview in 2015. 'It was insane, and it was a very hard test on a marriage. And, in fact, we all got divorced. A lot of people got very hurt.'

★ ★ ★

At the end of July, the band flew from Montserrat to Venezuela in an old DC-3. As if he wasn't having a bad enough time already, a window opened and Andy was almost sucked out of the aeroplane. Sting's heroic bodyguard, Larry Bernet, saved the day and managed to secure the window before the guitarist was lost. No foul play was suspected.

★ ★ ★

In Venezuela, they played two shows at the Poliedro de Caracas. The army turned up at the end of the second, rounded up a group of teenage boys at gunpoint and threw them into the backs of trucks. The boys had been press-ganged into the army. Andy said, 'You feel so impotent – it's hard to accept that you are just in a foreign country and that's the way it is.'

In Canada, at Le Studio in Morin-Heights, Quebec, they started mixing the new album. There was no doubt now that Stewart and Andy were regarded as Sting's backing band and that their say counted for little.

On 22 August, they played a new wave festival at Philadelphia's Liberty Bell Park – appearing with three horn players who called themselves 'Chops'.

'They are nice guys,' Andy said, 'but what it has to do with the Police beats me – actually I hate it, so does Stewart... What next? Nothing seems out in the open any more.'

Sting dug his heels in. 'When Stewart's good he's great and when he's bad he's fucking awful. The best drummers are orchestral. They play the song without losing the pulse. That's what I want from him – the pulse not the flash.'

On 23 August, they played their last gig for a month or so at the Grove in Oakville, Ontario, and were two hours late getting on stage.

Many of the crowd – there were 30,000 of them – had been waiting 11 hours, enduring various support acts. Some of them had to leave to catch trains and missed the Police entirely.

★ ★ ★

Back in London the band found it hard to settle.

Stewart felt out of place and out of sorts. He told *Creem* magazine:

> I went to an old friend's party recently, and all the people there were Police fans and I could hear them whispering, 'There's Stewart Copeland.' And I'd be introduced to somebody and it'd be like, 'Here's Shirley, she's a big fan of the band,' and Shirley would go 'Ooo,' and giggle and stuff.
>
> I have not failed to notice the absurdity of the way that I am now allowed to sit here and pontificate away, and everything I say is believed to be of immense value. The drugs, the marriage breakdowns, the ego – you know, when you have this image projected onto you, it's possible to forget your own personality that you started out with. You start believing in the image that shows up in the papers and that you see reflected in the eyes of the kids and you lose your own personality.

Meanwhile, Andy and Kate began the painful process of separation and divorce.

Sting's marriage was in trouble, too, although that, for the time being, remained a closely kept secret.

★ ★ ★

In 1979, *The Secret Policeman's Ball*, a charity benefit in aid of Amnesty International, had featured mostly comedians, including several Pythons, Peter Cook, Alan Bennett and (the outsider in the mostly Oxbridge gathering) Billy Connolly. To provide a bit of variety, Tom Robinson and Pete Townshend both did a short acoustic set. Townshend's duet with classical guitarist John Williams on 'Won't Get Fooled Again' provided possibly the show's most memorable moment.

In 1981, for a second Amnesty show, *The Secret Policeman's Other Ball*, the producers (Martin Lewis, Peter Walker and John Cleese) decided to bring in more musicians. Phil Collins, Eric Clapton, Jeff Beck, Bob

Geldof, Donovan and Sting all performed. Phil Collins sat at the piano and did 'In The Air Tonight'. Jeff and Eric did 'Crossroads'.

The show ran for four evenings and the juxtaposition of acts and charity appeals gave the whole a dream-like quality. Here's Donovan doing 'Catch The Wind', here's a film about people being horribly tortured, here's Rowan Atkinson pulling funny faces.

Sting was positioned in the middle of an empty stage. The voice came out of darkness before the spotlight hit him. 'Roxanne', he sang, and you could hear the hairs standing up on the backs of people's necks.

He'd become a fan of the newly emerged 'alternative comedy', and for a while befriended its chief exponent, Alexei Sayle.

Here's a story from Alexei's memoir, *Thatcher Stole My Trousers*.

'In December 1981, I was appearing on a mixed bill at the Albany Empire in Deptford. By then David Stafford, as well as writing with me, was providing the music for the songs I sang in my live act.'

Sting showed up at the Albany Empire to see the show.

My memory is that Sting got out of the car and so that he wouldn't be recognised by the public he put on a motorcycle helmet, which he wore as he walked to his seat before taking it off, at least I think he took it off because I've also got an image of him watching the entire show wearing a full face crash helmet.

Sting thought it was all brilliant, all the chaos was a reminder of his wilder past. Afterwards we went to the Joe Allen Restaurant, which they kept open especially for us. David Stafford was also in the party, but he was suffering from a cold and had drunk too much Night Nurse. Then we also drank a lot of champagne. At one point David tried to discuss guitar technique with Sting. 'Do you use open plangency?' he asked 'No, I generally play a curved fretboard in D.' 'Fucking hell!' shouted David. Then his second wife took him home, but on leaving the restaurant the night air hit him and he was sick all over the bonnet of Sting's limousine.

[Author's note: I used the bonnet of the car to support myself. A little may have splashed on the radiator grille and front bumper, but 'all over the bonnet' is an exaggeration. As I drew myself up from the semi-crouching position, I saw the look on the face of Sting's driver, sitting at the wheel of the car. There was murder in those eyes. Also, it's kind of Alexei to offer excuses, but I don't think Night Nurse came into it. I was just very, very drunk. Also, although I may briefly have made some unfocused comments about open tunings, I have never in my life used the word 'plangency'.]

The big news story that year was the marriage – or 'fairy-tale wedding' – of Charles, Prince of Wales, to Diana Spencer, Viscount Althorp's daughter. Her engagement ring had 14 diamonds and a 12-carat Ceylon sapphire set in white gold. Once she got photographed with the sun behind her so you could see a vague outline of her legs through her frock. They dug out the big 72-point type for that one and got quotes from top shadowy-leg experts. She won an award at school for taking good care of a guinea pig. She taught Charles how to tap dance. Diana's dress cost £9,000 and had a 25-foot-long train. On the big day, she got flummoxed and called her new husband 'Philip Charles' instead of 'Charles Philip'. Unemployment had reached three million. There was bitter civil war raging in Lebanon, with Syrian, Israeli and American troops engaged on one side or another. There was another civil war raging in Northern Ireland. And something close to a civil war was raging in Brixton in London, Chapeltown in Leeds, Moss Side in Manchester, Toxteth in Liverpool and Handsworth in Birmingham. In Liverpool, the police used CS gas in an attempt to quell the rioters, the first time ever on the British mainland.

For many, the enduring image of 1981 was not the fairy-tale prince and princess waving from the balcony at Buckingham Palace, but the haunting shots of Horace Panter, bass player with the Specials, driving the band around the streets of London in a 1961 Vauxhall Cresta with the rest of the band in the car with him, singing 'Ghost Town'.

★ ★ ★

'Invisible Sun', the first UK single from the new album, released at the end of September, was a song written about Frances's home town, Belfast. 'The Troubles' that had been going on since either the mid-1960s or the early 17th century, depending on your point of view, had reached a terrible impasse.

In HM Prison Maze, a hunger strike by Republican prisoners, held in protest against the withdrawal of their special category (effectively political prisoner) status, had ended after 10 had died of starvation, including Bobby Sands, who had recently been elected Member of Parliament for Fermanagh and South Tyrone.

Explosions and gunfire had become part of everyday life, always terrifying but no longer remarkable.

The song was not partisan. It's not even specifically about Northern Ireland. It simply expresses a faith that the 'invisible sun' exists, to bring hope and 'give its heat to everyone'.

Stewart identified the song as being about Beirut, where he had grown up. The Palestine Liberation Organization had its base there. The Israeli military laid siege to the town, which escalated to saturation bombing.

'My home town was being vilified by the media as a terrorist stronghold, and it was being blasted by bombs and napalm – 20,000 Lebanese were killed that year. And the Lebanese must have been feeling some heat from the invisible sun, because they were keeping their peckers up.'

A video for the song was put together by Derek Burbidge. It shows black-and-white scenes of the war-torn landscape in Northern Ireland, superimposed sporadically with images of Sting's blond loveliness.

★ ★ ★

The BBC decided that the subject matter was too controversial and banned the video, but the single still made number two in the charts.

★ ★ ★

The album *Ghost in the Machine* was released at the beginning of October.

'It would be pretty pompous if I turned round and said this album is going to change the way people think,' Sting said at the time, to pretty much universal agreement. The sleeve 'showed our three faces transposed into digital images' and this reduction is meant to suggest that they are the 'ghosts in the machine'. It takes a stretch to see them as faces at all, although they could be letters of an alien alphabet, signifying something appropriately enigmatic.

The press was good. Robin Denselow in the *Guardian* liked the new lyrical departure, comparing it to late-period Beatles. 'It's an album of thoughts and questions rather than simple answers, and these range from the semi-religious to the semi-political.' He liked the music, too, praising Andy's 'complex embroidery', admiring 'Sting's newly developed skill as saxophonist', and respecting the simplicity of, for instance, 'Demolition Man', 'so any new mysticism is offset with an Eighties' hard edge'.

Debra Rae Cohen, in *Rolling Stone*, found much to praise, too, claiming that although the Police of *Reggatta* and *Zenyatta* were 'relentlessly, calculatedly middlebrow', the ideas on the new album were 'strongly stated, consistent and compelling. The thrashing, denatured funk of "Too Much Information", the whirlpool riff that punctuates "Omegaman" and the oppressive, hymn like aspects of "Invisible Sun" all bespeak claustrophobia and frustration, and the lyrics bear them out.'

Robin Smith in *Record Mirror* said it was 'the best thing they've ever done' and called it 'thoughtful pop for now people'.

Most of the others piled in with the encomiums, leaving Charles Shaar Murray, in *NME*, pretty out on a limb with his doubts and criticisms.

'O Sting, where is thy depth? And whoever suggested that it was necessary or desirable to plumb it?' he began. And he ended with, 'The fact remains that – as far as this particular listener is concerned – "The Ghost In The Machine" is AMAAAAAAAAAZINGLY DULL. Sting is obviously a decent, intelligent chap and if we were debating politics and philosophy, I'd probably find large areas of agreement with him, but dull music with worthy sentiments attached is, ultimately, no more rewarding an aesthetic experience than dull music with foul sentiments.'

Shaar Murray's censure was pretty much par for the course for *NME*, which had developed a tendency to disagree on principle with anything the other music papers said.

Miles complained. 'Look at the NME Top 50 albums of last year, and the Police are not mentioned once. Yet we sold in the first three weeks of release of the last album more records than the rest of the Top 10 albums put together. It's almost unreal! Quite remarkable! The group has done more for the British music business than anyone in the last 10 years – than anyone since the Beatles, in fact. We brought the new wave to America!'

Ghost in the Machine went straight to number one 'in every country in the world' – to quote Charles Shaar Murray again – 'where Coca-Cola is sold.'

★ ★ ★

The second single, 'Every Little Thing She Does Is Magic', was the song that Andy and Stewart hadn't wanted to do, but Sting had said, 'But listen, it's a hit.' And he was right, damn him. Released at the beginning of November, it made number one in the UK, and, among other Coca-Cola-buying countries, only the Japanese were able to resist hurling it straight into the Top 5.

★ ★ ★

1981 was the year that MTV took to the air (or at least came down the cable) in the US, opening with the words, 'Ladies and gentlemen, rock and roll.'

Then, in a declaration of intent, it segued into the video of 'Video Killed The Radio Star' by the Buggles.

From the start, the station was music 24 hours a day, except for the occasional blackouts when an employee forgot to change the tape (which, in the early days, were not infrequent).

Eventually bands and record companies got used to the idea that every single release had to come with a video for MTV play, but in the early days this was still something of a novelty for US bands. This gave British bands, who for years had been producing videos for those difficult days when they couldn't show up at the *Top of the Pops* studio, an advantage.

Some say that MTV – not Miles and the Police – was responsible for the second 'British invasion' of America.

The Police had been making excellent videos, directed by Derek Burbidge, since 1978 and MTV ate them up.

Even before the record had been released in the US, MTV was showing the 'Every Little Thing She Does Is Magic' video practically on never-ending loop. Shot on Montserrat, it features Sting playing his Van Zalinge electric stand-up bass with a bow, an outdoor concert with lots of locals dancing around and a steel band playing pans, and much messing with the AIR mixing desk including a moment, which must have been harrowing for George Martin when he saw the video ('Do they have any idea how much it cost just to *transport* that thing to Montserrat?'), when Andy jumps on the desk and dances on the faders.

'We weren't aware of trashing it at all,' Stewart said. 'We were in the habit – because we were all very fit – of climbing over it, because it was very long. And, if you were over there and you wanted to get over here to hit a fader or something, we'd just climb over it.'

And, on the way, maybe, do a bit of dancing.

★ ★ ★

In the autumn, they kept themselves busy.

Sting started shooting another film – more of which in the next chapter.

Andy organised a photography exhibition in Dublin and worked with Robert Fripp on an album, *I Advance Masked*, released in the following year.

Stewart and Sonja bought a big old house in Bledlow Ridge, Buckinghamshire, and moved in.

★ ★ ★

The third single, 'Spirits In The Material World', was released at the beginning of December. The video, shot again at AIR in Montserrat, is subdued. Just the three of them miming to the track (and Andy miming to a guitar part that's no longer audible). Disappointingly, it didn't go Top 10 in the UK or US and didn't even make the Top 40 in Germany. The Human League had the Christmas number one – and it's not difficult to understand why a song bewailing the fact that there wasn't really a solution to our dire political situation might not have the edge over one about meeting someone who was working as a waitress in a cocktail bar.

★ ★ ★

Then they were back on tour again.

★ ★ ★

On 12 December, they played the Marquee in London. It was a closely guarded secret, with tickets only available to the official fan club.

Jayne Hawkins, aged 14, braved the icy weather to come down from Coventry. She was one of the first to get in and bagged a place at the front, right next to where Sting would stand.

'I could not believe my eyes when the band came on stage and launched into the first song. Was I really here, was it true that my heroes were here right in front of me? YES, it was. I was literally a few inches away from Sting! What a night that was, and what a gig!'

Then, by way of contrast, they did three nights at the Wembley Arena, the size of three or four aircraft hangars but with much worse acoustics. They played in front of a massive back-projection screen which, during

'Invisible Sun', showed the bleak black-and-white footage of the wrecked streets of Belfast that the BBC had banned.

'Of course, the ultimate irony is that you'll get Legs & Co. fucking dancing to it [on *Top of the Pops*],' Sting announced at the concert, 'in sombreros and suntan oil thinking it's about the sun. I don't give a shit.'

At one of the Wembley concerts, Sting was heard screaming at Stewart, 'If you speed up any more, you'll fly up your own arse.'

The *NME* commented that Stewart had descended to a 'taciturn, vaguely sulky presence' when he's not 'birching his gear with desperate conviction, as if determined to drive it to the front of the stage'. And adding that 'Old Andy, with his baggy blue trousers and glittery jacket, seems to know he's the lottery winner of a sort. He does his best to forget those old guitar immortal posturings but when there's not much else happening he sidles to the front of the stage and leans tentatively back in a half-remembered gesture of heroics.'

But the *NME* had to admit that the concert, even if it 'panhandled the obvious, still managed exhilaration in heavy doses'.

The fans felt only that exhilaration and screamed themselves hoarse for encores.

And the Police donated the profits from their British shows to charity. Just from these few gigs, the Outlandos Trust made £60,000.

★ ★ ★

At the end of 1981, you could barely turn the telly on without one or more of the Police cropping up.

At the beginning of December, they did *The Kenny Everett Television Show*, the comedy/pop/mildly pornographic entertainment that had the youth of the nation in its thrall, and Mrs Mary Whitehouse, national scourge of filth, up in arms. Kenny interviewed Sting (who was wearing a drapey shirt open to the navel) for his 'Sex Symbol Request Spot', for which viewers had supposedly written in asking Kenny to take liberties with Sting on their behalf. Thus, on behalf on Barbara of Birmingham, he caressed Sting's nipples; on behalf of Cotty of Colchester, he kissed his ear; and, on behalf of Agnes of Aberystwyth, he wrestled him to the ground and simulated sex.

Just before Christmas, the BBC aired a 40-minute documentary, *The Police – Montserrat '81*, presented by Jools Holland, directed again by Derek Burbidge. The programme was mostly the videos already seen, and shot in Montserrat, of their latest hits, but in between Jools interviewed the three of them.

Everything is pally and cheerful. Nothing is in evidence to suggest that these lovely chaps have ever had a cross word or disagreed about anything – other, perhaps, than the fact that Jools never speaks to them as a group, just one by one. Jools talks to Andy about his guitar pedals, to Sting about his songwriting techniques and to Stewart about the construction of the reggae rhythm.

You can just about see that Stewart has something written in large letters on his tom-toms, but the camera angle makes it impossible to read. The letters in fact spell 'FUCK... OFF... YOU... CUNT...' and they remained a feature of the kit for a good while, ensuring that every thwack was a protest and every fill a bitter harangue.

'That was for me,' Sting said, later. 'He was hitting me with the drumsticks.'

★ ★ ★

Artemis 81, the BBC film that Sting had been involved with in April, was aired on 29 December.

The synopsis in *Radio Times* said: 'A Danish museum case shattered, the pieces of a pagan statue hidden in cars on a North Sea ferry, the subsequent deaths of ferry passengers, an old musician terrified that a curse upon him will cause the devastation of the Earth.'

At various times, Sting has described this plot as 'sub-*Star Wars*' and 'a balls-up'.

It wasn't well received.

Melody Maker said, 'Old Stingo carried himself not half badly, though he didn't have that hard a task, mostly staring with vacant love, being generally beneficent and uttering lines like "I am not of your earth... I do not know this 'cold'."

'There's no disputing his stage and camera presence. His mere appearance on the horizon seemed enough to make a whole Dormobile explode. But while *Artemis 81* bought him a few more pages of script than the Face in *Quadrophenia*, a few meatier parts wouldn't go amiss.'

He was already at work on a meatier part, playing a Satanic rapist in the film of *Brimstone and Treacle*, written by Dennis Potter, directed by Richard Loncraine, and co-starring Denholm Elliott and Joan Plowright, all Premier League players at the tops of their games and very distinguished company for a popster who'd neither been to RADA nor done rep.

During the filming, Denholm Elliott, playing the dad, had the hots for his co-star.

'Sting was a gorgeous lad,' he told Wensley Clarkson in his book *A Tale in the Sting*. 'I fancied him like crazy, but I usually had a rule not to get involved with any fellow actors. I thought he was coming on to me. I was probably wrong, but I convinced myself that he wanted to go to bed with me. I did everything in my power to lure him into bed, but I failed miserably.'

It was while working on *Brimstone*, at the end of 1981, that Sting nearly ended his bass-playing career for good by smashing his fist through a window and lacerating his hand.

The following night, the Police played the Birmingham Exhibition Centre. Sting had his arm in a sling, but he could sing, so Danny Quatrochi was brought on to play bass.

There were other problems that night, too. Andy wasn't feeling well when the car picked him up to take him to the Birmingham gig. By the time he got to Hammersmith, he was in severe pain. At Hammersmith Hospital, they diagnosed kidney stones. They did things to him to make the stones go away. Then, still groggy from the operation, he was bundled into the back of a car and ferried to Birmingham, where 14,000 fans greeted their crippled heroes.

★ ★ ★

1981 had been the year of Sting. He was everywhere, glowering moodily out of the pages of glossy magazines, sharing the secrets of his sex life in the tabloids and talking philosophy and politics in posh Sundays.

'I have a pressure cooker existence,' he said, 'and every so often it explodes. People see the glamorous side of things, but my life is not easy. I am propelled by rocket fuel and those around me are inclined to get burned. I can't change myself.'

CHAPTER SIXTEEN

I AM A ROCK'N'ROLL ASSHOLE

'The trouble with society these days is ignorance – from the Third World, who are ignorant about birth control and farming, to the kids in the streets of Manchester who don't know what to do with themselves,' Sting told the *News of the World*. 'They have a really tough time with unemployment and no prospects. It doesn't surprise me there's vandalism and violence.'

The Police were doing their bit to address the problem. 'The band's British earnings are poured into a trust fund for youth clubs. We'll buy equipment for aspiring musicians to help them along the road because I feel it's a crime to see so much talent go to waste.'

He was in his thirties now and, like a proper Geordie down the pub, was fond of sounding off about any number of pressing issues. 'Women should stop relying on men, and stop blaming us for everything,' he said. 'I've no time for those who can't change a wheel or mend a broken window. That's their fault. They owe it to themselves to learn. After all, men can do traditionally female jobs. I can cook. I wasn't taught to.'

The Police were selling newspapers nearly as successfully as Princess Diana. A pic of one or the other – or, even better, an interview – could do wonders for a flagging circulation.

When interviewed, they were rarely more than two questions in before they found themselves batting away rumours of a break-up. 'That's not true,' Andy told *Creem*. 'There's always tensions and difficulties. There's a lot of pressure in a situation like this. There are huge flare-ups. But we never hold grudges.'

Sting picked up the theme:

Journalists are always trying to get into the politics of the group, trying to get dirt on how I supposedly ride roughshod over the others, because it makes good copy…

It's not as if we're bound together in financial brotherhood. We're all very free; the group could end tomorrow without damaging any of us.

I'm not irresponsible; I'm not just gonna walk out. But if something really interests me, and I see the group standing in my way… I know it sounds really callous, but…

★ ★ ★

They were A-list superstars. On tour, 5,000 or 6,000 was a boutique gig. Mostly it was stadiums, with the full priest-god treatment.

On 15 January, they played the Boston Garden for the first night of a tour of the Americas that lasted till 22 April.

They'd flown out that morning. To save his jet-lagged voice, Sting kept the chat between numbers to a minimum, but still got the 15,500-strong audience chanting 'when the world is coming down, you make the best of what's still around', and 'one world is enough for all of us' – proselytising the philosophy of the new album to the true believers.

And he had a word for the punters sitting behind the stage.

'I hope you like our arses,' he said.

And the punters sitting behind the stage cheered their arses.

At the end, they did the full rock star number – 'they ran off stage, were wrapped in blankets held by their security crew, into the limousines, and off to three hundred dollar a night hotel suites', it said in the *Bostonian*. 'And the story goes that four years ago when they came to Boston to play at the Rat they slept in their van.'

All of their last three albums had gone platinum in the US. They were voted Band of the Year in *Rolling Stone* and Sting tied with Mick Jagger for the title of Best Singer.

In New York, New York, Sting's vagabond shoes took him to see Frank Sinatra at Radio City Music Hall. Afterwards, Frank signed an autograph for him. It said, 'to the new Blue Eyes'.

He was A number one, top of the list, king of the hill.

When they played Madison Square Garden again, he looked up and said, 'It seems very curious that this roof on Madison Square Garden has been here so long. I realise tonight's the night it goes. Help us raise the fucking roof of Madison Square Garden in New York, New York,' and for a breath-stopping moment everybody thought he would actually do it.

The dissolution was turned up a notch or two.

'Everywhere we turned up there was a party. The rot set in. You know, the water keeps hitting the rock and it finally starts to crumble.'

John Blake, then editing a celeb gossip column for the *Sun*, joined them at an after-show party and provided a lurid (although probably accurate) description.

★ ★ ★

Next to him [Sting] a marshmallow-breasted blonde is whispering of the things she could do if only he would let her. Though Sting doesn't appear to be listening, she looks furious when her burblings are momentarily interrupted by a fat man, sweat dripping from his face on to his solid polyester suit, who muscles in to tell the singer of the new film he wants him to star in.

'It's made for you... made for you...,' he splutters.

Close by, like a vulture hovering, is a cross-eyed drug dealer waiting his moment to try to offer the star the little envelope of cocaine crystals he holds in his hand. And every few seconds a fresh, nervous supplicant arrives to plead an autograph, a picture, or simply a gawp. To the victor, truly, belongs the spoils.

Not all the praise was unstinting.

The *Washington Post*, for instance, was sniffy about their show at the Capital Centre: 'When the band played melodic, up-tempo songs like "De Do Do Do, De Da Da Da", they were as refreshing as the Bee Gees, the Jacksons or Elton John. When they played slower, artsier material, they were as pompously dreary as Yes or the Moody Blues.'

Trudie and Sting celebrating at Stringfellows nightclub, 1982. Sting introduced her as his 'mistress'.
RICHARD YOUNG/SHUTTERSTOCK

Sting using his powers to fascinate on Paula Yates on *The Tube*, 1982. SHUTTERSTOCK

The Police at the Shea Stadium, 1983. 'What else was there to do after reaching this peak?'
EBET ROBERTS/REDFERNS

Sting surrounded by the press at Sydney Airport, 1984.

Andy comparing calluses with Robert Fripp after the release of their album *I Advance Masked.*

Stewart playing polo, 1984.
THEODORE LIASI/ALAMY

Sting recording 'Feed the World', 1984. STEVE HURRELL/REDFERNS

Sting on stage for the finale of Live Aid, 1985. MIRRORPIX

'We've been very lucky.' A rather tense band and their manager collecting their Brit Award for Outstanding Contribution to Music, 1985. STEVE FENTON/SHUTTERSTOCK

Sting and Quentin Crisp in the film *The Bride*. When Stewart mocked his performance it was the final straw for Sting. AF ARCHIVE/ALAMY

Sting and the musicians that he marshalled for the Blue Turtles tour, including Kenny Kirkland, Branford Marsalis and Omar Hakim, 1986. DAVE HOGAN/HULTON ARCHIVE/GETTY IMAGES

Sting and Stewart joshing around at the Whisky a Go Go after announcing their comeback tour, 2007. 'I am certifiably insane,' Sting said. HECTOR MATA/AFP VIA GETTY IMAGES

The Copelands, the Summers and the Sumners all in one room to be made Knights in the Order of Arts and Letters by the French government, 2007. JULIEN HEKIMIAN/GETTY IMAGES

The final concert of the reunion tour in Madison Square Garden, 7 August 2008. 'We went out and creamed everything in sight.' ZUMA PRESS, INC./ALAMY

The Police – the band that did everything right. KEVIN MAZUR/WIREIMAGE FOR KSM

On some of the gigs they were supported by the Go-Go's, the 'all-girl' group fronted by Belinda Carlisle. The Go-Go's had had a million-selling album in the previous year, and, later in 1982, were nominated for a Grammy. Andy was a fan. 'I rode in a limo with them tonight and blushed to the roots at their absolutely filthy conversation – they make us look like choirboys.'

On the longer hops, these days, they travelled in a private jet. 'Basically a Holiday Inn with wings,' Andy said. 'It comes with a stewardess who is falling over herself to please us – this might include a sandwich or a blowjob.'

Jack Nicholson showed up to the party after the show at the Forum in Los Angeles, along with Michael Douglas and (of course) John Belushi.

The moved down to South America.

In Brazil, they fooled around with Great Train Robber Ronnie Biggs, self-exiled beyond the clutches of the UK filth. Ronnie had recorded a few tracks with the Sex Pistols and had become an obligatory landmark on the rock-star tourist itinerary.

'Sting is a good guy,' Ronnie said. 'We played some table tennis, supped a few beers, got a little sloshed. It was all very civilised. He was bloody determined not to let me win a game of table tennis. That guy's a fierce competitor and I can fully see why he's become such an incredible success story.'

The South American leg of the tour moved on to Chile. The Police played two nights. The fact that they played there at all was widely criticised. Sting had done concerts for Amnesty International. Chile was the land where human rights had been forgotten.

It was a desperate time in the country's history. Under the military dictatorship of Augusto Pinochet, the national congress was dissolved, union activities banned, and tens of thousands had been imprisoned, tortured and/or killed. People – 'the disappeared' – were taken and simply never heard of again. The economy had meanwhile been trashed. Inflation was running at 20 per cent, unemployment at 43 per cent.

'I don't believe we condoned the regime by playing in Chile any more than by playing in England we'd be condoning the regime of Margaret Thatcher,' Sting said. 'It's different in South Africa, where there's a white elite that craves acceptance and the performers who go there provide that acceptance. I'd never go to South Africa. In Chile, we played to 30,000 kids. I didn't see any political torturers among them.'

Amnesty had given him a message, in Spanish, to read out. It wasn't much. Just: 'This next song is for the "disappeared".'

'Looking at all the machine guns that were surrounding the place, I decided not to read it. I've been in those countries before. I know how instant the violence can be. What we took to Chile was the message of the music, which is, anyway, pretty rebellious. It's like giving out pamphlets, but cleverer.'

Later in the year, when the touring ennui got bad, Andy said, 'I have a very strong urge to empty a bottle of vodka over the sheets and toss a match in it… I am a rock'n'roll asshole.'

★ ★ ★

After life on the road, with roadies and staff to pander to every passing whim – 'He wants a frozen Jubbly in here, now. I don't care if they went out of production in 1968, get them to reopen the factory or something' – home, reality, domesticity, normal life, is a cruel wake-up.

During a quick break in the tour, Sting went home to Frances and Joe in Ireland. Frances was heavily pregnant.

In the local, he offered to buy a round for the entire pub. It didn't go down well. He was taunted by another drinker. Afterwards, he got a (possibly unrelated) threatening letter. He put the house on the market and went back on the road.

In April, Sting got the call that told him that their daughter, Fuchsia Katherine, had been born at the Royal Free Hospital in London. It was a week before the tour finished and he could fly home.

★ ★ ★

He and Frances both knew the marriage was over. Sting had been having an affair with Frances's friend, Trudie Styler.

Shit happens. People fall in love. They fall out of love. They act ungraciously and ungratefully, and their timing is execrable. Hearts get broken. People get irreparably damaged. It's the price of being human.

The only difference money and fame make is that every step they take, every move they make, is watched and reported. Judgements are passed. The humiliations are compounded, the guilt intensified.

Often, when talking about artists and musicians, much is made of the relationship between the emotional life and the work, but it's never simple.

Knowing that 'Hungry For You' or 'Every Little Thing She Does Is Magic' may have been inspired by Trudie is interesting, but no more so than knowing that 'Roxanne' was inspired by a theatre poster or 'Walking On The Moon' was inspired by a drunken wobble in a hotel room.

Ultimately, a song is about whatever the listener thinks it's about. If a listener gets more enjoyment out of 'Mull Of Kintyre' if they think it's about hot spiced wine, or if they believe that 'Waterloo Sunset' is a coded celebration of the defeat of Napoleon's army in 1815, or if they prefer 'White Christmas' to be thinly veiled racism, that's up to them. The Sistine Chapel, if you think it's about Santa passing the Christmas spirit to his Chief Elf, is still an impressive and moving work of art.

And, even if there is a link between inspiration and art, it's by no means inevitable that *this* inspiration will lead to *that* art.

Seeing a poster for *Cyrano de Bergerac* and then going for a walk in a red-light district might easily have inspired another songwriter to compose something about a prostitute with a big nose ('it really is quite sizeable, is surgery advisable?').

'Inspiration' is one tiny factor in the making of a work of art. It might start the process off, but without huge dollops of craft, experience, influence, theft, taste, slog and various indefinable qualities that get called 'talent', the song could never happen.

And songs are never about one thing. They're about all things. 'When you're writing a song,' Sting told Phil Sutcliffe, 'you're looking for the meaning of life.'

Love and heartbreak can, of course, affect the artiste's ability actually to get any work done at all. Andy, in his autobiography *One Train Later*, tells of how the phone call from Kate asking him for a divorce that came while he was in Montserrat recording *Ghost in the Machine* left him dazed and frightened. He found it hard to relate to what was going on in the studio. It seemed distant, irrelevant.

But you'd be hard-pressed to hear that in his playing, and probably fooling yourself if you thought you did. Maybe, if the phone call hadn't come, he would have argued more vehemently to retain his guitar part on, for instance, 'Spirits In The Material World', but that's not to say he would have won the argument.

On the other hand, love and heartbreak provide rattling good copy for journalists: true-life romances with cracking headlines, strong narrative twists and breathtaking reversals. National treasure turned love rat, TV's sweetheart revealed as no better than she ought to be, bishop caught dogging, perfect couple in violent break-up – this is what people want with their mug of brown tea and their oily rag.

'The marriage of rock star Sting and actress Frances Tomelty has run into problems, I am saddened to learn,' John Blake reported in the *Sun*. 'The pair have argued and spent little time together recently – partly because of Sting's fondness for a 27-year-old blonde actress, who was a friend of his wife until recently.'

After that, every scrap of a rumour became sellable copy. A photo of Sting with a 'companion' of some description – anybody other than his wife – was gold.

★ ★ ★

Financially, the band were in great shape.

Andy had been house-hunting. Among those he viewed was that of Bill Oddie, on the market in Hampstead. Bill, as it happened, had just opened the mail when Andy called, and found he was being done for a parking offence. His teenage daughter answered the door. 'Dad, it's the Police,' she said. And Bill wondered when double yellow lines had become a matter for the serious crime squad.

Stewart and Sonja were now lord and lady of the manor in Buckinghamshire. They made everything formal by getting married on 16 July 1982 (Stewart's birthday) – a quiet do at a register office.

Sting – now commonly referred to in the press as 'millionaire popster Sting (30)' – had been doing some serious shopping.

Alexei Sayle, in *Thatcher Stole My Trousers*, remembers popping round to see him.

He didn't seem that pleased by my impromptu visit, which caused me to congratulate myself on how far I'd come. A few years ago, I'd been dropping in unwanted on art students in Maidstone, now I was dropping in unwanted on the biggest pop star in the world. We chatted uneasily for a while. Sting had just bought himself a clavichord, a predecessor of the piano, which had once belonged to Dr Johnson.

'Did it cost a lot?' I asked.

'Well I had to bid for it against the Smithsonian Museum,' he replied.

This was something I'd begun to notice that rich people did. They bought stuff that was the same as ordinary stuff but cost a lot more. So, if you wanted a piano you could either get a nice cheap electric one in a shop or you could be like Sting and buy a piano only if it had first been owned by Dr Johnson. I wondered how far down that road he'd go, if he'd end up only buying things that'd been owned by a famous historical figure, so his knives and forks were Shakespeare's and his underpants had once belonged to Einstein.

Along the way, Sting also acquired a couple of racehorses, Sweetcal and Sandalay, stabled near Newbury, Berkshire, and trained by Peter Cundell.

'Sweetcal is just a bit of fun for Sting,' Cundell said. 'But Sandalay is a really good horse – I have high hopes for him this season.' The high hopes were borne out when, in the following year, Sandalay won the Queen Alexandra Stakes at Ascot.

Stewart, too, acquired horses. He liked to relax by playing polo on his country estate.

He did the place up to suit his taste.

'I've got a 24-track studio at home and I can spend hours there. But that's really doodling, entertaining myself. It really is a power rush to play everything yourself in your own studio.'

Later in the year, the doodling started to pay off when Stewart was commissioned to write the score for a movie, and not just any movie. *Rumble Fish* was a Francis Ford Coppola movie starring Mickey Rourke and Matt Dillon.

★ ★ ★

Sting turned his attention to the Virgin publishing contract he'd signed in 1976 and which had been diverting substantial amounts of his royalties from his pockets into those of Richard Branson's company ever since.

It was an advert that tipped him over the edge. Virgin had licensed 'Don't Stand So Close To Me' for use in a Right Guard deodorant advert. Sting, incensed, was granted an injunction to stop it. He was counter-sued by the manufacturers of Right Guard and the ad agency. It cost him a lot of money, but the ad was pulled.

In July, he and Miles took Virgin to the High Court. The original contract had given Virgin 50 per cent of Sting's publishing earnings on the first two Police albums and 40 per cent on the third, a deal which had, so far, cost Sting an estimated £700,000.

Frances, despite the problems they were having, went into the witness box to testify.

'We were a very naive bunch of people,' she said. 'Just a bunch of idiots really... He [Sting] took his usual attitude of not being interested in anything but singing and playing.'

The case was settled out of court after two weeks to prevent huge legal costs, which had already reached £300,000. Virgin agreed to pay an extra 7.5 per cent on all the songs going back to 1976, in return for guaranteed rights on the next album.

When the negotiations were over, the judge, Mr Justice Mars-Jones, said, 'If I had known it was going to take so much time, I would have written a couple of songs while I was waiting.'

A&M had, in fact, already offered the Police a £1 million advance on the next album.

'It's a great temptation to present them with an album of farting – and they'll be legally bound to give us the money,' Sting said.

★ ★ ★

Americans, it's often reported, admire success. The British – particularly those outside the Home Counties – like their stars to be slightly too small for their boots.

The Police, it was decided, had outgrown theirs. The tall poppy syndrome demands that anybody perceived as having become too rich, too famous, too bloated or too bland must be cut down to size.

It's not just a matter of schadenfreude. It's a question of narrative. Maybe the Americans never tire of the story in which the hero endures the occasional setback but generally stays on an upward track until he gets to heaven, meets God, and God says, 'You're a hero.' But the British like more of a twist. After a while, the story about the good guy who makes a success of it needs pepping with a bit more dramatic oomph. We need to learn that this guy we thought was a hero is actually the villain. We need to know he cheated on his wife, took drugs, hit his dog, neglected his children.

And perhaps the British – the middle-aged newspaper-buying British – need the reassurance, as they read their morning papers, swallowing regret and ruefulness with every mouthful of cornflakes, that you have to be a bastard to get on in this world. 'You see? I never stood a chance. I'm far too nice.'

Sometimes Sting seemed deliberately to set himself up for the put-downs.

On 24 July, he went to the ritziest of ritzy parties hosted by the notorious Saudi Arabian arms dealer Adnan Khashoggi – another of Miles II's acquaintances when the Copelands were kids.

'I got this request and he sent a jet to pick us up and fly us to Monte Carlo,' Sting later told the *Face*. 'I was fascinated by this excess, this madness… and frankly if it was wrong for my public image, well tough.'

He went with Trudie. They signed into the Hermitage Hotel as 'Mr & Mrs Sumner'. At the party they hung out with Ryan O'Neal (star of *Love Story*, *Paper Moon* and *Barry Lyndon*) and Farrah Fawcett (one of the original *Charlie's Angels*).

'Sting's companion,' said the *Daily Mail*, 'wearing a lavish white mini-dress, giggled delightedly when a tribute to the Police was played and a soup, named "Material World" after one of the band's songs, was served.'

They shared their private jet back to London with Christopher (*Superman*) Reeve.

Paparazzi got wind and were waiting for them at Heathrow. The paps got their photo; it was gold. 'Anger As Sting Flies in with a Mystery Blonde.'

Then, even better, a 'bodyguard' pushed one of the photographers down some steps. A photo and a story.

There'd been a war in the Falklands that year, but that had only lasted a couple of months or so. Other national and international disasters had come and gone. Now here was Sting in a love triangle. News editors must have rubbed their hands together in glee knowing that this one would run and run.

Open season on Sting and Trudie was declared.

★ ★ ★

A few days later, they were snapped at the second birthday party for Stringfellows, the Covent Garden club which still advertises itself as 'nothing like your typical London strip club, or lap dancing club'.

Sting, said one of the reports, 'wore the hunted look of a man who suspects everyone and everything'. He introduced Trudie as his 'mistress'.

A few days after Sting came back from Khashoggi's party, the Police played Gateshead Stadium. They were accompanied by an extraordinary array of supports: U2, the Beat, Gang of Four, Lords of the New Church.

Ticket sales were disappointing – between 6,000 and 15,000, depending on who you believe, in a 25,000-capacity venue remained unsold.

'Seven years ago, I left this town and I said I would make it. It's nice to come back and make you part of the success,' Sting said.

Unemployment in the North-East had doubled since Thatcher came to power. Shops were boarded up. And, anyway, it wasn't like Sting had come from Gateshead in the first place. He was from Newcastle over the river. How dare he claim to have 'left this town seven years ago' when he did no such thing.

(There is a joke told about a man who stopped a passer-by in Newcastle and asked how you get to Gateshead. 'You go over the bridge,' came the reply, 'and you think, "This can't be Gateshead." But it is.')

A lot of the reviewers reckoned that U2 – soon to become the tallest of poppies themselves – stole the show. They played a three-song encore.

'The Police were totally predictable,' wrote the *Record Mirror*. 'Coming on over a tape to ecstatic applause from the half-empty stadium, Sting yodelled and changed basses for every other song in sight… I can't say that they played badly – they're much too professional and slick for that – but their many hits were trotted out with a lack of excitement which suggests that their days as a group may be numbered.'

Sting wasn't in a good mood that night. Between songs he railed against press intrusions into his private life, against Virgin and against the music business in general.

And suddenly the difficulties of living on the dole in Gateshead were put into sharp perspective.

★ ★ ★

It must have been with some sense of relief that the band returned to the US. All the gigs now were in arenas – some even transcended the arena description and passed themselves off sometimes as amphitheatres, sometimes as coliseums. Big places, anyway. Massive places. Accessed in big limos which took them to and from big hotel suites and then maybe to a big private jet.

They were back in England on 9 September and, late that same day, Sting went to the opening of his latest film.

★ ★ ★

Brimstone and Treacle was originally a TV play, made in 1976 by the BBC. Since the subject matter was somewhat controversial, it was referred to the (then) director of television, Alasdair Milne. It made him, he said, 'almost physically sick', and, on the grounds that the viewing public would find it equally repugnant, he withdrew its transmission.

So, a feature film version, starring Sting, was made instead.

It's a nasty tale of a young man – who may or may not be an agent of the Devil, or even the Devil himself – who worms his way into the home of a nice middle-class Christian family: mum, dad and daughter. A car accident has left the daughter paralysed and unable to speak. The young man rapes the daughter. This 'heals' her, enabling her to reveal the family's hypocrisies.

Though the novelty of a top popster doing the dirties in such a vile way attracted plenty of publicity ('That Old Devil Sting – He's So Evil in New Film Shocker', *Daily Mail*), the reviews were less than ecstatic.

The Times had a few crumbs of comfort for the actors, including Sting, 'who looks the part and holds his own creditably against such seasoned expertise', but wondered why the director, Richard Loncraine, got 'carried away with Hammer horror in an overwrought and overlong dream sequence'. (To be fair, the same review was iffy about *Blade Runner*, too – there's clearly no pleasing some people.)

The revered Roger Ebert, of the *Chicago Sun-Times*, wasn't completely won over, either: 'What happens in this movie is so bizarre that if this were an American film it would have been a Dead Teenager movie. Only the British could turn it into a stylish allegory.' But, ultimately, he concludes that it is 'primarily an exercise in style' that doesn't deliver much in the way of content. He does, however, praise Sting for being appropriately 'unctuous, slimy and wonderfully ingratiating'.

A&M released a 'soundtrack' album of the film, which didn't include much of Michael Nyman's score, but did include tracks by A&M artistes, including Squeeze and the Go-Go's, who were featured in the film. Sting and the Police had a few tracks on there, too, including 'I Burn For You', one of the old Last Exit songs that had been a rejected contender for *Zenyatta Mondatta*, and 'Spread A Little Happiness', a song from the 1928 British musical *Mr Cinders*, which Sting sings to an arrow-straight orchestral arrangement.

In October, 'Spread A Little Happiness' was released as a single – Sting's first as a solo artiste – and went to number 16.

★ ★ ★

Earlier in the year, Sting and Trudie had taken a holiday at Goldeneye, Ian Fleming's old house on Jamaica, where Fleming had written all of the James Bond novels. In 1976, the property had been acquired by Chris Blackwell, founder of Island Records. Sting found the place conducive to songwriting and came home with three hits in his pocket: 'Every Breath You Take', 'Wrapped Around Your Finger' and 'King Of Pain'.

'Every Breath You Take' came to him in the middle of the night – the title, anyway. It took half an hour's work at the piano to get it done and dusted.

One day he was sitting watching the sunset in the garden, noticed sunspots and remarked, 'There's a little black spot on the sun today.' Then added, for no particular reason, 'That's my soul up there.' To which Trudie, who knew her man, replied, 'There he goes again, the king of pain.'

Back in London he recorded demos and played them to Miles and Hugh Padgham. Miles was impressed, particularly with 'Every Breath'.

'This will be a massive hit,' he said to Hugh, 'so don't fuck it up, boy!'

On 3 December, Stewart and Sting flew out to Montserrat. Andy followed the next day.

Hugh Padgham hadn't seen much of the band since the *Ghost in the Machine* sessions the year before. He was shocked by how badly relations between the three of them had deteriorated.

'By now,' Hugh said, 'they were all really tired of each other – Sting and Stewart weren't getting on well and, although Andy didn't show as much venom, he could be quite grumpy – and there were both verbal and physical fights in the studio.'

'Often, when these would take place, I'd try to be Mr Producer and get in the way, saying, "Come on, do you have to kick the shit out of one another?" but they'd just turn around and shout, "Get out of it! What do you know? You don't know anything about us!"'

Part of the problem (or maybe the solution) was a physical separation that emerged between Stewart and the rest of the band.

The main studio, it was decided, was not the best acoustic for his drum sound. Accordingly, the drums were set up in the dining room with long cables feeding the mic signals to the desk. A video camera was set up in front of the kit, with a monitor in the control room, so that Hugh, and Sting and Andy, could see Stewart. But Stewart could not see the others. And, while Hugh, Sting and Andy could speak to Stewart over the talkback in his headphones, he could only talk to them if they deigned to open the faders to the drum mics. This meant that, often, after a take, he would be left for an age while the others discussed its merits before they passed down their judgement.

And, on top of that, the dining room didn't have much in the way of air conditioning. Sometimes Stewart got so sweaty, the sticks flew out of his hands. They had to be gaffer-taped in place.

The recording of 'Every Breath You Take' brought a low point.

'Sting wanted Stewart to just play a very straight rhythm with no fills or anything,' Hugh said, 'and that was the complete antithesis of what Stewart was about. Stewart would say, "I want to fucking put my drum part on it!" and Sting would say, "I don't want you to put your fucking drum part on it! I want you to put what I want you to put on it!"'

After 10 days, they had nothing on tape that they could agree was worth keeping.

Miles Copeland was sent for, and a meeting was convened by the swimming pool to try to work out a compromise. Sting did not want to compromise.

There is a story, possibly apocryphal, that Miles, given the choice between a proven business asset and filial loyalty, might have said to Stewart, 'Just fuck off and play the drums!'

Keith Altham, the band's PR, reckons that Stewart felt that 'Every Breath You Take' was not 'in keeping with the group identity'.

Whereas Sting (and probably Miles) knew it was a number one.

Eventually – after two weeks – they managed to get bass and drums down with a guide vocal. Andy was sent in to make some magic happen.

'It has to be something that says "Police" but doesn't get in the way of the vocal. I play it straight through in one take. There is a brief silence, and then everyone in the control room stands up and cheers.'

★ ★ ★

Looking back on 1982, Sting said, 'I behaved like a complete cunt during this year.'

CHAPTER SEVENTEEN

SYNCHRONIZITÄT ALS EIN PRINZIP AKAUSALER ZUSAMMENHÄNGE

In 1982, the Beat had a hit (number 22, anyway) with 'Stand Down Margaret', a song calling for Prime Minister Margaret Thatcher to, well, stand down.

Despite earlier punk approval, by 1983 the general consensus was that liking Margaret Thatcher, with her fibreglass hair and weaponised handbag, was not rock'n'roll. Her presence, policies and attitudes were at odds with hippy idealism, with (certain species of) punk protest, with the spirit of ur-Gong, with the loose-limbed ecstasy of jazz and with every characteristic of reggae, soul and the then newly emerging hip-hop. The jury's out on dinner jazz.

Thus, in the build-up to the 1983 general election, when the Young Conservatives were looking around for entertainers who might appear at their annual conference and get the kids on board, they were hard pushed to find any takers.

Eventually they signed up drippy girl singer Lynsey de Paul, who wrote a special song, 'Vote Tory, Tory, Tory/For Election Glory', comedians Bob Monkhouse and Jimmy Tarbuck (both well advanced into middle age), swimmer Sharron Davies, wrestler Mick McManus, cricketer Freddie Trueman (52) (the young folk do like their sport, don't they?) and – at last a real coup – DJ and edgy TV favourite Kenny Everett, the man who had caressed Sting's nipples on behalf of Barbara of Birmingham.

Kenny, whose political understanding was that of the average newborn calf, got the measure of the crowd straight off. The more outrageous he got, the better they liked it. One of the characters he played in his TV show was an American hawk by the name of General Marvin D. Bombthebastards. Kenny faced the massed ranks of Young Conservatives and adopted the persona.

'Let's bomb Russia,' he shouted.

The Young Conservatives brayed and cheered.

'Let's kick Michael Foot's stick away!' he yelled.

And they brayed some more.

Michael Foot, the Labour leader, walked with a limp – the result of a traffic accident.

The following day, Thatcher had to assure the press and public that nuclear war with Russia was not part of the Conservative manifesto.

Kenny picked up some bad press for his questionable taste and one or two voices pointed out that the real horror was the triumphant braying of the audience.

None of it made any difference. The Conservatives won the 1983 election with their biggest margin since 1959, because – though their policies had plunged the country into recession and doubled unemployment – in 1982, Thatcher (or rather the British armed forces, but she preferred to take the credit) had won an undeclared war with Argentina over possession of the Falkland Islands. The tabloids had stoked anti-'Argie' sentiment and rampant jingoism. When British torpedoes sank the ARA *General Belgrano*, with the loss of 363 lives, the *Sun's* headline was just one word: 'GOTCHA!'

Victory in the Falklands allowed Thatcher to further adorn her Iron Lady image with the mantle of Winston Churchill.

The election made her the 'great leader' and turned her cocktail of hard-line free-market capitalism, privatisation of anything that looked vaguely public and the erosion of the nanny state into a gospel to be embraced even when it led to cruelty and disaster. It still largely is.

The Police were never a political band – not in the party political sense, anyway.

Sting was broadly of the Left and was often critical of Thatcher's policies.

Andy kept his mouth shut about such matters.

The Copelands were a different matter. They were Americans. Even Stewart – albeit jokily – kept to the faith of flag and free markets.

Miles rarely joked about such matters, not so as you'd notice, anyway. At a later Tory Party conference – yes, he spoke at Tory party conferences – he said, 'I believe I have never met a socialist in the music business... It's the free enterprise system at its best.' Which suggests either that his definition of 'the music business' was limited or he didn't get out much.

At one time or another he had a go at Paul Weller for championing the working class while being a hard businessman negotiating his contracts and fees – as if the two were somehow in contradiction. And he had a go at Billy Bragg for being Billy Bragg.

(Paul Weller's feelings about Sting ('Fucking horrible man. Not my cup of tea at all. Fucking rubbish. No edge, no attitude, no nothing') are well documented. He's also not too keen on Bob Geldof ('Boomtown Rats? Fuck off'), James Blunt ('I'd rather eat my own shit than duet with him') and Queen (when Freddie Mercury said he wanted to bring ballet to the working classes, Weller's response was, 'What a cunt'). He did, however, have some good things to say about David Bowie ('I like about three records of his. The rest of it's pish').)

Sting called Miles 'the most right-wing person I know... but Miles is a force to be reckoned with. He's the kind of person you need on your side when the going gets tough. People are frightened of him, which keeps them off balance.'

Miles on Sting sounds eerily similar: 'Sting can be very opinionated and, if I have any value for Sting, it is that I can criticise him and he will listen... He is surrounded by others who are too scared to tell him for fear of losing their jobs.'

A symbiosis, then.

★ ★ ★

1983 was the year the Police reached, as John Lennon used to say, 'the Toppermost of the Poppermost'. The Beatles comparison was frequently made. The Police were spearheading the second 'British invasion' of America. They were making more money than the Beatles, selling more records, causing more hysteria – by all sorts of measures, the Police were outdoing what everybody, up until then, had seen as the band that could never be outdone.

And, like their forebears, they were discovering that the Toppermost of the Poppermost is actually a fairly shitty place to be.

This is what happens. Somebody designs a brilliant product. It sells by the truckload. Fortunes are made. Thousands of people are employed to make, market and distribute the product. Those thousands of people come to depend on the success of that product to put their kids through college, pay off mortgages, fund Granny's hip replacement. Thus, nobody can afford to take the risk of changing the product. Maybe they can make the flanges slightly smaller, or adjust the flow ratio, but essentially it has to be the same product, because, if it even looks like a different product, people will stop buying it and then Granny can't have her hip replacement.

And this is the point where the entire venture gets boring. There's nothing interesting there for the designers and the clever R&D people who designed the product in the first place. They go off to join another company or get down to that time machine they had an idea for or take up performance poetry, leaving the company in the hands of accountants and management people.

And then the diminishing returns kick in. The product becomes old hat. A rival comes up with a better one. The product is superseded by digital technology and the managers and accountants don't know what to do about it, because they're managers and accountants. Product design and innovation have never been in their skill set.

And so it was with the Police, with the added complication that, as well as being the designers and clever R&D people, they were the product. And, as a product, they were – in line with the 1980s zeitgeist – subject to the tyranny of the bottom line and the vicissitudes of the free-market economy.

Stewart had already begun to feel the pressure three years earlier, when A&M, in financial straits, fired 180 people: 'So many people earn a crust from my activities. Occasionally I get vertigo.'

Now they were up there beyond the stratosphere and thousands depended on their coming up with the product – themselves, their image and their music.

And the real sod of it was that nobody could reliably identify the unique selling points of that product. Was it Andy's shimmering guitar? Was it Stewart's skittery drums? Sting's soaring voice? The lyrics? The taking off of the shirt? What could they change without bringing the whole edifice tumbling down? Or were they, like so many before them, condemned forever to churn out the same clutch of hits to ever-decreasing effect until they're being mauled by pensioners at a Prestatyn Pontins 'Remember the Eighties' weekend.

★ ★ ★

The band stayed in Montserrat until the second week of January. At the end of the month, Andy took a little R&R time in New York, booking a suite at the American Stanhope and cruising Studio 54, Limelight and Area 51 – in his words, 'packing the girls in the back of the limo'.

Then Hugh and the band reconvened at Studio Morin-Heights, in the Laurentian Mountains in Quebec, to mix the album.

Sting and Stewart enjoyed skiing – but not together.

The usual routine was that Sting would go skiing and, while he was away, Stewart would, say, overdub a hi-hat part.

Then Stewart would go skiing, and Sting, fresh from the slopes, would wipe the hi-hat part.

It was not a productive workflow.

They'd hit the brick wall again. The Police had been a messy, screaming collective for a little bit, but that was then. Now the only way forward was for somebody to take the helm. Stewart had effectively lost control of the band the day Henri had left. It just took a while for it properly to sink in.

Years later, Stewart, looking back, said, 'Here I am, the musical truth has been revealed to me, and here I am with somebody that I know is really, really talented and has all kinds of musical truth that they bring to the party. But it's just this relentless, unbending acceptance of the fact that *my* musical truth could be *the* musical truth, and this can be frustrating. I'm being ironic here, of course. It's not that the other ideas were wrong. In fact, in many cases, it is that they were right. It was just that, what made the Police what is was, was three different sensibilities.'

In the end, Hugh, forced to take sides, decided they were, after all, Sting's songs, with the result that, by the time it was all over, 'Stewart and I weren't on each other's Christmas card lists.'

Like Ringo and George on Beatles albums, Stewart and Andy got one song each – 'Miss Gradenko' was Stewart's and 'Mother' was Andy's.

'Mother' was never a well-loved track.

Rob Siegel, writing about the history of the cassette on the Hagerty website, talks about the joys of making your own 'road mix' tapes to play in the car.

'I vividly remember driving with friends in Austin, Texas, in 1983. The Police's album *Synchronicity* had just been released. I slid my copy into the cassette deck. My friend Josiah wagged his finger and pulled his copy out of his coat pocket. I didn't understand. "I'm already playing *Synchronicity*," I said. "Yes," he replied, "but my copy has 'Mother' left off it." (It was a truly horrible song.)'

Another of Andy's songs, 'Murder By Numbers', co-written with Sting, made it onto the cassette and CD versions of the album.

Gratifyingly, 'Murder By Numbers' invoked the ire of US TV evangelist (and Jerry Lee Lewis's cousin) Jimmy Swaggart, who, with a doggedly literal reading of lyric, condemned it as the work of Satan. (More acute spotters of Satanic conspiracies have probably already noted that 'Andy Summers' is an anagram of 'My Damn Ruses', and 'Gordon Sumner' of 'Go, Demons! R-Run!' 'Copeland' = 'Plan Code' belongs to a different kind of conspiracy entirely.)

★ ★ ★

In the outside world, now a faraway place that had to be managed rather than engaged with, it seemed that the rumours of the band's imminent break-up had become all anybody wanted to talk about.

'The Police to Split?' asked the *Evening Standard*.

'Why I May Quit the Police,' said the *Sun*, next to a fetching picture of Sting.

Miles, in the *NME*, vehemently denied the rumours, pointing out that the band would definitely be touring the UK in December, but then left the door ajar by adding, 'The Police was never constituted as a prison. Every member has always been free to do whatever he wanted.'

The fan club, too, would have none of it.

'First of all, let us put some of you out of your misery! THE POLICE ARE NOT SPLITTING UP! O.K.?' said the official fan club letter of 1 April, adding its usual promiscuous exclamation marks. 'NO REALLY! The rumours have been quite unfounded! We decided to wait for Miles and Stewart to return from America to get our news first hand and they are both amazed that such a story should have been spread.'

Press scrutiny of every breath they took and every move they made became intrusive. The feasting on every blessed detail of the Sting/Frances/Trudie mess was particularly hard to bear.

In January, Frances released a statement saying, 'I'm still very bruised by what has happened. But there's no question of us being reconciled. Instead there will be a divorce. I want to bring to a close a part of my life which is finished forever... I told myself I had to face it. I wasn't the only single parent in the country, and I didn't have a copyright on pain.'

Confusingly, in an interview that could hardly have endeared him to Trudie, and certainly didn't impress Frances, Sting told the *Sun* on 24 May that he still loved his wife and even though Trudie was a 'great friend', that was all she was.

'I'm not planning on marrying her. I'm already married... I know I had an overblown ego when the Police took off but that wasn't the problem with my marriage. It was a geographical problem in that I was strung out all over America the whole time. It's hard to keep together relationships when you are 5,000 miles apart... To be honest I hope there is a possibility we may get together again one day – but that really is my business, nobody else's.'

There was speculation about how much Sting was worth and how much of it Frances would get in a divorce settlement.

'Will Sting Be Stung for £5m', asked the *Sun*, reporting that, according to their 'spies' at the record company, he was worth £10 million. 'A top London lawyer,' they said (as if they needed to assure readers that they would never rely on a middle-ranking lawyer from Stoke-on-Trent), had told them that 'Frances has an excellent case to claim half of Sting's fortune'.

The same report also mentions that 'a source close to the group' had said that 'Sting has set his sights on a Hollywood career and is pursuing it with fury. The other members of the band just don't know what's going on.'

★ ★ ★

The early 1980s were a time when, if, say, an advertising exec, a music business high-flyer and an up-and-coming Bullingdon-boy politician met in some fancy restaurant, the talk would inevitably turn to the health of their nasal septum – the cartilage that separates the nostrils and which gets eroded by prolonged cocaine use.

North America and Europe were awash with charlie.

As Harry Shapiro notes in his book *Helter Skelter*, 'given that the music business thrives on aggression, hard partying and bullshit, it is hardly surprising that cocaine became the *sine qua non* drug of the industry, not only for musicians but company executives, producers and managers alike. Cocaine imbues the user with a supreme self-confidence, an illusion of clear mindedness, a manipulative power over people, a control of yourself and a loathing for any kind of etiquette.'

Which, as a summary of what certain parts of London were like in the early 1980s, cannot be bettered. Indeed, sometimes the world seemed so deep in minted knob-ends with tiny pupils, big mouths and stupid ideas, it was hard to believe that there was anybody left to listen any more.

Sting told *Rolling Stone* that he'd given up drugs a year earlier: 'one day I realised that I was saying they weren't a problem for me, and I stepped back and thought, "That's a very sad psychology. I'm kidding myself." So, about a year ago, I decided to stop them altogether. I wasn't a heroin addict or anything like that, it's just that drugs are around and you take them, and then you start taking them on your own as well, and that's dangerous.'

Then he said, 'I don't believe people who say, "I can handle it. I've been taking drugs since I was twelve." It's wrong, and as puritan as it might sound, they're not even that much fun.'

And, of course, both the *Daily Mirror* and *Woman* magazine reported him as having said, 'I've been taking drugs since I was 12.' Which, of course, he hadn't.

He complained. The *Daily Mirror* published a retraction, but headlined it 'Sting on Drugs'. You can't win.

★ ★ ★

The new album was to be called *Synchronicity*, a title nicked from *Synchronizität als ein Prinzip akausaler Zusammenhänge* (*Synchronicity: An Acausal Connecting Principle*), by the analytical psychiatrist C. G. Jung, which advances the theory (in a nutshell) that events we call coincidences are in fact manifestations of a deeper order that may be able to transcend the known dimensions of time and space.

A lot of the songs are vaguely informed by this metaphorical view of reality. 'Synchronicity II' links a domestic situation where a family is falling apart with a monster appearing in a Scottish loch. 'King Of Pain' talks of a black spot on the sun, dead salmon in a waterfall and butterflies in spiders' webs.

The themes of pain and damage crop up a lot.

'*Synchronicity* is really more autobiographical,' Sting told *NME*. 'It's about my mental breakdown and the putting back together of that personality.'

'It's been a year of hell and torture for me,' he told *Musician*. 'And I know that without that torture and without that pain – without that awfulness – those lyrics wouldn't have been as good. So, in a sense I'm very suspicious of myself. I wonder if I manufacture pain in order to create.'

Q magazine, 10 years later, came straight to the point that was on everybody's minds at the time and asked him how he felt about being perceived as a 'pretentious wanker'.

'I can't help that. I read books. What can I do? And it's a perfectly valid source.' (He was referring to *Synchronizität als ein Prinzip akausaler Zusammenhänge*.)

'But they were seen as pretentious books.'

'That was the critics' problem,' countered Sting. 'That whole pretentious wanker campaign. Their problem.'

★ ★ ★

Following the established pattern, the single 'Every Breath You Take' was released before the album.

Earlier in the year, in March, while they were in Los Angeles, they shot a video for the song. It was directed by Lol Creme and Kevin Godley, who, after their adventures in 10cc and Godley & Creme, had become hotshot video directors.

It was they who had Kate Bush and Peter Gabriel cuddling in front of an eclipse for 'Don't Give Up', who had supermodels mixing it with sumo wrestlers in Duran Duran's 'Girls On Film', and who had Ronald Reagan and Konstantin Chernenko fighting in talcum powder for Frankie Goes to Hollywood's 'Two Tribes'.

Inspiration for the 'Every Breath' video came from *Jammin' the Blues*, a 1944 black-and-white short featuring Lester Young, Harry Edison, Illinois Jacquet, phenomenal lighting and camera angles, and some fierce jitterbugging.

Godley & Creme set the song in a shadow-filled ballroom. Sting plays an upright double bass. Four elderly gentlemen play violins. Behind the huge, ornate window, a window cleaner goes about his work.

'The window washer felt right for that kind of noir feel,' Godley explained. 'But it also may be somebody who you don't expect to be watching the process, which refers to that sense of surveillance that the song is really about.'

Or, as George Formby put it, 'I go window cleaning to earn an honest bob / for a nosey parker it's an interesting job.'

The camera dwells on Sting's face. He has never looked more beautiful nor more menacing.

It is often cited as one of the best pop videos ever made. Daniel Pearl, who shot it, would win the first MTV Best Cinematography award for his contribution.

A&M Records executive Jeff Ayeroff reckoned the video probably cost $75,000 to $100,000. 'With a good video, the return on your investment was phenomenal.'

And, to prove the point, MTV put it into heavy rotation and sales rocketed.

★ ★ ★

It was first single (in the UK, anyway) the band had released in nearly two years. In mid-May, Miles launched it with a lavish event at the Kensington Roof Gardens.

After an interview with Peter Powell for TV's *Get Set*, the doors were flung wide and the Fleet Street hacks, the media freeloaders and a German film crew trooped in.

It was a busy news day. Earlier, the Conservatives had launched their election manifesto. 'Together, we have achieved much over the past four years,' said Margaret Thatcher. 'I believe it is now right to ask for a new mandate to meet the challenge of our times.'

Which was pretty much what Miles and the Police were up to with their launch party.

The press showed signs of churlishness, and perhaps with good reason.

Miles had spent the past year putting some effort into shielding the band from too much press intrusion. It was never going to work. The rows, splits and divorces had still made the headlines, but Miles, with

222

no product to sell, had been generally uncooperative and sometimes downright obstructive.

Now there was product and he was courting their attention. You can't have it both ways.

Trevor Dann of the *Sunday Telegraph* was particularly aggrieved:

So, about a hundred underdressed hacks and photographers were accorded the dubious pleasure of mingling with the blond trio, pausing only to enjoy sausages on sticks – described as a finger buffet – and watch interminable reruns of the promotional video for the new single 'Every Breath You Take'.

The results will be splashed over the music press during the next few days, fulfilling Miles Copeland's desire to persuade us all that the Police are still as newsworthy and important as they ever were. But chatting with Stewart Copeland made it clear that he was there not out of duty to the fans but rather to get exposure with the least effort. 'If we don't do this, we have a non-successful Police album.'

None of the press were actually allowed to hear the new album. Its 'worldwide consolidated air date' was not for another month.

The hostile press made no difference. The single went to number one, stayed there for a month, got kicked off by Rod Stewart's also slightly stalkerish ('Don't forget I know secrets about you') 'Baby Jane', but still hung around the Top 40 to the end of summer. And it was number one, or at least Top 10, in most other places.

Billboard and *Rolling Stone* both judged it their number one single of 1983, and 36 years later, in May 2019, BMI (Broadcast Music Inc., one of the US equivalents of the British Performing Rights Society, responsible for collecting artists' royalties) handed an award to Sting recognising 'Every Breath You Take' as the most-played song in the history of radio. Up to that date, it had received 15 million plays and had already generated over a third of Sting's music publishing income.

Sting has always been mystified by people's reactions to the song. He has called it a 'nasty little song' about obsession, jealousy and surveillance.

Others have pointed out its liturgical resonances. The repetition is prayer-like, similar to cadences of the traditional Catholic prayer that goes 'God be in my mouth / And in my speaking; / God be in my heart / And in my thinking; / God be at mine end / And at my departing.'

It's also faintly reminiscent of the prayer of St Francis, quoted by Margaret Thatcher when she first went into Downing Street: 'Where there is hatred, let me sow love / Where there is injury, pardon / Where there is doubt, faith / Where there is despair, hope / Where there is darkness, light / Where there is sadness, joy.'

And when the altar boy sneaks a crafty smoke behind the choir stalls, the omniscient God sees every puff he takes, every cough he makes.

As the saying goes, you can take the boy out of the Church, but you can never take the Church out of the boy.

Seven years earlier, Sting had made a sacred vow, before God, in Our Lady and St Oswin's Catholic Church, Front Street, Tynemouth. Every bond you break, every step you take.

'One couple told me,' Sting said, '"Oh, we love that song; it was the main song played at our wedding!" I thought, "Well, good luck."'

★ ★ ★

Sting was out of the country when the single hit the charts, pursuing, as the *Sun* had inaccurately suggested, 'a Hollywood career' 'with fury'.

He spent the next five weeks in Mexico, filming the screen adaptation of Frank Herbert's sci-fi bestseller *Dune* with David Lynch, who had worked miracles directing *The Elephant Man* and *Eraserhead*.

It was a huge project – two years in the making, with a screenful of big names and a $45 million budget (the first *Star Wars* film, six years earlier, had cost a quarter of that).

Sting plays the nephew of Baron Vladimir Harkonnen, head baddy. A character called Feyd.

'He's a homosexual killer with a huge codpiece,' Sting said. 'I really act it up. It has to be a special event. It could be appalling; it could be brilliant. If anyone can pull it off, it's Lynch. I have high hopes for it.'

★ ★ ★

Synchronicity, the album, reached its 'worldwide consolidated airdate' in mid-June. It went straight to number one in the album chart (making a run of five consecutive number ones – the Beatles scored either seven or 11, depending on how you're counting, and 16 altogether) and stayed in the Top 100 well into the following year.

For the first time, the album cover featured the three band members photographed separately. They chose their own images to illustrate the idea of synchronicity.

Sting mostly chose to be photographed with bones, human and dinosaur, and Stewart with clocks. Andy came up with the idea of being surrounded by butterflies. They're hard to come by in New York in January, but somehow they got hold of a batch of frozen ones, hoping that cryogenics worked. They tried a hairdryer and everything, but the poor little bugs wouldn't wake up. One or two of them fluttered a wing for a moment, but that might just have been the breeze from the anti-frizz nozzle. Otherwise, they remained resolutely moribund. So, the butterflies were axed, and Andy settled for dark glasses and a telephone.

In at least two of Sting's photos, the *NME* noted, the 'eyes are secretly murderous. He smiles with a mouth that looks like it's about to bite the head off a baby doll.'

★ ★ ★

Derek Green, then the head of A&M, was said to be disappointed by the album. He described it as falling between a Police and a solo Sting album.

But Stewart thought it was slick, 'We took off the raw edges – got rid of the stuff that Middle America couldn't handle.'

The jury's out on whether this was a good thing or a bad thing.

'In the lyrics, paranoia, cynicism and excruciating loneliness run rampant,' *Rolling Stone* said. 'The end of this bleak brilliant safari into Sting's heart deposits us at the edge of a desert, searching skyward our cups full of sand.'

Again, it's hard to say whether this is supposed to be a good thing or a bad thing.

The *Chicago Tribune* went for a less lyrical sort of cynicism, saying, 'the band has not only perfected mass marketing but found a mass market. In the past, the Police's mix of pop and reggae seemed uncomfortably close to the sort of synthetic calypso one could imagine being played at a Club Med. These days the trio has broadened its musical base and sounds much the better for it.'

Robin Denselow in the *Guardian* started with: 'For a band rumoured to dislike each other, to be past their peak and on the verge of breaking up, the Police aren't doing too badly.' And finished: 'The Police shouldn't be written off quite yet.'

Adam Sweeting, in *Melody Maker*, damned the lyrical content as 'Drivel, mostly, but it gives that patina of books having been read', praised Hugh Padgham's production and made the Marks & Spencer comparison that Sting had already mentioned a couple of years earlier, saying, 'The retail business isn't renowned for its daredevil adventure, nor for its profound emotional content, and however impressive bits of *Synchronicity* might sound, I could never fall in love with a group which plans its every move so carefully and which would never do anything just for the hell of it.'

Richard C. Walls, in *Creem*, referred to Sting's 'humdrum depressions' and 'grandiose glumness', and concluded that it was 'limp, but catchy (as opposed to catchy, but limp)'.

But what do critics know? By October, the album had sold 11 million copies. So, what the hell, what the hell.

★ ★ ★

On 8 July, the second single from the album was released.

'Wrapped Around Your Finger' – about being controlled by someone in a relationship and then turning the tables – was a sensual and meandering track that Andy hated.

For the B-side, Andy had written 'Someone To Talk To'.

Sting hated that and refused to sing it.

So, Andy had to.

The single was also released as a picture disc. Significantly, 10,000 copies were pressed bearing Sting's face, but just 1,000 featuring Stewart's and 1,000 with Andy's.

At the time of writing, on eBay, a Sting one was going for £19.99 and a Stewart one for £29.99. So there.

Godley & Creme were hired again to make the video. They decided to use candles, ordered up 1,000 of them, along with fancy six-foot stands, and arranged them in a sort of maze. In the reverse of an effect that Stewart had used in one of his Klark Kent videos, they played the track for miming at a fast speed so that the action would appear slightly slo-moed. All the same, Sting, dressed in what looks like martial arts formal wear, dances like somebody who forgot to take his Xanax.

After a 12-hour shoot, the producers, worried about spiralling costs (1,000 candles with fancy matching stands do not come cheap), called a wrap.

Sting wasn't happy and called for one more take (that he offered to pay for). Halfway through the take, he started knocking the candles over, which is what fans of the domino effect had wanted to happen all along.

'Sting got to shoot his part last in that video and made a meal of knocking all the candles out,' said Andy. 'Fuck him.'

★ ★ ★

On 30 July, Sonja gave birth to a son, Daniel Jordan James. When the baby was just three weeks old, Daddy had to go on tour.

CHAPTER EIGHTEEN

I'D LIKE TO THANK THE BEATLES FOR LENDING US THEIR STADIUM

The most prestigious of all their US tours kicked off at Comiskey Park, Chicago, with Joan Jett and the Blackhearts and A Flock of Seagulls as support.

Most of the venues on that tour held 30,000 plus and they inevitably sold out. Kim Turner was still tour manager, but the roster of roadies, techs and other personnel had swollen to 75. Andy bemoaned the fact that it was the first time they'd travelled with a crew many of whose names they did not know.

To ensure they got enough rest between shows, Miles had rented a mansion in Bridgehampton, Long Island, at a cost of $15,000 a week. Private planes and helicopters were on hand to ferry them to and from gigs.

★ ★ ★

'Every top group gets exhausted and run down by all the travelling, changes of hotels and airports,' he said. 'At least this way they feel happy and comfortable. It makes good sense.'

The second 'British invasion' was well under way. Most weeks, half of the Top 10 singles in the Billboard Hot 100 were from British acts. The Eurythmics, Dexy's Midnight Runners, the Human League, Duran Duran, ELO, Kajagoogoo, Culture Club and David Bowie were all enjoying major US hits, and the Police were everywhere.

'Every Breath You Take' was top of the Billboard Hot 100 for eight weeks. *Synchronicity* was top of the US album chart, fighting hard to keep Michael Jackson's *Thriller* at bay, for 12 weeks.

Their videos, old and new, were shown so frequently on MTV that some wags had begun to call it the Police Channel.

Later that year Sting would make the cover of *Time* magazine and the cover of *Rolling Stone*.

The 'bigger than the Beatles' tag was on everybody's lips, but mostly it was on Miles's.

'We're the biggest band in the world,' he said. 'Bigger than the Beatles.'

It was a theme picked up by the *Boston Globe* when they played the Sullivan Stadium, and 'Sting led the crowd through inspired singalongs while the younger teens in the audience shrieked as though he were John Lennon in the prime of the Beatles'.

They had put wacky mop-top-style moments into the show, too.

Sting had taken to using a little trampoline to make his onstage jumps just that little bit more spectacular.

At one point during the Boston concert, they left the stage followed by a video camera, which showed them on the massive screen.

'They went into a rear dressing room,' the *Globe* reported, 'and literally took a British tea break. They all put on stovepipe dunce caps, mugged for the camera and sipped politely until Sting, with a fiendish smile, yanked the white tablecloth and upset all the cups as the crowd roared with laughter.'

★ ★ ★

On 15 August 1965, 18 years earlier, TV host and entrepreneur Ed Sullivan had announced, at Shea Stadium, home of the New York Mets and the New York Jets, 'Now, ladies and gentlemen, honoured by their country, decorated by their Queen, and loved here in America, here are the Beatles!'

More than 55,000 screaming fans were in the audience. It was the biggest concert of the Beatles' career and at the time the biggest rock concert ever. It was also the first time pop music had set foot in a sports stadium.

John Lennon later said, 'At Shea Stadium, I saw the top of the mountain.'

Forever after, or at least until the place closed in 2008, even though there were gigs at much bigger venues, and festivals attended by hundreds of thousands, symbolically Shea Stadium was still 'the top of the mountain'.

Tickets for the Police at Shea Stadium sold out within five hours.

The Beatles had played with a stage set up at Second Base, with what seemed like acres of grass between them and the fans in the stands. The Police fitted in an extra 15,000 seats on the pitch. This meant that, in fact, they were playing for around a quarter more people than the Beatles had.

Like the Beatles, they arrived at the stadium by helicopter.

'I sat with Andy and Stewart,' Sting said, 'and I said, "This is as good as it gets. We're playing Shea Stadium, this is where the Beatles played. We're the biggest band in the world this year. After this it's going to be diminishing returns. I think we should stop now, at the top."'

Andy remembers no such thing. 'I have no clear memory of sitting down and discussing that it was all over.'

Then again, helicopter engines are very loud.

The show nearly didn't happen.

'And so, we were doing a photo session with the three of us,' Stewart told Gert-Peter Bruch. 'They were all joking and laughing around... I had my *New York Times* and Sting grabs it off me and I grab it back, he grabs it again... It's just like the Monkees or something like that, or the boys having fun!'

It was par for the course. They wrestled a lot. 'I use Syrian army wrestling tactics on Sting. He's very strong, so the key is to get him on the floor and twist him out of shape. I find a foot on the head works pretty well too.

'Finally, I get him down on the ground with the knees in his chest and he screamed. So I said, "Oh shit, sorry man!"'

They played the show but, for several days afterwards, Sting complained of pain in his chest.

After a somewhat truncated concert at the Met Center in Bloomington, Sting checked into the United Hospital in St Paul, Minnesota, for an X-ray. He had a cracked rib. A hairline fracture. They kept him in for 12 hours or so.

Like Watcyn Thomas, the hero who scored the winning try in a Wales versus Scotland rugby match even though he'd broken his collarbone, Sting played Shea Stadium with a busted rib.

And... 'It was our best show ever.'

The Beatles, when they played Shea Stadium, were working with an embryonic sound system which would have made a horrible noise if anyone could have heard it over the screaming (the much better sound on the movie of the Shea Stadium concert has little to do with the noise that would have been coming out of the speakers). The Police had many thousands of watts of state-of-the-art technology and three huge video screens to make sure they could be heard and seen.

All the same, 'everyone in the stadium seems to want to get closer to them', said *Smash Hits*. 'Kids with tickets for the top levels of the stadium want to get to the lower levels. Kids on the lower levels want to be on the pitch. Kids on the pitch want to get in front of the stage and a lot of kids want to get backstage.'

Crowds gathered outside the stadium, hoping at least to hear some of the concert but the cops moved them on. Warnings were issued on local TV stations not to turn up if you didn't have tickets.

'It all seems to have happened step by step,' Sting told *Smash Hits*, 'and this time everything fell into place. We've got the biggest album, the biggest single, the biggest video, the biggest concert tour. It's the result of hard work – we've done about nine or ten tours here. It's just a logical progression.'

After a muted first three tracks from *Synchronicity*, Sting led the audience in singing 'Message In A Bottle' and they went wild. After 'Don't Stand So Close To Me', he addressed the adoring crowd.

'I'd like to thank the Beatles for lending us their stadium.'

Then they went into the encores – 'Roxanne', 'Can't Stand Losing You' and 'So Lonely'. Sting with his shirt off, his rib hardly hurting at all, doing what he does best in front of 70,000 worshippers.

'What else was there to do after reaching this peak?' he said.

Truman Capote, William Burroughs and Andy Warhol (who had the temerity to accuse Sting of looking old and tired) came to the after-show party, as well as hordes of journalists.

'We talked to *Time* and *Newsweek*,' Stewart said, 'and both of them let slip the fact that "Look, look, what we really want, the editors in New York, what they're really after is a story on the conflict within the group." And if that's the story you want... you know? I mean, it's boring, but they've written their stories before they even get here.'

★ ★ ★

They got back to London on 13 September, to discover that, just as their career had reached its pinnacle in the US, in the UK, it seemed, they were on the wane. Despite the candle-smashing video, 'Wrapped Around Your Finger', released in August, peaked at number seven and stayed in the Top 10 for only two weeks. 'Synchronicity II' was released in October. Again, it came with an elaborate Godley & Creme video, influenced by *Dune* or *Mad Max*. The band are stationed on separate scaffolding towers, over a pile of junk, broken guitars and drums and bits of cars and wires. Scraps of paper and rubbish fly about in the air and dry ice rises up from the floor. Sting does his best beautiful but evil eyes. His hair alone could sell out Shea Stadium. During the filming, it's said, Stewart's tower caught fire. Lol Creme told the cameraman to keep on filming.

Even so, the single limped to number 17 for one week, and three weeks later had vanished without trace. In the US it scraped number 16.

On 17 September, they embarked on a mini German tour as part of the sixth Golden Summernight Festival.

It had been a lovely summer, but now the weather had turned cold and wet. The Rosenaustadion in Augsburg was only a quarter full. Sting looked out at the sparse audience, huddled in the damp, and asked whether they were cold. 'Ich bin warm,' he said, to startled looks. Sting had just told 7,000 people, 'I am gay.'

Though the European concertgoers and record-buyers seemed to be deserting them, the press still clung like leeches to every breath, move, bond and step.

Sting was going to become a father again in the new year – Trudie was expecting her first child. Even though she was pregnant, she travelled with Sting most of the time – joking that the baby would probably be born on a plane.

'I know that last year I was a rat as far as the public were concerned,' Sting told Annie Nightingale in the *Daily Express*. 'I could feel it when I walked down the street.'

The press, he said, are 'a bunch of stupid idiot liars as far as I'm concerned. The *Sun* is written by buffoons for buffoons.'

'Actually,' he told *Creem*, 'I'm fairly immune to what the press says. Particularly in England, where they invent a private life for you and then proceed to comment on it. It's a joke, really – it's not me they're writing about, they're writing about some invention. I bait the press a lot. Somebody slags me off, I'll slag them back. I quite enjoy that privilege. I like the right to say what the hell I like. They say what the hell they like.'

Sting's brother Phil, who was still a milkman in Whitley Bay, had given an interview to the *Sun*: 'Everyone talks about Sting... it puts me on edge. Some people can be heartless and cruel.'

Andy and Stewart, meanwhile, were courting a bit of press attention for projects they had to publicise.

★ ★ ★

Rumble Fish, the Francis Ford Coppola film about bad boys and gang fights in Tulsa, Oklahoma, starring Matt Dillon and Mickey Rourke, and with music by Stewart, was released in November. It was Stewart's first of many film scores. Stewart had initially been approached for an advisory role. Coppola had intended to compose the music himself and sent the tunes, which he'd whistled, on a tape to an arranger.

'So, some guy had to listen to those whistling things and have a violin play them,' Stewart said, 'and they were awful. The arranger kept talking about "sweetening" everything. I got rid of him pretty quick by out-concepting him!'

Instead, Stewart composed a full experimental score, using an early form of sampler to integrate disparate sounds into sometimes reggae-ish/ Police-ish contexts. It is the perfect score for the jagged story shot in stark black and white, and proved, just in case anybody had any doubts, that Stewart had not been hired in the cynical hope of luring a few Police fans into the movie theatre. He was a talented and responsive composer who knew movies as well as he knew music.

A single from the soundtrack album, 'Don't Box Me In', with Stewart on guitar, bass, drums and keyboards, and vocals from Stan Ridgway from the band Wall of Voodoo, got a lot of airplay on MTV and momentarily sneaked into the Top 100.

★ ★ ★

In 1984, when Nick Rhodes of Duran Duran published a book of his photographs, he called it *Interference*. When David Sylvian of Japan published a book of his photographs, he called it *Perspectives*. When Andy Summers published a book of photographs, he went for the more pithy *Throb*.

He flew out to the US to talk about *Throb* on *Late Night with David Letterman* and appeared swamped by an eccentric get-up of flappy red trousers and a voluminous black felt Japanese jacket. He twinkled saucily when asked about the photographs – there were a lot of bare-naked ladies posing in hotel rooms among the many pictures of Sting and Stewart on tour, by swimming pools or in hotel corridors.

As Miles told the *Sun*, 'Andy's hobby is photography. His other hobby is girls. He is recently divorced and has been labelled "Randy Andy" for good reason. He has a very interesting life with women. The truth is never as great as the fiction, but you can say that Andy has a very active sex life.'

At the end of October, the second leg of the US tour kicked off at Orange Bowl in Miami. The weather was warm. The 49,000 seats had all sold. The support act was the Animals – the band that Andy had played with years earlier – now featuring the entire original line-up, including Eric Burdon and Alan Price, together with Andy's old pal Zoot Money on keyboards. As well as stuff from a newly recorded album, *Ark*, they treated the folks to a selection of their old hits – 'House Of The Rising Sun' and 'We Gotta Get Out Of This Place'.

The Police flew back to the UK a month later and, after a week's rest, kicked off a UK tour, not at a stadium but at the 3,000-seat Playhouse Theatre in Edinburgh.

'It is commendable to see the Police undertaking a British tour which takes in small provincial theatres,' said the *Daily Mirror*, then went on to note that they showed signs of fatigue during their performance.

The *NME*, which caught them at Nottingham City Hall (2,500 seats), also noted the battle fatigue: 'It could just be the Mad Max-goes-New Romantic togs that fail to convince, but the routine of performance has caught up with him [Sting]. His little-boy-blue antics and gestures towards rock theatre look tired. A forced affability ill-masks the gulf between the man and his audience.

'Nottingham's smoothly square young adults are here for the "moons" and "Da Doos", the chunes they made out to before the first down-payment. They are not here for "King Of Pain".'

The Police had become what all bands become when the iconic status takes precedence over music or genuine joy. They had become a tribute band to themselves. The Bootleg Police, running through the hits, wearing the clothes, removing the clothes, saying the lines, coaxing the singalongs. Sometimes older members of the audience, the ones who'd been out of touch for a while, came in flying suits with their hair bleached.

After Cornwall, Birmingham and Brighton, the band got a few days off for Christmas and then did four straight sold-out nights at the Wembley Arena.

'Hello, Wembley...'

'Yaaaaaa-y.'

'Raaaaah-x...'

'Yaaaaaa-y.'

Miles warned in the *News of the World*, 'The fans will have to make the most of the British tour because when it finishes at Wembley on New Year's Eve, the Police plan to take nearly all 1984 off. The time has come to pull back from work and publicity. Too many groups make the mistake of over-exposure and they become boring and fade away.'

But the noises that they might take 1985 off too, and every year after that, were growing louder. Sting said, 'The only reason we'd stay together is if there's a further challenge for us as a group. I find it a little difficult to think of something at this particular moment. Our LP is a phenomenal success – we could regurgitate the same thing and be big stars for years and years. America is like that, it's so reactionary and slow. Once you reach a level you stay there. It kind of bores me.'

And he spelled it out even more plainly to *You Magazine*: 'As soon as the group is no longer useful, I'll drop it like a stone. I'm out for myself – and the other two know it. A Sting is dangerous and painful. I'm ruthless so far as my work is concerned. If you care what you're doing you've got to fight no holds barred. When I fight it's like gelignite.'

CHAPTER NINETEEN

ANDY, STING AND STEWART HAVE NO INTENTION OF DISBANDING!

'King Of Pain', the fourth single from their album *Synchronicity*, was released on 6 January 1984.

Apart from later re-releases and re-packaged product, this was their final flourish as a singles band. It made number three on the Billboard Hot 100 and number one in Canada, but in the UK, like 'Synchronicity II', it crept up to number 17 for one week in the UK chart, then vanished from the Top 20, giving 'Synchronicity II' and 'King Of Pain' the distinction of being their lowest-charting singles since the early days of 'Fall Out'.

It had very little promotion. No video was shown in this country or the US, although there was one cobbled together for Australian TV with stills from the album, things on Roman plinths and, oh, a telephone that goes on fire.

Top of the Pops played the single over the credits on 14 January, but Frankie Goes to Hollywood's 'Relax' came along accompanied by ads announcing 'All The Nice Boys Love Sea Men' and made all other records seem strangely tame.

★ ★ ★

Sting and Trudie had moved into 2 The Grove, Highgate, London, bought from the violinist Yehudi Menuhin. (Doctor Johnson's clavichord, Yehudi Menuhin's house – could Einstein's underpants be far behind?)

The baby, Brigitte Michael, was born on 19 January. Sting missed the birth – again – having popped out for something to eat.

★ ★ ★

The tour continued, 10 days after the birth, starting with two nights in Rome, followed by a quick hop over the Atlantic to play to 41,500 people at the Carrier Dome in Syracuse, New York.

The following night, at the Providence Civic Center (now the Dunkin' Donuts Center) (12,400) on Rhode Island, they failed to impress Steve Morse of the *Boston Globe*. 'Sunday's show,' he said, 'was saddled with slow, ponderous moments and a disturbing lack of unity between singer Sting, guitarist Andy Summers and drummer Stewart Copeland. Where they played like symbiotic teammates last July, they played this time like three strangers who will be glad to take some time off from each other.' Steve also took issue with the number of smoke bombs let off during the show.

At Chicago (18,500) on 19 February, it wasn't so much the smoke bombs that got on the *Chicago Tribune*'s nerves as the audience participation. The Police had indeed turned into their own tribute band: 'There comes a point where a band's popularity becomes so widespread that its concerts take the form of mass singalongs. The Police have clearly reached that point, as their sold-out Sunday night concert at the Rosemont Horizon easily proved. In one hit after another, one could hear less of the band and more of the fans, who sang along in a variety of keys and intonations. The effect was something like a massive try-out for an opening in the group, as if this inventive and persuasive rock trio needed one.'

After the Buffalo Memorial Auditorium (14,500), they played one night in Hawaii, then on to New Zealand, where Sting and Andy nearly died.

It was leisure activities that did it.

Sting went hang-gliding or parascending – one of those things – and Andy hired a catamaran. The wind got up. Andy was swept out to sea, where the waves were cresting at four metres, while a sudden updraught sent Sting high into the air.

He couldn't get down. Andy couldn't turn round.

Just as Andy's boat was about to be smashed to matchsticks and Sting was about to trespass into flight lanes, the wind changed again. Both were blown back to shore – Andy back to shore and safety; Sting back to shore, but still 200 feet in the air. It took another 90 minutes (or 60, or 30, depending on which account you believe) to get him down.

Stewart, meanwhile, was off playing polo, his passion. Earlier in the year he'd popped over to the Dominican Republic for a game or two. Mike Rutherford of Genesis was another keen player – as, of course, were Prince Charles and, incongruously, Tommy Lee Jones, the Man in Black, who fields two teams, owns a string of 50 ponies and often regrets the extent to which the movie business eats into his polo time.

In Australia, the band played the Sydney Showground (30,000).

Philip Stafford, of *RAM* (*Rock Australia Magazine*) wondered 'just how much of the Police Phenomenon has to do with form, style, image over substance, meaning content. There's no doubting Sting's personal magnetism – his demigod-like allure hung over this event like the dark clouds overhead.'

After the last gig, at the Melbourne Showgrounds (a paltry 4,300), they were presented with an end-of-tour cake. Sting picked it up and smashed it over Stewart's head.

They had done their job. They had thrilled. They had delighted. They had been worshipped and adored. And they knew that definitely, maybe, probably, it was over.

On 5 March, the Police fan club Outlandos released a newsletter:

Panic has struck our American and Australian friends as overseas Press reports say once more the band is about to break up! Maybe these reporters believe their own lines or is it they get a bonus for a good story?

We can definitely say that at the present time ANDY, STING and STEWART have no intention of disbanding THE POLICE as a group.

Touring means working travelling and living together in close contact and as they have been on the road continuously since July 1983 not only the band but the managers; Miles, Kim, the crew: Billy,

Danny, Jeff, Tam, Joe and all the others are ready for a rest from each other.

They left Melbourne separately. Stewart left for Fiji, then Tahiti and California. Andy went to Sri Lanka to decompress.

And Sting flew back to London to face divorce proceedings – from Frances, not the band.

'When I divorced Frances,' he later told the *Sunday Express*, 'the press really carved me up. I was a drug-taking philanderer and those were the nice things they said about me!... None of it was true. Sure, I'd had my share of pharmaceuticals. But that's in the past. And I'm certainly not a philanderer. There's no way someone as well-known as myself can avoid publicity. It's an occupational hazard. I'm just sorry for my parents because it can't be much fun for them to read those things about their son and then have to face the neighbours.'

On 10 March, *The Times* – with no mention of philandering or pharmaceuticals – reported: 'Frances Tomelty, the actress, was granted a *decree nisi* in London yesterday from Gordon Sumner, better known as Sting, from the Police music group.'

Frances was in rehearsal for productions of *The Merchant of Venice* and *Richard III* with the Royal Shakespeare Company in Stratford, playing Portia opposite Ian McDiarmid's Shylock and Elizabeth opposite Antony Sher's Richard. Her reviews were excellent.

Sting, meanwhile, took off for the Caribbean with Trudie and baby Bridget. Rumour has it that, somewhere around this time, he had a nose job. Other rumours say he had it much earlier. And others still say he didn't have one at all. If it matters, look at the before-and-after pictures and decide for yourself.

The band was still being showered with awards: they got two Grammys for *Synchronicity* and 'Every Breath', and Sting got one for his *Brimstone and Treacle* music.

In May, Sting took his mum to the Ivor Novello Awards, so that she could be proud while he picked up a couple of trophies for 'Every Breath You Take'. They won a Canadian Juno award for *Synchronicity*. At the first MTV Awards ceremony, Andy and Stewart, no Sting, tried to look like good losers as the 'Every Breath' video, nominated for eight different awards, won just one, for Daniel Pearl's cinematography.

But the crowning glory came when Sting was voted *Woman's Own*'s 'Man with the Sexiest Bum', beating off firm competition from rival 'Mr Bumbums' Rod Stewart and Daley Thompson.

★ ★ ★

They did their own things.

Andy had given up trying to find spiritual healing in Sri Lanka and was looking for it in Bournemouth instead. He and Robert Fripp worked on their second album together, *Bewitched*, recording at Arny's Shack, a studio in Poole, just round the coast. There were other musicians involved, but it was mostly awash with new technology. One cruel observer noted that it sounded like a demonstration disc for the Roland product line.

Stewart took himself off to Kenya, Tanzania, Burundi, Zaire and the Congo to shoot a film with Jean-Pierre Dutilleux about the search for the African roots of American music called *The Rhythmatist*. It is cutting edge in its use of the (then) near-miraculous portable digital technology to make field recordings that were later sampled and reassembled using a Fairlight – an early computer music device that could do things that were so miraculous (and so phenomenally expensive) that no phone could do them until about 2002.

Stewart, in black trousers, black shirt and black flamenco dancer's hat, is shown intrepidly rowing up rivers, playing a mini Yamaha keyboard to hippopotami, crossing sand dunes by undersized donkey, navigating windswept lakes in a dhow and, most notably, insouciantly playing his drums in a flimsy wire cage while lions charge at him (ravenous lions clearly holding no fear for a man who's worked with Sting).

The film also incorporated an undoubtedly bizarre and arguably inappropriate 'plot line' involving encounters with a beautiful blonde, the ghost of a dancing musicologist that sometimes appears to a remote tribe of 'pygmies', and the smoking of ritual 'weed' – 'fortunately my college education in California has prepared me for this trial'.

An album of music related to the project was subsequently released. It's better than you might have been led to expect – but didn't make much of a dent in the market.

In May, Sting flew off to New York to discuss a new film role with Franc Roddam, who had directed him in *Quadrophenia* back in 1979. He agreed to play Baron Frankenstein opposite Jennifer Beals (welder by day, exotic dancer by night star of *Flashdance*) in *The Bride* – a British/ American horror film in which the Baron decides to create a bride for his monster but (spoiler alert) loses his life in the end.

It had a sensational cast, including Timothy Spall, Phil Daniels, David Rappaport, the *Vogue* cover model Veruschka von Lehndorff and Alexei Sayle.

Part of the action took place in a circus tent, erected at Shepperton Studios. There was a slight setback at the start of October, when, during the filming of a trapeze scene with David Rappaport, a light fell over and the tent caught fire.

It burned to the ground, according to the *Sun*, in four minutes flat, but miraculously no one was hurt, although an estimated £1 million of damage resulted. Sting wasn't there, having finished his bits the day before.

The film, released a year later in August 1985, was widely ridiculed. Franc Roddam did all right for himself, though. He came up with the format for *MasterChef*, one of BBC's biggest franchises, at the time of writing broadcasting in 26 countries.

When he wasn't filming, Sting was writing songs. These were not, however, songs for the Police, but for a solo album he was planning.

'I have to say,' Sting wrote in *Lyrics*, 'the sense of freedom in not having to tailor songs to accommodate a three piece, even one as versatile as the Police, was like opening a window in a closed room. Although I believed that the Police had thrived on the limitation of being a small band, I was more than ready after seven years to fly the coop.'

★ ★ ★

On 24 October, the BBC broadcast a harrowing news report from East Africa. The rain hadn't come that year in Ethiopia and starvation had reached what Michael Buerk, the BBC reporter, described as 'biblical proportions'.

The programme kicked the government, which until then had offered no aid at all to the starving, into coughing up £3 million and the use of a couple of Hercules aircraft, to distribute supplies.

Then, on 5 November, Sting got a call from Bob Geldof.

The documentary had turned Geldof's life around. He became a man with a mission and enlisted the help of Midge Ure of Ultravox, whose greatest hits album, *The Collection*, had just gone into the Top 10. Bob hadn't seen the Top 10 with album or single since 1981.

Geldof's idea was to make a charity single – all proceeds to go to the famine relief – and get Sting to record it.

Then the idea snowballed. Geldof, always prepared to talk both hind and front legs off not just donkeys but any other animal unlucky to find itself in the neighbourhood, barely had to ask before people said 'Yes'.

Trevor Horn, producer of Frankie Goes to Hollywood, offered his studio in Notting Hill.

Boy George flew in from New York to make the session.

Spandau Ballet flew in from Germany.

Status Quo brought their stash and shared nicely.

Phil Collins brought his drums.

Geldof had sold exclusive access to the *Daily Mirror* (who brought booze), and had sweet-talked retailers, including big shots like Woolworths and HMV, into chipping their mark-up into the kitty.

Artist Peter Blake, the man responsible for the Beatles' *Sgt. Pepper* sleeve, donated his services for the cover art.

The only skinflint in the equation was the British government, which refused to waive the VAT on the record. So Geldof kicked up a stink in the press, and eventually – in one of the U-turns she was famous for never doing – Thatcher relented and the starving got the VAT.

Sting went to see Midge before the session, to rehearse.

'Sting sang his harmony parts – "and there won't be snow in Africa this Christmas time" and "The bitter sting of tears" – to my guide vocal,' Midge said, 'but when we changed it, whoever sang that line – Glenn Gregory, Bono or George Michael – Sting's harmony still fitted perfectly. It was electric.'

'It was a funny day,' said Sting, 'like a school reunion for truants. All of us had a lot in common but had rarely been in the same room together. At first their very fragile egos walked through the door and I thought, is it going to be all right? But there was a lovely spirit.'

Pretty much the opposite, then, of a Police recording session.

The record, 'Do They Know It's Christmas?', released on 3 December, less than two weeks after the session, became the (then) fastest-selling single ever in the UK. It went straight in at number one and stayed there for five weeks. And it was number one in most other European countries, as well (except France, where Peter and Sloane's '*Besoin De Rien, Envie De Toi*' ('Euro-disco at its worst') reigned supreme until

Christmas, when it was displaced by Stevie Wonder's 'I Just Called To Say I Love You' while succour for the starving languished at 34).

★ ★ ★

From the end of November, you could barely move anywhere in the country without being confronted by huge posters showing a desert under a purple sky with two blue-green planets hovering, and the caption 'A world beyond your experience, beyond your imagination'.

Dino De Laurentiis, the big-shot movie producer, a man who never cared much for litotes, excelled himself, describing *Dune*, the film featuring Sting, as 'not only the greatest motion picture of my career – it's one of the greatest motion pictures ever made'.

It was released in December. Sting, Andy and Stewart all went to the premiere and stayed there for a very long time.

The rough cut had run to four hours. David Lynch, the director, had got it down to three. Dino and his cohorts had another hack at it and the final version ran at just over two and a quarter hours, but somehow it still made 10 minutes seem like a lifetime.

It was a mess – the redoubtable Roger Ebert said so. He also said it was 'incomprehensible', 'pointless' and 'the worst movie of the year', and most other critics agreed.

The Times (UK) bucked the trend a little by praising the cinematography and art direction, so 'at least there is something to look at while the players gabble on about their incomprehensible conflicts'.

Many of the reviews were accompanied by a photo of Sting, sometimes with shirt, more often without. 'Sting as the saucy catamite,' the caption in *The Times* read.

Since its release, some cinephiles have tried to reappraise *Dune*, claiming that investigation of its deeper resonances can be rewarding, but they're fooling no one but themselves.

Despite which, Sting's acting career was thriving.

He'd acquired the rights to Mervyn Peake's Gormenghast novels, the fantasy/comic stories of the Groan family, their grotesque castle and their curious realm. Movies had been mooted, but never materialised. In November 1984, however, he was heard in a two-part BBC Radio 4 adaptation of the stories playing Steerpike, the schemer, who 'if ever he had harboured a conscience in his tough narrow breast he had by now dug out and flung away the awkward thing'.

The Times found the production 'spellbinding', gasped at the impressive roster of names in the cast list – David Warner, Freddie Jones, Eleanor Bron, Judy Parfitt, Sheila Hancock, Bernard Hepton, etc., etc. and 'then, of course, there was rock star Sting, cast as Steerpike, and a bit of a director's gimmick you might think. He stood apart, certainly, and that was right for he was thinner, more metallic – a killer terrorist at large and unsuspected among a band of gaudy players.'

Even more impressive was his role in the film adaptation of David Hare's play *Plenty* playing Meryl Streep's lover. Again, the company – Streep, Charles Dance, Ian McKellen, John Gielgud, Sam Neill – could not have been more distinguished, and the film, when it was released the following year, was much admired. Sting said it was the 'best work I've done. It's the first chance I've had on screen to show a weak or sympathetic side.'

After filming, Sting, still sporting the short back and sides from the *Plenty* shoot, headed off to the Caribbean with his family.

On 20 December, they arrived in Montserrat and Sting started demos for his new project.

'Vocally I'm at the peak of my powers,' he told the *News of the World*, 'and to prove it I'm working on an album of my own songs. Whether or not I still have a career with the Police though remains to be seen.'

CHAPTER TWENTY

AMERICA LOVES A PILGRIM WHO ISSUES PRESS RELEASES ON HIS PROGRESS

Mark Knopfler, of Dire Straits, was a couple of years older than Sting, and had been at Gosforth Grammar in Newcastle (a five-minute walk from the Gosforth Hotel) at the same time as Sting was at St Cuthbert's.

His first hit, 'Sultans Of Swing', was on its way down just as 'Roxanne' had begun to climb.

One day he was thinking about a song he was writing for his new album.

'I'd seen the Police doing an MTV advert,' he said, 'saying "I want my MTV", just saying it all together; and I thought, "If I set that to the notes of 'Don't Stand So Close To Me' it'll work."'

He happened to be recording the new album on Montserrat at the start of 1985, which is when Sting also happened to be there, recording demos and windsurfing.

Mark confessed to Sting that he'd nicked his tune, but wondered whether he fancied singing it on the record. Sting was amenable.

There was an eerie moment as Sting came into the studio and looked around.

'What's wrong?' John Illsley, Dire Straits' bass player, asked.

'Nobody's fighting.'

He nailed the vocal in a couple of takes. Mark suggested that, since that bit of the song was his tune, he should accept a couple of percentage points on the royalties. Sting again was amenable.

The song was 'Money For Nothing' – but you knew that anyway. It went to number four in the UK, number one in the US and number 34 in France.

'His [Sting's] first royalty cheque, which he showed me,' says the Police PR man, Keith Altham, 'was for $1 million – with more to come.'

Whether this was before or after Virgin, who still owned a huge chunk of 'Don't Stand', had taken their sizeable cut remains unclear.

★ ★ ★

There was no Police in 1985. Whether there would ever be a Police again was a matter of some speculation. Only Miles spoke on the matter with any certainty.

'The group doesn't plan to be working together until 1986,' he told the *San Francisco Chronicle*. 'There'll be a studio album at the beginning of that year, and a live album at the end. We'll let the other bands play themselves out and then come back on top.'

In the same feature, Sting was rather more equivocal.

'It's a sabbatical,' he said. 'When we feel like working again with each other, we will. On my new album, I've written a couple of songs that have been influenced by Kurt Weill. I'm working with a full orchestra on those, and that wouldn't be suitable for the Police.'

Stewart, according to the *Daily Mirror* anyway, took a different line. 'The belief that we have taken a sabbatical is utter rubbish,' he said. 'We officially broke up at the end of our 1984 tour of America. I signed an agreement and there is definitely no decision to get back together again.'

The *Mirror* went on: 'Despite rumours that the group were always fighting among themselves Stewart says there was no row when they broke up.'

At around the same time, Stewart told *Record Mirror*, 'Sting not only hates humanity passionately, he also hates every individual within the species as well.'

Print, it should be added, isn't very good at conveying a twinkle in the eye, a note of irony or exaggeration for dramatic or comic effect.

Although, having said that, in a subsequent *Sounds* interview, Sting himself went some way to confirm Stewart's assessment of the situation.

'I was terrible to work with. Or be around. I was a complete nightmare: unsympathetic, aggressive, mean, selfish, egotistical. But so were the others.'

★ ★ ★

On 11 February, at the Grosvenor Hotel, the three of them assembled looking haunted in black ties, to pick up a Brit award for Outstanding Contribution to Music. Noel Edmonds, host of the evening, stood nervously behind them, as if he knew things could turn ugly in the blink of an eye.

'We've been very lucky,' Sting announced, 'We're a good team.' He looked round. Stewart nodded stiffly, agreeing not perhaps with the sentiment but with the idea that this is the sort of thing they should be saying. 'We have a lot of talent,' Sting continued, 'and inspired management. To solve the problem of dividing the trophy into three, we're giving it to Miles Copeland.'

★ ★ ★

Stewart was still living the life of a country gent at his spread in leafy Buckinghamshire.

He played polo – 'for a while, horses even crowded out my obsession with music' – and worked in his sumptuously equipped home studio.

In New York, he worked on the CBS TV series *The Equalizer*, starring Edward Woodward as Robert McCall – spy, vigilante, defective parent, accomplished classical pianist and maverick, who delivers rough justice to bad guys who thought they were going to get away with it. Stewart wrote the series sig and incidental music for 51 of the 88 episodes, using synths, samples (the Fairlight again) and what were described as 'world rhythms'.

He also released a single. 'Koteja', with vocals by Ray Lema, was a track from his album *The Rhythmatist*.

Despite an appearance on Channel 4's *The Tube* at the end of March, the single, like the album, had disappointing sales.

In an interview on *Music Box*, a cable TV show, Stewart, in between talking about the film and the album, mentioned that, although he'd seen Sting recently in America (he'd guested in a show with Sting in Salt Lake City), he hadn't seen Andy in a while and wondered if he was in Bournemouth…

★ ★ ★

Andy, in his sabbatical, staged an exhibition of his photographs at the Photographers' Gallery under the same title as his book – *Throb*.

'I have my guitar and my camera – they are the two constant things in a world of change,' he told *The Times*, fulfilling the by-now-familiar brief that nobody from the Police is ever allowed to say anything without appending a gnomic aperçu.

He toyed with the idea of acting.

'I've been offered a lot of stuff, but most of it I turn down because I don't really like the screenplays,' he told *Guitar Player*. 'Rock musicians tend to get offered fairly dumb, rock-type movies, and that's not what I want to do. I'd rather do stuff outside the rock'n'roll genre.'

He was 42 – the sort of age at which many a road-worn man starts thinking about settling down and having kids, or, if he's already settled down and had kids, he starts thinking about doing it again.

Andy achieved what is perhaps an ideal of sorts by settling down and having kids the second time with the same person as the first time. He started to see more of his ex-wife Kate.

'And we've been together ever since. Throughout that whole period, I never found anyone like her. We got back together and immediately had two more kids. She was who I was supposed to be with.'

★ ★ ★

Sting hogged the limelight.

In January, he flew to New York to recruit a new band.

'I guess what I'm looking for is jazz musicians who'll be willing play pop – and maybe stretch the boundaries a bit.'

With help from Vic Garbarini of *Sounds*, he ended up with as distinguished a line-up as can be imagined:

- Omar Hakim (drums) played with Weather Report for two years, was the drummer on Bowie's 'Let's Dance', and, brought in as a dep, knocked off all the drum parts on Dire Straits' *Brothers In Arms* album in a couple of days.
- Darryl Jones (bass) had, at the age of 21, landed a job as sideman to (speak his name with reverence) Miles Davis and held it for five years.
- Branford Marsalis (sax) had played with Miles, too, as well as with Art Blakey's Jazz Messengers, Clark Terry, Herbie Hancock and (all stand for Dizzy) Dizzy Gillespie.
- Kenny Kirkland (keyboards) had also played with Dizzy, as well as Elvin Jones, Carla Bley and with Branford's brother, trumpeter Wynton Marsalis.

Back in the 1970s, after a hard night of jazz/rock/pop at the Wednesday night Last Exit gig, Gerry and Sting might well have played 'fantasy band' and it's easy to believe that this would have been exactly the fantasy band they would have assembled. Maybe with Mozart doubling with Kirkland on keys, the horn section boosted by the angel Gabriel, Joshua (who fought the battle of Jericho) and Buddy Bolden, and the Little Drummer Boy on congas. And Maria Callas doing shoo-wap vocals.

The initial idea was to try out some of Sting's new songs for a few nights at New York's Ritz club and then see where it went from there.

★ ★ ★

He had had a dream.

In the dream, he was sitting in his garden. 'Suddenly the bricks from the wall exploded into the garden and I turned to see the head of an enormous turtle emerging from the darkness, followed by four or five others. They were not only the size of a man, they were also blue and had an air of being immensely cool, like hepcats, insouciant and fearless. They didn't harm me but with an almost casual violence commenced to destroy my genteel English garden, digging up the lawn with their claws, chomping at the rosebushes, bulldozing the lilac tree. Total mayhem.'

The dream, according to the lessons he'd learned in his Jungian analysis, was about unrealised potential – his subconscious, living under the sea.

'So, with the album I wanted to destroy a lot of preconceptions and expectations and do something unsettling, different. These blue turtles, these musicians, were gonna help me. And they did.'

As Keith Altham points out, Sting '[can] fall victim to his own intellectual conceit by assuming all reporters can be won over by erudition and intelligence when most just want a story that will keep them in their jobs. They appeal to his intellect and off Sting goes, seduced into an erudite discussion on anything that can be taken out of context and used to make him appear pretentious later.'

Sting played the three gigs with his new band at the Ritz, starting on 25 February, then flew off to the Caribbean for seven weeks to start work on an album with the fantasy band at Eddy Grant's Blue Wave Recording Studio in St Philip, Barbados (Eddy Grant himself put some congas on a couple of tracks).

Rolling Stone sent a journalist, who detected a certain tension in the studio. When Sting had trouble with his voice, he lashed out: 'Don't ever fucking tell me I'm fucking flat.'

But he insisted that this was the set-up he wanted.

'It's such a relief here not to have to fight battles about your role. The Police were formed as a tripartite democracy with an equal say and the roles weren't exactly defined […] This band is more clearly defined. I hired them to play and I'm the songwriter and singer. So, there are no more arguments about roles.'

Miles and Sting decided that the next step would be to make a film about his new direction.

Michael Apted, a British director (*The Triple Echo*, *Stardust*, *Coal Miner's Daughter*) was brought in to make a feature-length documentary, covering rehearsals at the Château de Courson, on the outskirts of Paris, followed by concerts at the Théâtre Mogador and the launch of the album.

Sting said. 'I wanted a film about the beginning of a band.'

It was unwise for Trudie to fly, being heavily pregnant with their second child, so she and Sting took the Orient Express to Paris to stay at the £1,000-a-night Hotel Le Royal Monceau.

Sting had missed the birth of his three other children and was determined not to miss the arrival of this one. He had promised to be at the birth even if it meant he had to walk off stage mid-note.

In the event, Jake was born the day after the first concert at the Mogador. Sting was present. So was the film crew, invited by Sting on the grounds that he wanted the film to be 'an honest account of that nine days of my life'.

A press conference at the Pompidou Centre was also filmed. Unfortunately, none of the journalists had been given pre-release copies of the album, which meant they couldn't ask questions about it. So, instead they asked personal stuff and the usual 'Is there any truth in the rumours that the Police have split?' ('There is no plan whatever for the Police to work again. Nor is there a reason to say we've broken up...,' Sting said, rigorously on message.)

'I hear you had a child today.'

'Yes, I get my figure back very quickly.'

The chap from the *Daily Star* seemed to enjoy calling Sting 'Gordon'. Sting pointed out that his mother called him 'Sting'. His children called him 'Sting'. The same chap then asked whether he was going to marry Trudie.

'You asked me that last week in Montreux,' Sting said, testily.

The world's top jazz musicians sit in line on either side of him, looking slightly bemused.

'What's it like playing with Sting?'

'Uuuh... It's great.'

'He's in competition with probably the greatest act in history, the Police,' Kim Turner says.

'That's the risk,' says Miles. 'The risk is being only on his own, where there's no cocoon. Every interview has to be done by him, whereas in the Police, he had only to do a quarter of the interview and the others would carry the bulk of it. Everything is now Sting.'

The great joy of the film is the music. Musicians of that standard could (and at one point do) play the theme from *The Flintstones* and it would be worth listening to. An hour of just Omar Hakim and Darryl Jones jamming rhythm tracks would provide as much musical excitement and satisfaction as you'd get from a week of, say, Vivaldi.

One telling moment comes when, in an interview, Darryl Jones says, choosing his words very carefully, 'I am not... so totally sure yet... that... er... this is a... *band*... in that... everyone... has... er... [*very long pause*]... a totally equal say in what happens.'

★ ★ ★

The album, *The Dream of the Blue Turtles*, was released in the UK on 17 June. Sting did the first single from the album, 'If You Love Somebody Set Them Free', on *Top of the Pops*. As is obvious from the title, it's the antidote to 'Every Breath You Take'. It slipped into the Top 30 for a couple of weeks but made number three on the Billboard Hot 100. The subsequent single releases (there were five in all) provided diminishing returns.

The album itself, though, was a huge hit. In the UK it spent a good 18 months in the Top 100, peaking at number three, and it made number two in the US (kept off the top spot by Bruce Springsteen's *Born in the USA*).

Rolling Stone described the album as 'a clutch of songs about materialism, the cold war, nuclear war, the plight of British coal miners, heroin addiction and the slaughter of innocents in World War One, as well as a few leavening cantos on love, possession and loss'.

He told them, 'What I'm out to do is challenge the autonomy of the current rigid form. Of course, I want it to sell like hot cakes,' to which the journalist added, 'America loves a pilgrim who issues press releases on his progress.'

★ ★ ★

Four singles were released from the album. Two of them, 'If You Love Somebody Set Them Free' and 'Love Is The Seventh Wave', briefly charted in the UK. Only one, 'Russians', made the UK Top 20.

It was, Sting said, 'a song that's easy to mock, a very earnest song, but at the time it was written – at the height of the Reagan–Rambo paranoia years, when Russians were thought of as grey subhuman automatons only good enough to blow up – it seemed important'.

It made number 12.

The French loved it even more – it got to number two for three weeks and remained in the Top 50 there for 19 weeks.

★ ★ ★

And, by such means, he stayed in the limelight for the rest of the year.

★ ★ ★

On 4 July, he showed up on stage with Dire Straits, singing his 'I want my MTV' line from 'Money For Nothing' at the Prince's Trust Concert at Wembley Arena.

On 13 July, he was back in Wembley again, at the stadium this time, for the massive Live Aid concert. Watched by a couple of billion people, he performed with Branford Marsalis and sometimes Phil Collins. And he showed up on stage with Dire Straits again to do his 'Money For Nothing' turn.

His movie, *The Bride*, was released in August. His other movie – the good one with Meryl Streep – came out in September.

And, from August to November, he toured with the Blue Turtles supergroup – more modest venues than those the Police were used to, but well received.

In September, he sold out Radio City Music Hall in New York for seven nights – a total of 41,000 tickets.

Elsewhere, the reception tended to be more muted, and in Charlottesville and Austin they only sold between half and three-quarters of the available capacity.

A double live album of the concerts – titled, like the film, *Bring on the Night* – was released the following year.

After the US, the tour moved to Europe and kept going until 23 December, when he returned to spend Christmas in London.

And, when it was all over, after rehearsing together, recording together and touring together for the best part of a year, Branford Marsalis commented, 'Guys like him, you never get to know.'

CHAPTER TWENTY-ONE

THERE WAS NO MORE UP TO GO

Some bands start with love affairs. A guitar player and a bass player will meet and find every kind of affinity. They sing impeccable two-part harmony without even thinking about it. They write songs together. They discover they can finish each other's musical sentences. Their ideas about arrangement, style and genre are identical in every respect.

Then they get too close. They get on each other's nerves. Or a drummer comes between them. Or maybe an actual wife comes between them. They bicker ('Why don't you get Brian to do the harmonies, if you think he's so clever!'), split and, likely as not, they sue each other into poverty.

The Police was always a marriage of convenience, a balance between three individuals. All they had in common was that they were good at this – although the 'this' that they were good at was never properly defined and thus was always a bone of contention. And, if they're to be believed, the heat of those arguments was what fired the engine that drove the whole thing. The finished product, rather than being the sum of three contributions, was rather what was left when all the compromises had been made. You can have 'Nabokov' if I can do a hi-hat splash.

Tortoises cannot live in the UK. The climate is no good for them. The fact that some of them live for years and years does not disprove this assertion. It's just that tortoises take a long time to die, just as they take a long time over everything they do.

Maybe they weren't Blue Turtles. Maybe they were blue tortoises, telling Sting that the Police had always been a tortoise band. It started dying as soon as it was born but took nearly 10 years to do it. And in the meantime – to stretch the analogy to breaking point and beyond – it did some brilliant tricks with lettuce leaves and bits of carrot.

Sting kicked off the UK leg of the Blue Turtles tour at the 4,000-seater Windsor Hall, Bournemouth, and found Andy there.

Just like Nigel Tufnel in *This Is Spinal Tap*, he joined Sting on stage for some of the old tunes – they did 'Message', they did 'Every Breath'. It was what the people of Bournemouth wanted to hear more than anything.

★ ★ ★

At Newcastle, local boy Sting announced that *The Dream of the Blue Turtles* had been nominated for six Grammy awards, adding, 'I'm only telling you this because I want to read it in the *Evening Chronicle*.'

Disappointingly, none of the nominations turned into an actual award.

On 21 January, the tour moved into the Royal Albert Hall for six nights. It was deemed an apt subject for the broadsheet's critics.

'From the very first note of his Albert Hall concert on Monday the audience was taken on an exciting journey,' said the *Financial Times*, 'which, while not breaking new musical ground, revealed just how powerful and varied jazz funk can be. Some of the songs boogied along for fifteen minutes with no jot of tedium.'

The *Guardian* disagreed. 'If he'd stopped an hour earlier it would have been a triumph…'

★ ★ ★

On to Ireland, back to Newcastle, Italy, France, Spain, Germany, the Netherlands, Australia, and back to France, finishing up on 3 May at the Palais Omnisports de Paris-Bercy. At the after-show party, he was presented with a gold disc, then pushed, along with Trudie, into the hotel's swimming pool.

★ ★ ★

1986 was Amnesty International's 25th birthday.

The tradition of rock/comedy concerts to raise money and publicise the work of the charity was well established by now, so it was decided to celebrate by holding a string of six multi-star concerts – the 'Conspiracy of Hope' tour – across the US: San Francisco; Los Angeles; Denver, Colorado; Atlanta, Georgia; Rosemont, Illinois; winding up at the Giants Stadium in East Rutherford, New Jersey.

Lou Reed, Peter Gabriel, Joni Mitchell, Joan Baez, Bob Geldof, Miles Davis, Jackson Browne, the Neville Brothers and U2 had all agreed to appear at one or more of the gigs. Sting was up for it, too.

Then Jack Healey, the director of Amnesty, asked him over for lunch and suggested that the event would be much bigger if Sting could pull Andy and Stewart in as well.

In the event, Sting played the first three concerts and the Police the second three.

There were wrangles. U2 were slated to top the bill and it was right that they should do so, having been involved with the project from the start. Miles wasn't happy with that. He was also worried about Japanese TV rights, which, he felt, might jeopardise a deal he was doing over there. Presumably somebody, somewhere along the line, would have said, 'It's for *charity*, Miles,' but the Police did not get to be the biggest band in the world by having a big wet nelly for management.

Compromises were made. U2 would close the first three concerts, the Police the last three. Actually, the show closed, like Amnesty concerts always did, with all the acts coming on stage, along with, in this case, '18 prisoners of conscience released because of Amnesty International', and joining their voices in Dylan's 'I Shall Be Released'.

★ ★ ★

For his 1983 album, *Trouble in Paradise*, Randy Newman wrote a song (a narration, anyway) called 'My Life Is Good', in which he adopts the persona (or perhaps this is the real Randy, it's always hard to tell) of a pampered, boorish Los Angeles rock star, boasting to his kid's schoolteacher about how wonderful he is and what fabulous things happen to him all the time. He tells the teacher that the other day he and his wife went to see 'a very good friend of theirs' at the Hotel Bel-Air.

'And the name of this young man is Mr Bruce Springsteen, that's right, yeah.' And Bruce says to him, 'Rand, I'm tired. How would *you* like to be the Boss for a while?'

★ ★ ★

At the last concert of the tour, at the Giants Stadium in New Jersey, U2's Bono joined the Police on stage to sing a couple of choruses of 'Invisible Sun'.

He's impressive, possibly because, being Irish, albeit from the Republic, the lyric belongs to him in a way it could never belong to a bloke from Wallsend.

'It was a very symbolic moment,' said Sting. 'We'd broken up, then sort of re-formed to do the Amnesty tour. U2 were there as well and as we closed our set with "Invisible Sun", Bono came out and sang it with us. And then we symbolically handed our instruments over to U2, because they were about to become what we were – the biggest band in the world.'

As Randy said, 'How would *you* like to be the Boss for a while?'

'It was very emotional for them,' Bono said, later in *Rolling Stone*. 'I think it was clear in Sting's eyes that he was not going to be in a band any more. They had come together for this tour and that was it. It was a very big moment, like passing a torch.'

(U2 didn't get to keep the instruments, by the way. Andy was playing the magic 1961 Telecaster he'd bought from a student for $200 all those years before. The Edge could play it for one number, but keepsies was out of the question.)

Anyway, it worked. A month after the tour, the membership of Amnesty International in the United States had increased by 45,000 members.

And that concert in New Jersey was, indeed, the last time The Police would play together in front of a public audience until their induction into the Rock and Roll Hall of Fame, 17 years later.

★ ★ ★

But there was still one last shake of the bag for the Police as a recording band. The tale of Sting, Andy and Stewart's final studio venture is one that has passed into music industry legend, and is well documented in interviews in *Rolling Stone, Guitar World, Sounds Magazine* and many, many other organs.

What follows is a summary of the major campaigns and battles. Three or four volumes would be required for a detailed account of the entire war.

First of all, a word about the weaponry. It's already been mentioned that Stewart was a big fan of the Fairlight system of computer music-making. Sting, on the other hand, had invested in a system known as the Synclavier, which performed similar functions to the Fairlight but used different circuitry and (fearfully complicated) programming. Both cost about the same as the average family home. Among many other functions, both could perform as drum machines that sounded a bit more like real drums than the standard dub-tish-cha-cha-cha of a Binatone home organ.

★ ★ ★

It all began when Miles went round to Sting's house in Highgate and made an impassioned plea for Sting to make just one more album with the Police so they could go out with a bang not a whimper. Miles acknowledged that it was all over for the band, but suggested that the record company would really go for a greatest hits album, especially if – and here Miles knew he was on shaky ground – Sting could come up with a few new tracks to ensure that it got some radio play.

It had been three years since the last Police single. The market was crying out for new product, but over time such demand peaks, then withers. It was essential, therefore, to move fast.

In the end Sting suggested a compromise – a greatest hits album with no new material but with new recordings and radical reimaginings of two of their hits – say, 'Don't Stand So Close To Me' and 'De Do Do Do, De Da Da Da' from *Zenyatta Mondatta*.

They booked RAK Studios, in St John's Wood, London, for three weeks from 21 July. (The Pogues had booked the place for August, to work on – an unlikely, not to say improbable, choice for them – a Christmas record. Now, 30-odd years later, singing along with Kirsty's 'Well, so could anyone' has become as much a part of Christmas as crackers and turkey.)

★ ★ ★

258

Stewart was busy in leafy Bucks. He and Sonja had another son, Scott, on 28 January. He had more composing opportunities than he could handle – up to his elbows in *The Equalizer*, the *Star Wars: Droids* TV series and God knows what else.

In the following year, he'd do the music for *Wall Street*, the 'greed is good' movie for which Michael Douglas won a Best Actor Oscar.

His dad had just told the *Sunday Times*, 'I predict that one day Stewart will be taken as seriously as Darius Milhaud, Edgard Varèse and Steve Reich as a leading innovator of this and the next century.'

Andy, too, was busy with a movie score for *Down and Out in Beverly Hills*, and had been working on his first solo album, *XYZ*, at Devo's recording studio in Los Angeles.

He'd also remarried Kate.

'A fancy Buddhist wedding on our lawn,' he said. 'Sounds very Californian, doesn't it?'

He agreed to the new Police album, but feared that getting back with the Police was going to be a good bit more risky and less fruitful than getting back with his beloved Kate.

★ ★ ★

Andy had got a few songs that might work on a new album.

Stewart had a few, too.

But Sting insisted on sticking to his plan of re-recording old numbers. He had a notion that 'Don't Stand So Close To Me' might work at a really slow tempo.

Andy had his doubts, but resigned himself to the notion that Sting would, once again, be calling the shots.

In *One Train Later*, he graphically describes a Police session as 'a group of unruly children locked in a small house with big shiny machines and a handful of explosives'.

★ ★ ★

The first big bang happened on 21 July, when Stewart turned up at RAK Studios with his arm in a sling. He'd fallen off a horse and fractured his collarbone. He would not be able to play drums. But he was sanguine about the matter (or possibly heavily medicated) and said he could program his drum parts into his Fairlight (see above), just as he did with his movie scores. His roadie was busy setting up the Fairlight at one end of the studio.

Ominously, Sting's roadie was setting up his Synclavier at the other end of the studio.

A drum pattern for the much-slowed-down 'Don't Stand So Close To Me' was agreed and programming began.

Andy kicked his heels and waited, disappointed that – instead of jamming together and working out the new arrangement collectively and creatively – everything had been reduced to pressing buttons.

Eventually they were ready, and they figured out a guitar part – 'we changed the key slightly, and Sting put in one or two chord changes'.

Andy nailed it in a couple or three takes.

Then Stewart collapsed in pain over his Fairlight. An ambulance was summoned, and he was carted off to hospital for surgery.

Stewart recalled that, while he was in hospital, under heavy sedation, he decided to clear the air with Sting. He'd point out that he was fine. He missed playing the drums in the Police. So, he would acknowledge that it was now Sting's band. He would be the drummer.

'If that's the only way you'll do the Police, then that's fine.'

The next day, Andy and Sting went back into the studio without Stewart. Sting started laying down backing vocals and, as he did so, realised that the rhythms Stewart had put down the day before weren't working. They'd have to be redone. On the Synclavier.

On day three, Stewart returned, full of optimism and painkillers. He heard the new drum tracks. It was, he later told *Reeling in the Years*, a Qantas inflight radio programme, 'the straw that broke the camel's back'.

Sting had not only changed the rhythms, but the sounds as well, replacing Stewart's trademark snappy snare sound with something Sting thought bigger and fuller but which Stewart called 'ugly, flatulent and sludgy'.

So, when Sting left the studio that evening, Stewart erased Sting's drum tracks and replaced them with his own.

On day four, they worked on 'De Do Do Do, De Da Da Da'.

Andy, gloomy and bored, went out to buy some magazines from the newsstand in St John's Wood. In one of the magazines he found a review of a film of Sting's that had just been released on video. It could have been *The Bride*, it could have been *Brimstone and Treacle*, accounts vary. Most probably it was *The Bride*.

The review was less than complimentary about Sting's acting. Andy showed it to Stewart. Stewart read it aloud to everybody in the studio. Sting, who felt he was being humiliated in front of strangers, was stung, but, to his credit, kept his peace.

But then it got worse. That night, Stewart and Sonja rented the new video release (it had to be *The Bride*), watched it and found it hilarious.

On day five in the studio, he mentioned his enjoyment, at which Sting turned on his heel and walked out.

Two days went by. Sting did not return.

Stewart got a furious call from Miles in America. He told Stewart that Sting was really pissed off with him for ridiculing his film and that he'd better sort things out.

Stewart phoned Sting's Highgate house but Trudie said that Sting was still really, really mad and didn't want to speak to him.

The next day, at the studio, a motorcycle messenger delivered a note to Stewart from Sting.

According to Vic Garbarini, it read: 'Stewart, you have always been jealous of me... I've had to put up with your petty cutting me off at the knees, your total disregard for my feelings and lack of respect... an unrelenting barrage of little innuendos and digs.'

Stewart wrote back an apology, acknowledging that he had slipped back into the old conflicts and bad behaviour. He did point out, though, that he was in quite a bit of pain and had been taking heavy medication over the last week, which may have clouded his judgement somewhat.

The tracks for 'Don't Stand' were all finished and ready to be mixed.

Miles (now back in the UK) put a deadline on Sting – either you come back to the studio by 10 o'clock on Friday or Stewart will mix the track without you.

Still Sting didn't show. The deadline passed. The hours ticked by. Eventually, Miles went round to Sting's house and somehow persuaded him back into the studio.

Vic Garbarini once again takes up the story.

'"Now, about that snare drum sound..." With those words Sting pulls out a 12-inch switchblade and flicks it under Stewart's chin. Everyone freezes. Simultaneously, Stewart and Sting break into convulsive laughter. It's as if the unbearable tension of the last seven days – and the last seven years – has been lanced.'

It got done.

And that was that. The next edition of the Outlandos fan club letter summed it up: 'We make no pretence about knowing what is going to happen in the future but will keep sending you news of all three of the Police in the hope that one day they will be back in the studio again.'

★ ★ ★

On 3 October, A&M released 'Don't Stand So Close To Me '86' as a single.

It was not the triumphant swansong that would have been a fitting ending. It's not that much slower than the original, just a lot less sparky. As if Dr Frankenstein had drained its life force for use in another project.

A video was made, exploiting the full potential of 1986 video hi-tech and including clips from previous videos. The single made number 24 in the UK and 46 on the Billboard Hot 100.

The track was included on the album, *Every Breath You Take: The Singles*, released at the end of October.

The other new recording, 'De Do Do Do, De Da Da Da', didn't emerge publicly until a much later compilation.

Critics were showered with copies of the album in the hope of gleaning some interest and quotable compliments, in response to which *Sounds* said, 'Some companies seem to think that the more copies of their record they send out, the better the review will be. Wrong! The first 27 people to want this record and yet don't already have it can each have one of my copies and be welcome to it.'

A&M needn't have bothered publicising the album at all, though. This was the Police they were dealing with. The songs were some of the best loved of the previous 10 years. The album went straight in at number one, stayed in the Top 10 until mid-January, and didn't leave the Top 100 until July 1987.

★ ★ ★

The world had changed – the technology, the style, the music, everything.

A new breed of human had emerged, the product of all that aspiration that Thatcher had encouraged, people who had benefited from her 'hard work pays and success is rewarded' promise. They were called yuppies ('young upwardly mobile professionals'). You saw them everywhere, mostly in wine bars, where they ate fancy quiche and banoffee pie and drank Beaujolais nouveau. Their role model was the man in the Renault 25 ad (played by the young Anthony Head), who, in the smuggest voice and with the smuggest face known to humankind, turned to his worryingly posh wife as he played with the electric windows and adjusted the climate control, 'I'm starting my own business. John's with me. Ian's with me. And we've got the backing.'

The men wore suits. Or Fiorucci jeans at weekends. Their neckties alone cost more than a punk would spend on clothes in 17 lifetimes. The women had hair like Princess Diana, and wore Betty Jackson blouses with pie-crust collars.

Yuppies did not buy records. They did not buy cassettes. They invested in the tiny, shiny perfection of the CD, then had to have their houses rebuilt to accommodate hi-fi systems accurate enough to capture those shimmering highs and mud-free lows. The CD played clean. No hiss, not clicks, no pops, no grunge. And they had the advantage of being a lot more expensive than records. Line them up on the shelf and it's like displaying actual currency for your friends to admire.

The latest must-have was the in-car CD player. Get one of those in your BMW (the Renault 25 was nice in the advert, but let's be serious) and you could glide along the M40 to see Boo and Ginny in Thame with hiss-free, click-free, pop-free music playing all the way.

And what was the perfect clean music to play all the way from Islington to Thame? You want to slam the greatest hits in, swing round the Hangar Lane gyratory, then on to the A40, put your foot down, hear the S38 unit deliver the revs, and, as it does so, you want the Blaupunkt to go 'Thwack! – "Every little thing she does is magic..."'

The Police, Dire Straits, Fleetwood Mac had all become CD music, yuppie music, BMW music. It wasn't their fault. Sting and Mark and Lindsey never meant it to happen. There was just something about Andy's shimmering guitar, Stewart's snappy snare and Sting's vocal register that suited analogue to digital to analogue reproduction in a luxury vehicle. Mark Knopfler's clean guitar tone was the same. Creeping up to 90 on the straight stretch after Heathrow when the fast diddles of the 'Sultans Of Swing' solo kicked in could provide the same sort of high that once had been available only from meditating in a yurt. And nothing on earth could match the ecstasy of 'Tusk' in the Dartford Tunnel.

As far as the rest of humanity was concerned, the poor people, still listening to C90s on their Boots music centres and Sharp boomboxes, the yuppie touch tainted everything. It gave the suggestion, first made five years earlier, that the Police were 'relentlessly, calculatedly middlebrow' some real traction.

And besides, in 1986, there was so much else available: the choice of stuff to listen to, even in the mainstream, was rich, varied and wonderful.

Prince from Minneapolis had been around since the late 1970s. By the mid-1980s he was simultaneously being original, technically breathtaking, phenomenally successful and very dirty. A couple of years earlier, his *Purple Rain* spent 24 weeks at the top of the Billboard 200 album chart.

Morrissey from Davyhulme was singing unhinged poems in a whiny voice, while Johnny Marr did jangly things with his guitar.

Kate Bush from Bexleyheath had started out extraordinary and remained remarkably consistent.

There was a whole new section in the record shop called 'world music' where you could discover Thomas Mapfumo, the Bhundu Boys and Nusrat Fateh Ali Khan filed cheek by jowl with Tibetan bowl music, stuff by Iceland's top langspil players, Mongolian throat singers and Welsh choirs.

Shane MacGowan and the Pogues from Kilburn had reinvented Irish music and married it to tough, literate, heartbreaking lyrics.

The Sugarhill Gang from New Jersey, Grandmaster Flash from Barbados and the Bronx, Run-DMC from Queens, Frankie Knuckles from the Bronx, Mikey Dread from Jamaica and a thousand others were reinventing the way in which music worked, the way it was made and what it actually was.

And it was all so incredibly *different*.

★ ★ ★

Stewart went back to his family, his horses and compositions.

Andy carried on working on his solo album, his film music and the production of twin boys.

Sting had a new family and a new album, too.

And Miles…

A group of musicians, including Billy Bragg, Paul Weller and Jimmy Somerville of the Communards, had joined forces under the banner 'Red Wedge' to chivvy support for the Labour Party. They toured, sometimes joined by an extraordinary range of musicians including Bananarama, Heaven 17, Elvis Costello and Prefab Sprout.

John Biffen, Tory MP, said, 'Central Office has been casting about like crazy for some top-heavy coal miner's daughter to take on Billy Bragg.'

Samantha Fox, the page-three stunner, was considered and rejected.

Toby Young, writing in *The Times*, reported that Miles had been recruited to the Conservative Party's campaign to win support from young voters: 'After an intensive search to find stars to match Labour's success with its Red Wedge campaign, headed by Billy Bragg, the Tory Party Youth Committee chaired by Mr John Moore, Secretary of State for Transport, has come up with a list likely to raise eyebrows among the party's old guard.'

The list included Bev Bevan, drummer with Electric Light Orchestra, formerly of the Move; gymnast Suzanne Dando; and dancer Debbie Moore.

Once again, they needn't have bothered. At the June 1987 general election, Thatcher and the Conservatives once again walked it.

★ ★ ★

At the end of 1986, the ever-optimistic Outlandos fan club newsletter letter said: 'Rumours have circulated about an autumn tour and even venues named but they were only the non-confirmed scoop of an overzealous newspaper columnist. Very early in 1986 we were all sure that the Police would be touring again before the end of the year but somehow the time skimmed by – the months have passed, and STING, ANDY and STEWART continue to be busy pursuing their own individual musical projects.'

★ ★ ★

They stayed busy with their own individual projects for a long, long time.

★ ★ ★

'There was no more up to go,' said Stewart. 'We had gone to clubs – containing 200 people – to theatres – containing 2,000 people – to arenas with 18,000. Where could we go?'

SOURCES AND ACKNOWLEDGEMENTS

A small selection of the many hundreds of books, periodicals, websites and other sources consulted.

NEWSPAPERS AND PERIODICALS

AND Magazine, Australian, Billboard, Boston Globe, Boston Phoenix, Bostonian, Chicago Sun-Times, Chicago Tribune, Classic Rock, Creem, Daily Mail, Daily Mirror, Daily Star, Daily Telegraph, Drum!, Egyptian Mail, Evening Standard, Fabulous, Face, Financial Times, Guardian, Guitar Player Magazine, Guitar World, Independent, International Musician and Recording World, Los Angeles, Los Angeles Times, Melody Maker, Musician Magazine, New Musical Express, New York Times, Newcastle Evening Chronicle, Newcastle Journal, News of the World, Q Magazine, RAM (Rock Australia Magazine), Record Collector, Record Mirror, Robert Christgau's Consumer Guide, Rock Milestones, Rolling Stone, San Francisco Chronicle, Smash Hits, Sniffin' Glue and Other Rock'n'Roll Habits (for Punks!), Sound on Sound, Sounds, Spare Rib, Sun, Sunday Express, Sunday Mirror, Sunday People, Sunday Telegraph, Sunday Times, Time, Times, Trouser Press, Washington Post, Woman, Woman's Own, You Magazine.

BOOKS AND ARTICLES

Carter Alan, *The Decibel Diaries*, Allen Press, 2017

Daevid Allen, *The Pocket Guide to the Planet Gong*, BYG Records, 1971

Keith Altham, *The PR Strikes Back*, Blake, 2002

Lawrence Black, Hugh Pemberton and Pat Thane (eds), *Reassessing 1970s Britain*, Manchester University Press, 2013

Marsha Bronson, *Sting*, Exley Publishers, 1993

Jake Brown, *Behind the Boards*, Hal Leonard, 2014

Wensley Clarkson, *A Tale in the Sting*, Blake Publishing, 2003

Ian Copeland, *Wild Thing*, Simon and Schuster, 1995

Miles Copeland, *The Police: A Visual Documentary*, Omnibus Press, 1981

Miles Copeland, *The Game Player*, Arum Press, 1989

Stewart Copeland, *Strange Things Happen: A Life with the Police, Polo and Pygmies*, HarperCollins, 2009

Jayne County, *Man Enough to Be a Woman*, Serpent's Tail, 1995

Jenny Fabian and Johnny Byrne, *Groupie*, Omnibus Press, 1969

Simon Frith, 'Look! Hear! The Uneasy Relationship of Music and Television', *Popular Music* 21(3), 2002: 277–290

Ken Garner, *The Peel Sessions*, BBC Books, 2010

Steve Gett, *Sting*, Cherry Lane Books, 1985

Ian Gittens, *Top of the Pops*, BBC Books, 2007

Luke James, *Stairway to Nowhere*, Brummie Git Press, 2010

Allan Jones, *Can't Stand Up for Falling Down*, Bloomsbury, 2017

Dennis Kavanagh and Anthony Seldon (eds), *The Thatcher Effect*, Oxford University Press, 1989

C. P. Lee, *When We Were Thin*, Hotun Press, 2007

Legs McNeil and Gillian McClean, *Please Kill Me*, Little, Brown and Company, 1996

Andy McSmith, *No Such Thing As Society*, Constable, 2011

John Otway, *That's Really Me*, Cherry Red Books, 2000

Henry Padovani, *Secret Police Man*, Pen Press, 2009

Henrik Paulsen, *1977: The Year of Punk and the New Wave*, Helter Skelter, 2006

James Perone, *The Album: A Guide to Pop Music's Most Provocative, Influential, and Important Creations*, vol. 3, Praeger, 2012

Greg Prato, *MTV Ruled the World*, Greg Prato, 2011

Danny Quatrochi, *Police Confidential*, MacDonald Queen Anne Press, 1987

Christopher Sandford, *Sting: Demolition Man*, Time Warner, 1999

Jon Savage, *The England's Dreaming Tapes*, Faber and Faber, 2009

Alexei Sayle, *Thatcher Stole My Trousers*, Bloomsbury, 2016

Robert Sellers, *Sting*, Omnibus Press, 1989

Harry Shapiro, *Helter Skelter*, Helter Skelter Publishing, 1999

Bruce Springsteen, *Born to Run*, Simon and Schuster, 2016

David and Caroline Stafford, *Fings Ain't Wot They Used T'Be: The Lionel Bart Story*, Omnibus Press, 2011

David and Caroline Stafford, *Cupid Stunts: The Life and Radio Times of Kenny Everett*, Omnibus Press, 2013

David and Caroline Stafford, *Big Time: The Life of Adam Faith*, Omnibus Press, 2015

David and Caroline Stafford, *Maybe I'm Doing It Wrong: The Life & Music of Randy Newman*, Omnibus Press, 2016

David and Caroline Stafford, *Halfway to Paradise: The Life of Billy Fury*, Omnibus Press, 2018

Sting, *Broken Music*, Simon and Schuster, 2003

Sting, *Lyrics*, Simon and Schuster, 2010

Andy Summers, *I'll Be Watching You*, Taschen, 2006

Andy Summers, *One Train Later*, Portrait, 2006

Philip Sutcliffe and Hugh Fielder, *The Police: L'Historia Bandido*, Proteus Books, 1981

John Taylor, *In the Pleasure Groove*, Sphere, 2013

Kieron Tyler, *The Damned*, Omnibus Press, 2017

Cherry Vanilla, *Lick Me*, Chicago Review Press, 2010

Aaron J. West, *Walking in Their Footsteps, Sting and the Police*, Rowman & Littlefield, 2015

Michael Worly, *No Future*, Cambridge University Press, 2017

DVDS

Police Around the World, Thorn EMI, 1982

The Police Live: Ghost in the Machine Tour, A&M, 2001

Every Breath You Take: The Videos, A&M, 2003

The Police: Synchronicity Concert, Universal/Island, 2005

Everyone Stares: The Police Inside Out, Universal Music, 2006

The Police: Greatest Video Hits, IMC, 2007

The Police: Certifiable, Universal, 2008

Can't Stand Losing You: Surviving the Police, Bob Yari Productions, 2012

WEBSITES (A TINY SELECTION)

thepolicewiki.org
sting.com
songfacts.com
songlines.co.uk
rockhistory.co.uk
soundvapors.com
revolvermag.com
spin.com

SPECIAL THANKS TO...

Keith Altham, David Barraclough, Laura Beaumont, Susannah Buxton, Chris Charlesworth, Tom Climpson, Dietmar Cloes, Charlie Dore, Mark Ellen, Vic Garbarini, Jimmy Hibbert, Bill Oddie, Chris Petit, Alexei and Linda Sayle, Philip Sutcliffe, Kipper Williams

And to the many journalists and commentators whose work we consulted, including...
Philip Bashe, John Blake, Cody Brooks, Richard Buskin, Harry Callaghan, J. D. Considine, Richard Cook, Hugh Fielder, Ian Fortnam, Richard Grabel, Jim Green, David Hepworth, Paolo Hewitt, Rob Hughes, Chris Iley, Nick Kent, J. Kordoush, Paul Lester, Tim Lott, Chris Morris, Philip Norman, Pierre Perrone, John Pidgeon, Kelly Pike, Greg Prato, Chris Salewicz, Sylvie Simmons, Adrian Thrills, Keith Waterhouse, Mark Williams

(VERY) LIMITED DISCOGRAPHY (JUST THE OBVIOUS ONES)

Singles (UK Releases)

Fall Out / Nothing Achieving, 1977
Roxanne / Peanuts, 1978
Can't Stand Losing You / Dead End Job, 1978
So Lonely / No Time This Time, 1978

Roxanne [reissue], 1979
Can't Stand Losing You [reissue], 1979
Message In A Bottle / Landlord, 1979
Walking On The Moon / Visions Of The Night, 1979
Fall Out [reissue], 1979
Six Pack (So Lonely, Roxanne, Walking On The Moon, Can't Stand Losing You, Message In A Bottle, The Bed's Too Big Without You + B-sides), 1980
Don't Stand So Close To Me / Friends, 1980
De Do Do Do, De Da Da Da / A Sermon, 1980
Invisible Sun / Shambelle, 1981
Every Little Thing She Does Is Magic / Flexible Strategies, 1981
Spirits In The Material World / Low Life, 1981
Every Breath You Take / Murder By Numbers, 1983
Wrapped Around Your Finger / Someone To Talk To, 1983
Synchronicity II / Once Upon A Daydream, 1983
King Of Pain / Tea In The Sahara, 1984

Studio Albums (UK Releases)

Outlandos d'Amour, November 1978
Reggatta de Blanc, October 1979
Zenyatta Mondatta, October 1980
Ghost in the Machine, October 1981
Synchronicity, June 1983
Every Breath You Take: The Singles, November 1985

FAN CLUB

Outlandos – official fan club, formed in April 1979
Sting.com – replaced Outlandos in 2003

INDEX

271